You Can't Win

Jack Black

AK Press / Nabat

Edinburgh, London, and San Francisco

2000

This edition copyright © 2000 Nabat/AK Press
2nd Edition

First published in 1926.
Republished in 1988 by AMOK Press. Thanks AMOK!

Introduction © 1988, 1999 by the William Burroughs Trust

Jack Black 1926, p. 14, Photograph by Edward Weston
© 1981 Center for Creative Photography, Arizona Board of Regents

You Can't Win

ISBN 1 902593 02 2
ISBN13 978 1902593 02 9

AK Press
674 A 23rd Street
Oakland CA
94612-1163 USA

AK Press
PO Box 12766
Edinburgh, Scotland
EH8 9YE

A catalogue record for this title is available from the Library of Congress

Series editor: Bruno Ruhland
Cover, cover art, book, and series design donated by fran sendbuehler, mouton-noir – montréal
fran@mouton-noir.org

Prisoners can receive this book by sending $10.00 to A.K. Press at the Oakland address noted above.

ABOUT NABAT BOOKS

Nabat books is a series dedicated to reprinting forgotten memoirs by various misfits, outsiders, and rebels. Nabat books are based on a few simple propositions:

That to be a success under current definition is highly toxic – wealth, fame and power are a poison cocktail; that this era of triumphal capitalism enshrines the most dreary human pathologies like greed and self-interest as good and natural; that the "winners" version of reality and history is deeply lame and soul-rotting stuff. Given this it follows that the truly interesting and meaningful lives and real adventures are only to be had on the margins of what Kenneth Rexroth called "the social lie". It's with the dropouts, misfits, dissidents, renegades and revolutionaries, against the grain, between the cracks and amongst the enemies of the state that the good stuff can be found. Fortunately there is a mighty underground river of testimony from the disaffected, a large cache of hidden history, of public secrets overlooked by the oppressive conventional wisdom that Nabat books aims to tap into. A little something to set against the crushed hopes, mountains of corpses, and commodification of everything. Actually, we think, is the best thing western civilization has going for itself.

FROM REVIEWS OF THE FIRST EDITION

Much of this book is about loneliness. Yet its pages are bracingly companionable. It is one of the friendliest books ever written. It is a superb piece of autobiography, testimony that cannot be impeached. While it is a statement of an American tragedy, it has laughter, brevity, style; as a book to pass the time away with, it is in a class with the best fiction.

Carl Sandburg, *New York World*

Nothing half as rewarding has come down the highway of books about thieves, tramps, murderers, bootleggers and crooks in years... Jack Black's story combines so many things: the carefully worked out detail and suspense of a detective story, the sharp eye and ears of a collector of fellow characters, all very different and alive, the naked, honest, unfevered revelation of the autobiography of a man's heart and mind.

New Republic

I believe Jack Black has written a remarkable book; it is vivid and picturesque; it is not fiction; it is a book that was needed and it should be widely read.

Clarence Darrow, *New York Herald Tribune*

Despite the fascination of these picaresque adventurings, the most nobly exciting thing in the book is the revelation it gives of the unbreakable spirit of Jack Black himself.

The Nation

Authenticity aside, this book is a most efficient thriller; and those readers – and they are very numerous – who enjoy hairbreadth captures and hairbreadth escapes, court trials and prison floggings, burglary and sudden death, vividly brought before them on the printed pages, are here provided with a satisfying and sufficiently gruesome meal.

London *Times Literary Supplement*

YOU CAN'T WIN

DEDICATION

This book is dedicated to Fremont Older, to Judge Frank H. Dunne, to the unnamed friend who sawed me out of the San Francisco jail and to that dirty, disreputable, crippled beggar, "Sticks" Sullivan who picked the buckshot out of my back – under the bridge – at Baraboo, Wisconsin.

The Author

FOREWORD

I first read *You Can't Win* in 1926, in an edition bound in red cardboard. Stultified and confined by middle-class St. Louis mores, I was fascinated by this glimpse of an underworld of seedy rooming-houses, pool parlors, cat houses and opium dens, of bull pens and cat burglars and hobo jungles. I learned about the Johnson Family of good bums and thieves, with a code of conduct that made more sense to me than the arbitrary, hypocritical rules that were taken for granted as being "right" by my peers.

A Johnson pays his debts and keeps his word. He minds his own business, but will give help when help is needed and asked for. He does not hold out on his confederates or cheat his landlady. He is what they call in show business "good people."

Re-reading the book fifty years later, I felt a deep nostalgia for a way of life that is gone forever. Scenes and characters emerge from the pages, bathed in the light of past times:

This young gay cat starts bad-mouthing Salt Chunk Mary and old George – a railriding safecracker with two fingers missing from crimping blasting caps – says to him: "'You were a good bum, but you're dog meat now', and shot him four times across the fire at a hobo jungle, and I could feel the slugs hit him. He fell down with his hair in the fire." Turns out Salt Chunk Mary is George's sister. Sister or not, the gay cat was out of line to talk against a woman like Salt Chunk Mary, Mother of the Johnson Family....

Half a century later, I was to use characters and scenes from the Good Red Book, quoting the prose of Jack Black from memory, occasionally word for word, and when you can remember a passage of prose after fifty years, it has to be good.

A two-story red brick house down by the tracks in Junction City, Idaho...Salt Chunk Mary, Mother of the Johnson Family... train whistles cross a distant sky.

Mary keeps a pot of pork and beans and a blue porcelain coffee pot always on the stove. You eat first, then you talk business, rings and watches slopped out on the kitchen table. She names a price. She doesn't name another. Mary could say "No" quicker than any woman Kim ever knew, and none of her no's ever meant yes. She kept the money in a cookie jar, but nobody thought about that. Her cold gray eyes would have seen the thought and maybe something goes wrong on the next lay. John Law just happens by, or John Citizen comes up with a load of double-zero into your soft and tenders.

And the Sanctimonious Kid, soft-spoken and sententious: "It's a crooked game, kid, but you have to think straight. Be as positive yourself as you like, but no positive clothes, and no off calibers like 41." The Sanctimonious Kid was later hanged in Australia for the murder of a police constable.

Jack Black dedicates *You Can't Win* to "that dirty, drunken, crippled beggar Sticks Sullivan who picked the buckshot out of my back under a bridge at Baraboo, Wisconsin." Sticks was a Johnson.

Looking back over the years, I remember the Johnsons....the old Mexican druggist who filled a morphine Rx after ten shits had snarled it back at me: "We do not serve dope fiends!" Yes, I remember the Johnsons, and I remember those of another persuasion. As a wise old black faggot said to me, "Some people are shits, darling."

And likely to remain so. A basic split between shits and Johnsons has emerged. I see the world as a stage on which different actors are assigned to different roles. Joseph Conrad arrived at a similar concept. Of course, any Johnson does do shitty things at times. But he knows enough to regret such actions. It is very rare that a hardcore shit acts like a Johnson. He simply does not understand what it means to be a Johnson, and is irrevocably committed to a contrary viewpoint. A direct confrontation of the shits and the Johnsons could be as drastic as the conjunction of matter and antimatter: POOF! No reconciliation, no agreeing to disagree, is possible.

Jack Black calls his book *You Can't Win.* Well, who can? Winner take nothing. Would he have been better off having spent his life at some full-time job? I don't think so. He has recorded a chapter of specifically American life that is now gone forever. Where are the hobo jungles, the hop joints, the old rod-riding yeggs, where is Salt Chunk

Mary? Where is the Johnson Family? As another thief, Francois Villon, said, "Where are the snows of yesteryear?"

In the words of poets and writers, in the pictures of painters.

— WILLIAM S. BURROUGHS

Jack Black, 1926 — Photograph by Edward Weston.

ONE

I AM now librarian of the *San Francisco Call.*

Do I look like one? I turn my chair so I can look in the mirror. I don't see the face of a librarian. There is no smooth, high, white forehead. I do not see the calm, placid, composed countenance of the student. The forehead I see is high enough, but it is lined with furrows that look like knife scars. There are two vertical furrows between my eyes that make me appear to be wearing a continual scowl. My eyes are wide enough apart and not small, but they are hard, cold, calculating. They are blue, but of that shade of blue farthest removed from the violet.

My nose is not long, not sharp. Nevertheless it is an inquisitive nose. My mouth is large – one corner of it is higher than the other and I appear to be continually sneering. I do not scowl, I do not sneer; yet there is something in my face that causes a man or woman to hesitate before asking to be directed to Dr. Gordon's church. I can't remember a time that any woman, young or old, ever stopped me on the street and asked to be directed. Once in a great while a drunk will roll over to where I am standing and ask how he can get to "Tw'-ninth 'n' Mission."

If I gaze into the mirror long enough and think hard enough I can conjure up another face. The old one seems to dissolve and in its place I see the face of a schoolboy – a bright, shining, innocent face. I see a mop of white hair, a pair of blue eyes, and an inquisitive nose. I see myself standing on the broad steps of the Sisters' Convent School. At the age of fourteen, after three years' "board and tuition," I am leaving to go home to my father and then to another school for "big boys."

My teacher, a sweet, gentle Sister, a madonna, is holding my hand. She is crying. I must hurry away or I will be crying, too. The Mother Superior says good-by. Her thin lips are pressed so tightly together that I can barely see the line where they meet. She is looking into my eyes intently and I am wondering what she is going to say to me when the crunching of gravel warns us that the old coach is ready and I must be off. The Mother takes my teacher gently by the hand. I see them go through the wide door and disappear silently down the long, dark hall.

All the boys in the school, and there were fifty of them, lined up and gave me a noisy send-off. The old coachman clucked to his horses, and I was off for the train – and the world.

Any reader with a spoonful of imagination can picture me going home, then to other schools in turn, then to some sort of an office job; advancement here and there, always leading a well-ordered, quiet, studious life, until he finally places me in the respectable and responsible position of librarian of a metropolitan newspaper. That's the way it should have been, but wasn't.

The course I followed from that convent school to this library desk, if charted on a piece of paper, would look like the zigzag line that statisticians use to denote the rise and fall of temperature or rainfall or fluctuations of business. Every turn I made was a sharp one, a sudden one. In years I cannot remember making one easy, graceful, rounded turn.

It has often been a question with me just how much the best of it a boy has, who has his mother with him until his feet are well planted under him; who has a home and its influences until he gathers some kind of a working philosophy that helps him to face the world. There is no substitute for the home and the mother.

It may not mean much to the average chap to have a friend say: "John, I want you to meet my mother." To me it means more than I can put on paper. It seems to explain to me why the man who so proudly says, "This is my mother," is so many things that I am not and never can be. The insurance people have not yet got to the stage of insuring a man against a lifetime of failure, but if they ever do, I imagine the chap who can guarantee them that he will keep his mother with him until he is twenty will have a shade the best of it when he pays his premium.

I am not lugging in the fact that I was left motherless at the age of ten to alibi myself away from anything. Nevertheless I think a fellow has the right to ask himself if things might not have been different. My mother died before I got very well acquainted with her– I doubt if any child gives its parents much thought before the age of twelve or thirteen.

I probably thought that my mother was a person put into the world to scrub my face and neck and to be screamed and kicked at; to put scratchy, flannel rags around my neck with smelly grease on them when I had the croup; and to stand by the bed and keep me in it when I had the measles. I can remember distinctly how angry I became when she brought me a nice, new toothbrush and showed me what to do with it.

This was the greatest indignity of all – the last straw. I threw the thing away and refused to use it; told her up and down that I was "no girl" and wouldn't have any "girl things." She did not get angry and scold; she just went on with her work, smiling. She may have been pleased with my manly outburst. I don't know.

I don't remember that I was shocked or pained when she was buried.

I cried, because it was expected of me. Mother's relatives, a couple of sisters, whom I never saw before or since, were crying. I saw tears in my father's eyes. So I tried to cry, and did. I know my father realized what we had lost and his grief was genuine, but I could not feel it then.

A few days later father sold our little cottage home and furnishings and we moved into the only hotel in the little town. Schools were few and far between for poor children then. I played around the hotel all day, running wild, till father came home from work. He would have his dinner, read a paper, and then put me to bed. After that he would read a book for an hour and go to bed himself. We lived this way for almost a year. Some nights he would put down his book and look at me strangely for minutes at a time. I was a problem, undoubtedly, and he was trying to decide what to do with me. A ten-year-old boy without a mother is a fit problem for any father's mind, and my father was a thoughtful man.

Looking back at it, it seems to me that I was blown here and there like a dead leaf whipped about by the autumn winds till at last it finds lodgment in some cozy fence corner. When I left school at fourteen I was as unsophisticated as a boy could be. I knew no more of the world and its strange way than the gentle, saintly woman who taught me my prayers in the convent.

Before my twentieth birthday, I was in the dock of a criminal court, on trial for burglary. I was acquitted, but that is another story. In six years I had deserted my father and home, gone on the road. I had become a snapper-up of small things, a tapper of tills, a street-door sneak thief, a prowler of cheap lodging houses, and at last a promising burglar in a small way.

At twenty-five I was an expert house burglar, a nighttime prowler, carefully choosing only the best homes – homes of the wealthy, careless, insured people. I "made" them in the small hours of the night, always under arms.

At thirty I was a respected member of the "yegg" brotherhood, a thief of which little is known. He is silent, secretive, wary; forever traveling, always a night "worker." He shuns the bright lights, seldom straying far from his kind, never coming to the surface. Circulating through space with his always-ready automatic, the yegg rules the underworld of criminals. At forty I found myself a solitary, capable journeyman highwayman; an escaped convict, a fugitive, with a background of twenty-five years in the underworld.

A bleak background! Crowded with robberies, burglaries, and thefts too numerous to recall. All manner of crimes against property. Arrests, trials, acquittals, convictions, escapes. Penitentiaries! I see in the background four of them. County jails, workhouses, city prisons, Mounted Police barracks, dungeons, solitary confinement, bread and water, hanging up, brutal floggings, and the murderous straitjacket.

I see hop joints, wine dumps, thieves' resorts, and beggars' hangouts.

Crime followed by swift retribution in one form or another.

I had very few glasses of wine as I traveled this route. I rarely saw a woman smile and seldom heard a song.

In those twenty-five years I took all these things, and I am going to write about them.

And I am going to write about them as I took them – with a smile.

Two

I WAS a problem to my father, running loose about the hotel while he was at work, and finally he took me to a Catholic school one hundred miles away. On that short trip my father and I got to be good friends, and I think I was closer to him that day than on any other of our lives. Father left that evening and told me to be good, mind the Sisters, and study hard.

I fell into my groove in the school with other boys of my age. Our days were passed pleasantly with our small studies, many prayers, and daily attendance at mass. The food was coarse but wholesome.

I never went home at vacation time. I spent those days in exploring near-by orchards, gardens, and fields, picking up fruit, vegetables, and berries, and other things that help to take the edge off a small boy's appetite.

I spent much time about the barns and stables with Thomas, the coachman. I was an expert listener, a rare talent, inherited from my father, no doubt. Thomas was a ready talker. This is a combination that never fails to make firm and lasting friendships, and we became friends. He was a veteran of our Civil War, had been on the losing side, and came out of it full of hatred, lead, and rheumatism. His heroes were not Lee or Stonewall Jackson, but Quantrell, the guerrilla, Jesse and Frank James, Cole and Bob Younger.

I never tired of listening to his war stories, and often found myself piecing them together in the schoolroom when I should have been active with my studies.

I believe I was the only boy at the school who never went away on holidays and vacations to visit parents or relatives. The Sister Superior, probably realizing that my life was a bit too drab, often gave me the privilege of going to the village for mail and papers. This was a rare treat, and much sought by all the boys. It meant a long walk, a stroll down the village street, a chance to see people, maybe to buy a fat sandwich, a bag of peanuts, or a bottle of pop – small things in a boy's life. It also meant authority and responsibility, good things for a boy. I looked forward to these journeys. I always had a little small silver, for spending, from my father.

The time passed quickly and pleasantly enough. I learned many prayers, practiced for singing in the church choir, and became an altar boy, serving the priest at mass. I liked learning the prayers and the Latin responses to the priest, but did not make much headway with my other studies.

I liked the dear, simple old priest to whom I made my first confession, and at times thought I would like some day to be a priest myself. Between my admiration for old Thomas, the coachman, with his stormy stories of the war, and my love for the quiet old priest, my mind was always pulling me this way and that – whether I should become a priest, or a soldier like Tommy, limping around with his short leg and his rheumatism.

One day when I was waiting for the mail I heard a nice old lady ask the postmaster whose boy I was.

He said, "That's one of the boys from the convent. You can tell them a block away. They are all perfect little gentlemen. They say 'Please' and 'Thank you.' I do not know how the Sisters do it, but they can surely bring boys up. I wish I could do it with mine."

When I returned with the mail I told the Superior what I heard the postmaster say about her and her boys. She seemed very much pleased, smiled, and said: "Boys are good when they are taught to say their prayers and to fear God." Shortly after, I was appointed "mailman." I went to the village every day after school. When the weather was fine I walked; if it was bad, I rode in or on the coach with Tommy. This was the first and only "appointment" of my life. I did not think it over then, but I know now I was not given it because I said "please" or my prayers – I got it because I had told the Superior the nice things the postmaster said. "Please" is a good word in its place; but it does not get one appointed to anything. It has a proper place in a small boy's vocabulary. And it is also much used by a certain class of prisoners and supplicants who are always "pleasing" somebody and are never pleasant to anybody.

Your capable beggar on the street does not say "please." He rips off his spiel in such exact and precise language that he gets your dime without it. You so admire his "art" that you do not miss the "please." His is an art. He omits the "please" because he knows you do not use it except when you want the mustard.

Looking back, it seems to me that our life in the convent was not properly balanced. We had none of the rough, boisterous times so dear to the small boy, no swimming, baseball, football. We were a little too cloistered, too quiet, too subdued. There was no wrestling, no boxing, no running and jumping and squabbling and shuffling and shouldering about. Of course I learned all those later. But I learned them quickly, too quickly – all in a bunch. That put me out of balance again. Those exercises should have been mixed in with my studies and prayers.

One stormy day I came out of the post office and as usual handed up the paper to Tommy, whose habit it was to glance at the headlines and return it to me. This day, however, he found something that interested him. He put the horses' lines between his legs and crossed his knees on them. I sat beside him on the box and shivered in the wind. He read on and on, column after column, then turned to an inner page, fighting the paper in the wind.

At last, and it seemed an hour, he folded it up carefully and returned it to me. "Good news to-day, Tommy?" "No, boy, no good news. Bad news, awful news, terrible news." He spoke in an awed voice, a voice that carried reverence. "Terrible news – Jesse James has been murdered, murdered in cold blood and by a traitor."

He fell silent and spoke to me no more that day. Later he told me many things about Jesse James. He worshipped him, and like many other good people of Missouri firmly believed that neither of the James boys ever fired a shot except in defense of their rights.

I delivered the mail and hastened to tell the other boys that Jesse James was dead, "murdered." Many of the older boys knew all about him – he was their hero, too – and the things they told me made me decide to get the paper and read his story myself. The next day, strangely enough, I passed the Superior's office when she was out to lunch. The paper was folded neatly, lying on some older papers on the corner of her neat desk. I walked in and took it. I put it away carefully, but many days passed before I got to the reading of it. I was so occupied with my duties as altar boy, and so busy with preparing for my first communion and learning new prayers, that the James boys and all other worldly things had no place in my mind.

Those were intense days. I lived in another world.

At last I found time to read my paper. On my way for the mail I slowly dug out the story of Jesse James' life and death, word by word. How I studied the picture of this bearded and be-pistoled hero! And the sketches of his shooting and the house in which it was done. Then came the story of his bereaved mother. How my boyish sympathy went out to her, as she wept for her loss and told the story of the lifelong persecution of her boys, Jesse and Frank, and how she feared that the hunted fugitive, Frank James, would also be dealt with in the same traitorous fashion. How I loathed the traitor, Bob Ford, one of the James boys gang, who shot Jesse when his back was turned, for a reward! How I rejoiced to read that Ford was almost lynched by friends and admirers of Jesse, and had to be locked in the strongest jail in the state to protect him from a mobbing. I finished the story entirely and wholly in sympathy with the James boys, and all other hunted, outlawed, and outraged men.

When I had done with the paper I passed it along to the other boys, who read it and handed it about till it was finally captured by the Superior. It was limp and ragged from usage. The Superior promptly traced it back to me. When asked where I got it, I told her I had taken it from her desk. I was lectured severely on the wrong of taking things without asking for them. I told her I did not ask for it because I was afraid she might refuse me. She said nothing, and did not offer to give me any, from which I understood that we were not to have papers. I was also relieved of my job as mailman. I was no longer to be trusted.

My teacher heard of my disgrace. She took me into her study, and we talked the thing over. The loss of my job was nothing; I would be going home soon, anyway. I must not feel bad about the lecture, I had done nothing wrong. I would have returned the paper, only the other boys wanted to read it. I discovered that she looked at it the same way I did.

She asked me if I wanted more papers. I was on fire for papers and told her so. She promised to get me one every day, and did. When I read it I returned it to her.

The James boys' story ran on for days and I followed it word for word, sympathizing with the hunted fugitive, Frank, wishing I were old enough and strong enough to find him and help him escape his pursuers and avenge his brother's death.

When that story was over I turned to other crime stories and read nothing else in the papers. Burglaries, robberies, murders – I devoured them all, always in sympathy with the adventurous and chance-taking criminals. I reconstructed their crimes in my boyish mind and often pictured myself taking part in them. I neglected my studies and prayers to rove about in fancy with such heroes as Jimmy Hope, Max Shinburn, and "Piano Charlie," famous "gopher men," who tunneled under banks like gophers and carried away their plunder after months of dangerous endeavor.

Looking back now I can plainly see the influence the James boys and similar characters had in turning my thoughts to adventure and later to crime.

THREE

AT last the day came for me to go home, for I had passed my fourteenth birthday and was too old to stay at the Sisters' School.

I wanted to kiss my favorite teacher good-by, but didn't quite dare do it. So I rode down to the station with Tommy, who bought me a fifty-cent knife, out of his salary, only twelve dollars a month, and went away to join my father.

Father took me back to the same hotel, to the same room. He had occupied it during the three years I had been away, and the only change was that he put a small bed in it for me. Everything was new and strange to me. Men coming and going all day, eating and drinking. Everything was noise and bustle, and it took me a few days to get used to this new life.

I found lots of papers lying around – some cheap novels, Police Gazettes, etc. – and I read them all, everything I could get hold of. I saw my father only at night, and occasionally we would take a walk then for an hour.

One evening as we were returning from our walk, we came upon a man whose team of horses was stalled in a mud hole. He was beating the horses, and cursing them with the most fearful oaths. I stopped still in my tracks and began praying for him. Father looked back, saw me standing still, and said: "What are you doing, John, listening to that mule skinner swear?"

I finished my prayer and caught up with him.

"You will learn to swear soon enough, John, without stopping to listen to these teamsters," he said a little severely.

In self-defense I told him I was not listening to the man, but praying for him. "The Sisters taught us to do that," I said. "They taught us to pray for all sinners."

Father wore a long beard, the custom of his day. When he was very thoughtful or vexed with some problem, he had a habit of twisting up the end of his beard into a pigtail. He would then put the pigtail between his teeth and chew on it.

After I explained what I had been doing, he looked at me strangely, twisted up his beard, put the end in his mouth, and began chewing. He took my hand, something he never did before, and we walked home in silence. He went straight upstairs, and I found some fresh papers, which I read downstairs. When I went up to go to bed he was sitting in his chair, staring at the wall and still chewing his beard. My coming aroused him. He said, "Good night, John," and we went to bed.

The next evening he came in as usual. He read his paper and I read whatever came to my hand. When we went upstairs, he said: "John, the Sisters taught you many prayers, did they?" "Yes, sir, all the prayers. I know them all," I said proudly.

"How about reading?" he asked. I read him a piece from a newspaper fairly well.

"And writing, John? Yes, I know you learned to write and spell. Your letters to me were very good. How's your arithmetic, John? How many are eight times nine, John?"

I was stuck. I hesitated and blushed. He saw my confusion and gave me an easier one. "Seven times six, John?"

I was stuck again and got more confused. "Start at the beginning, John, maybe you can get it that way."

I started at seven times one, got as far as seven times four, and fell down. This was torture. I think he saw it, too, for he said, "Oh, well, John, that will come to you later. Don't worry about it; just keep on trying."

He was a sharp at mathematics, and I think my failure to learn multiplication hurt him more than if he had caught me spelling bird with a "u," or sugar with two "gs." After a month of idleness it was decided that I should go to the district school, which had been built in our town while I was at the Sisters'. I got a new set of books and started bravely off.

We had a woman teacher, very strict, but fair to us all. I learned rapidly everything but arithmetic, which did not seem to agree with me, nor does it yet, for that matter. I also learned to play ball, football, marbles, and, I must admit, hooky, the most fascinating of all small-boy games. These new games, and so many other interesting new things, soon crowded the prayers into the background of my mind, but not entirely out of it. I said them no more at night and morning, nor any other time. But I still remember them, and I believe now, after forty prayerless years, I could muster a passable prayer if the occasion required it and there were not so many people about who could do it so much better.

After school, having no chores to do, I loitered around the hotel office. One day I found a dime novel entitled, "The James Boys," I seized upon it and devoured it. After that I was always on the lookout for dime novels. I found a place where they were sold. I would buy one and trade with some other boy when it was read. If I could not trade it, I took it back to the store and the woman gave me a five-cent one for it. The nickel one was just as thrilling, but shorter. I read them all. "Old Sleuth," "Cap Collier," "Frank Reade," "Kit Carson." Father saw me with them, but never bothered me. One day he brought me one of Fenimore Cooper's Leatherstocking tales. I read it and was cured of the five- and ten-cent novels. Between going to school and to the depot in the evening to see the train come in, and hanging around the hotel bar watching the town's celebrated ones, especially the "bad men" who had killed or shot somebody somewhere some time, I put in fairly busy days. The time flew.

I got to be quite looked up to by the other boys of my age. I "lived at the hotel," had "nobody to boss me around," didn't have to "run errands and chop kindling and go after the groceries and carry milk." When a new boy showed up, I was the one to show him around. I remember distinctly, now, that in less than a year after I left the Sisters, I was going down the street with a new boy when we came upon one of the town drunkards and bad men. I pointed him out with pride. "See that old fellow? That's old Beverly Shannon. He's been out to Leadville. He killed a man out there and nearly got hung. You ought to hear him swear when he gets drunk and falls down and nobody will help him up."

There was admiration in my voice. Our town was full of bad men. All had been in the war on one side or the other. Everybody had a pistol or two, and a shotgun or a rifle. Everybody knew how to use them. No small boy's outfit was complete without a pistol. Usually it was a rusty old "horse pistol," a cap-and-ball affair, some old relic of the Civil War. By a great stroke of fortune I got two of them. I was helping an old lady to move some things out of her cellar when we ran across them in a trunk.

"Lord, Lord," she said, "are those awful things here yet? I thought they had been thrown away years ago. Johnnie, take them out and bury them somewhere. Throw them away so I will never see them again."

These two old pistols made me feel important, established. I began to look about me. It was time I began to be somebody. My latest hero was the man that kept the bar in the hotel. He owned the building, leased the hotel, and ran the bar himself. He was a fat man, and he wore a fancy striped vest with a heavy gold watch chain across it and a twenty-dollar gold piece dangled from the chain for a charm. He had been out to California. It was the only twenty-dollar piece in the town. He was a small politician, the town fixer. When anybody got into any trouble and had to go before the justice of the peace, he went down to the hotel and saw "Cy" Near. Cy would say, "Leave it to me, that's all, leave it to me." When it was all over the fellow would come down to "Cy's" and order drinks for everybody in sight, several times. Then he would say, "What do I owe you, Cy"

"Owe me? Owe me for what?"

"Why, you know, Cy, for fixing up that little trouble."

"Oh, that's what you mean. Say, you don't owe me a thin dime, not a greasy nickel." Cy would wave a fat arm in the air. "I don't take money for helping my friends. I sell licker, good licker; that's my business."

The chap would buy a few more rounds of drinks, thank Cy again, and start for the door. Cy would shout, "Hey, George, I forgot to tell you. I'm rafflin' off a hoss an' buggy and you'd better take a half dozen tickets. You stand to win a good rig."

Around election time Cy would round up all the fellows he could, remind them that he had befriended them, and say, "What do we care who's President of the United States? What we want is a decent justice of the peace and town marshal."

I decided to pattern my life after Cy's. He was a popular, successful man. I began swinging my arms about, talking in a loud, hoarse voice, wearing my hat on the back of my head. Cy smoked big cigars. I tried one, and gave up the notion of smoking, at least for a while.

It was not long till my fancy for the saloon keeper changed. One evening when the train came in a single traveler got off. He was a tall, lean man, who walked like a soldier, erect and with a confident step. He had a short, stubby gray mustache. He wore a gray suit, a gray hat, and held a pair of gloves in his hand. He walked quickly toward the front of the train and waited by the baggage car till a trunk was tossed out. An express man near by was told to take the trunk over to the hotel.

I followed the gray man to the hotel. Presently the trunk was left in front and I went to inspect it. It was a leather trunk, with brass fittings, plastered over with stickers from many hotels and steamship lines. It was scratched and battered and travel-stained. The thing fascinated me. I stood around and felt it, read the stickers, some of them from foreign parts of the world, and wondered what kind of man he could be that possessed such a wonderful trunk.

I was restless and disturbed when the porter took it upstairs and out of my sight. It had roused strange thoughts and longings in my mind that I did not understand then. I know now that it suggested travel, adventure by land and sea – the world.

I now pulled my hat down from the back of my head and wore it properly. I straightened up, kept my hands out of my pockets, walked with a quick step, and assumed a confident, positive manner. I even began to think about a mustache, bristly, cut down like the gray man's. I must have a gray suit, gray hat, gloves, and a leather trunk. A big problem for a boy with no income.

I determined to earn some money and looked about for after-school work. After my father, I thought the saloon man, Cy, was the wisest man in our town. For some reason which I never could figure out, I did not submit the matter to my father, but went to the saloon man. Maybe it was because he was easier to talk to. We went over the situation carefully. There was no job in sight that either of us could think of. At last Cy said, "Well, if you're so crazy about a job, I'll make one for you."

Cy was a bachelor, and lived in a single room in the hotel. He opened and closed his bar, did all the work, was always drinking, but no one ever saw him drunk.

"You can come in here in the morning before school and clean the place up. Sweeping out ain't no man's job, anyway, and I'm tired of it. You can wash up the glasses and dust up around the bar. In the afternoon when you come home from school, you can be around in case there's any errands. At night you can look after the pool table, collect for the games, and see that they don't steal the balls. You can serve the drinks when there's a card game, and bring a new deck when some sore loser tears the old one up."

I was so grateful to Cy that I give him my very best "thank you." Here was a chance to get on in life, to have my own money, and be independent and mix around with men – to learn something of the world. I was so taken with this notion that I hunted up the broom, which was worn down to the strings, and began sweeping out the barroom. There were no customers in the place. Cy stood by, his hat on one side of his head, a big cigar in the opposite side of his mouth, hands in pockets, and eyed me thoughtfully. When I had the place about half swept out, Cy came over and took the broom out of my hands. He turned it about, examined it carefully. "Johnnie, I think you're on the square with me, and I'm going to be on the up and up with you. You go to the store and get yourself a new broom."

I did that, and swept the place all over again. Having started to work without my father's permission I decided to say nothing till I got well settled in my job. I had a feeling that he might veto the whole thing if I told him at the start, but if I waited a while and had a few dollars saved up he might let me continue.

Father knew Cy very well. On rare occasions he went into the bar and had a drink and a talk with him.

I worked faithfully, early and late. At the end of the week, in the afternoon when there was no customer about, Cy mysteriously beckoned me into his "office," a small closet of a room at one end of the bar. It was simply furnished – a table, a chair, a large spittoon, one picture on the wall opposite the desk. A picture of the mighty John L. Sullivan in fighting pose. Cy seated himself at the table, put on a pair of glasses, and drew out a small notebook. He looked carefully about the room. Seeing the door of his office open, he told me to close it.

To me Cy had always been much of a mystery. He had been "Out West" – to Leadville, Deadwood, and San Francisco. He owned the latest pattern of repeating rifle and a couple of "forty-fives." He played poker. I thought I was now to be initiated into some of the secret activities of his life. Maybe he would ask me to do something dangerous. Well, whatever, it was, I would do it. He wrote something in the notebook, then took three silver dollars out of his pocket and put them in my hand, carefully, without clinking them.

"Johnnie, this is pay day."

I went back to work happy. Pay day, three dollars of my own money. I would have a gray suit, gray hat, gloves, and a leather trunk in no time. I would soon be a tall, handsome, distinguished-looking gentleman, on Cy's money. I jingled my three dollars loudly and could hardly wait for my father to come home so I could tell him about my working and ask him to mind my money for me.

The possession of three dollars changed me at once. I became independent, confident, secure. When father came in I went to him without a single misgiving, feeling sure he would approve. I had my money in my hand and my spirit was high. I told him I had been working for Mr. Near all week; that I had three dollars in wages and wanted him to take care of them for me. He took the money and put it in his pocket, saying: "All right. Let me know when you want it."

"And you don't mind my working for Cy?"

"No. I don't mind. Cy told me all about it. You will have to learn to work some time. And you will have to learn lots of other things. So you may as well start at Cy's."

He turned to his paper, and I thought the thing was settled, but as I went out of the room I saw him twisting up the end of his long beard.

The school work was no trouble to me. I put in a year, and vacation time came along almost before I knew it. I was saving all the money I earned as assistant to Cy, and was looking forward to earning more during vacation. I brought home to my father a report from the school which seemed to show that I had made good progress. He glanced at the card and threw it to one side.

"I suppose you have the multiplication table this time, John?"

"Oh, yes, I learned it at last."

"How many are eight times nine, John?"

"Seventy-two, sir."

"Good. Seven times six?"

"Forty-two, sir."

"Correct, John."

He did not seem to be much interested in my correct and prompt answers; kept on looking at his paper. Finally he looked at me and said: "And eight times thirteen, John?"

I was stuck again. This one froze me stiff. I got mad, red in the face. I took pencil and paper out of my pockets, figured it out, and give him the result. It seemed that he was taking advantage of me. Nobody at school had ever asked me that question. I felt wronged. I thought of my money and my two big horse pistols. If I was to be treated in this way I would take my money and pistols and go away where I could get a square deal. And if I did not get a square deal, I'd take it.

Father looked at the paper I gave him. "Why, you have it right, John. That's good, very good." He was stroking his beard thoughtfully, and I could not tell whether he was smiling or making a face.

Vacation was almost over. I needed new books for the coming season and spoke to father about them one night.

"Never mind them now. We will see about them later. We are going away, going to Kansas City. I have been promoted after all these years."

"But I will lose my job," I demurred.

"I'll get you another job. Don't worry. Do you want a regular job, working all day, or would you like to go to school some more?"

I decided to have an all-day job, and let the school go.

"All right," he said, "we'll see about it."

My father made no fuss about leaving the small town where he had spent ten years of his life. He had no close friends or cronies. After my mother died, he seldom spoke to any one but me, and I think he was glad to go away. He was a cold, hard, silent Scotch-Irishman. He took no part in social doings, never went to church, belonged to no clubs; nor was he enough interested in politics to become a citizen and exercise the high privilege of voting on election day.

My good-bys did not take much time. Cy was sorry to have me go. He laboriously wrote me a fine letter of recommendation which he gave me along with a large, worn silver watch, that wound with a key. It weighed almost a pound, and I was proportionately proud of it. My boy friends envied me in going away to a big city and impressed upon me the necessity for taking my pistols with me. Unnecessary advice; I had no intention of leaving them behind.

And last of all I hunted up old Beverly Shannon, the bad man. He was a hooknosed old man with hard eyes and a long chin whisker dripping tobacco juice. He had worn the Northern blue, and drew a small pension for a "bad leg." Times when he was half drunk, limping around town in search of more drinks, some one would say: "Look Out, 'Bev.' You're limpin' on the wrong leg." This always brought a string of eloquent curses from him, and a warning that they had "better be keerful. I hain't stopped killin' jest 'cause Abe Lincoln says the war's over."

In those days all roads led to the harness shop, and there "old Bev" was always to be found when sober, outside the shop on a bench under a tree. There he met all the droughty farmers and entertained them with war stories and tales of his wanderings "out West." He was always invited to drink with them. His pension kept him in food. His life held no serious problem.

I found him on his bench, sober and sorry for it. He passed the time of day with me, and I told him I was going away and had come to say good-by.

"Goin' to the city, huh? Well, don't let 'em rub it into you. You ain't a very strong boy." He was a foxy old man. He leered at me out of his cunning eyes. "Have you got any shootin' irons?" Long John Silver, the pirate, could not have done any better in the way of complimenting a boy. I was fairly hooked. I assured him that I was well heeled, having two pistols.

"That's good. You'll git along all right. Now you run along. I've got to git me a farmer. I ain't had my whisky yet."

I hastily dug up enough silver out of my small pocket money for a couple of drinks, and gave it to him. As I went away I thought he looked like an old spider watching his web for a fly.

FOUR

IN his new position father was forced to travel much, often leaving me to my own devices for weeks and sometimes months. I was put up at a small boarding house kept by a widow, who had two children. She was over-worked, sickly, and cranky. She had half a dozen boarders. Before he left, father gave me the money I had saved up, and told me to look about for a job.

There was nobody at the hotel that interested me. The widow was always whining and I kept away from her. Her children were too small for company, and I saw nothing of the other boarders except at meal-times when they ate much and talked little.

The widow gave me a trunkful of books she had taken for a board bill. Among them I found a battered old volume of Dumas' "The Count of Monte Cristo," on which I put in many nights. This sharpened my appetite for reading, and I went around secondhand bookstores, and got hold of the D'Artagnan tales and devoured them. Then "Les Miserables," and on to the master, Dickens. The books so fired me with the desire for travel, adventure, romance, that I was miserable most of the time. As my money dwindled I resolved to find a job. I'd ask the landlady for advice.

I found her out in front, scrubbing the steps, red in the face and vicious looking. I told her I was thinking of going to work.

"Well, it's about time you thought of that," she snapped, "layin' around here readin' and eatin' up your father's money. You can get a job just like I did when my husband run off and left me with two brats on my hands. I just started out and asked for it at every place I come to till I got it, that's all. And you can do it, too, if you got the gizzard."

I left her and started my search. If there was a job in the city I determined to get it. I went through block after block, store after store, hour after hour. I got mostly "Noes" but some answered pleasantly, taking my name and address. I kept going until one morning I stopped in front of a cigar store – a dead-looking place, no customers. A man was reading a paper spread out on the counter. I went in and put my question to him. When he stood up I saw he was very tall and very thin. He looked sick. I had never seen an eye like his. It attracted me strangely. I could not have described it then, but I can now. It was a larcenous eye. He was very nice, asking many questions. How old was I? Did I ever work before? Where?

I handed him Cy's letter. He read it and asked me more questions. I have never answered so many questions since, except in a police station. At last he quit, and snapping himself together like a man coming out of a trance, he rapped his knuckles on the counter.

"I'll tell you what I'll do with you, kid. You come down here at nine o'clock every morning, open this joint up, and stay here till one o'clock. Then I come on and you go off till six in the evening. At six you come on and stay till ten, and call it a day. You can go to work right now. The sooner the better. In a week you will know the prices of the different things as well as I do, and I can leave you by yourself. Your wages will be three dollars a week and all the cigars you can smoke."

"But I do not smoke."

"Well, that's your bad luck, kid, not mine. What do you say? Want to chance the job?"

I got right in behind the counter and he showed me the different cigars, cigarettes, and tobaccos, and told me their prices. In a week I knew all about the "store" and had learned to serve the few customers that came in, and to make change properly. I further learned that the store was but a "front" or blind for a poker game and dice games in the back room, and that I was a part of the "front." My business was to sweep the place out in the morning, stand behind the counter in case any one wanted a cigar, and to keep an eye out for "new coppers on the beat" in the evening. The job was interesting. I soon came to know the poker players, crap shooters, and dice sharks who brought their victims into the back room to "clean" them. I often spent my afternoons in the back room watching the games and learning the life.

When there was no game, the sharks sat around practicing their tricks and bewailing their bad luck. Sometimes a poker player would show me how to "shuffle up a hand," or cut the cards at a given place or "go out" with a hand. The dice shakers and crap shooters showed me their favorite "shots." I was an apt scholar, absorbing everything like a young sponge. "Tex," my boss (if he had any other name I never heard it), admonished me never to gamble. "Lay away from it, kid; it's a tough racket. Look at me and my gatherings of forty years. I ain't got a white quarter to my name; if it was rainin' soup I couldn't buy myself a tin spoon, and I've got a string of debts longer than a widow's clothesline."

Next door to the cigar store there was a small milk depot kept by a man and his wife. I used to go in every day for a glass of milk, and got acquainted with them. He delivered milk around his routes and the wife minded the shop. He was forever complaining about not being able to collect his money from "them women." "Them women" were women who kept "parlor houses" in the Tenderloin district a few blocks from his milk store. They were good pay, but he could not get away from his work at the right hour to find them.

One day he told me he would pay me well if I would take the bills and go to the places and stay till I got the money. Here was a chance to earn more money, and I grabbed it. I went in and asked Tex, my boss, when would be the best time to call at those places to collect the milk bills.

If Tex had not gathered much of worldly goods in his forty years, he had at least learned something of the habits of "them women." "I'll tell you," he said. "If you go in the morning you'll find them asleep; in the afternoon they are out riding or shopping; and at night they will be either too busy or too drunk. Take my advice and go about five o'clock in the evening and you will catch them at dinner, or breakfast, or whatever they call it."

I followed Tex's advice that evening and collected three bills out of five. The milkman was pleased with my enterprise and gave me a dollar. Thereafter I collected his bills in the Tenderloin. I visited certain places weekly and was paid promptly. The women I met were nice to me, and I saw nothing of the other side of their lives. I worked faithfully at my two jobs, saved my money, and began looking in the store windows for my gray suit and gray hat. My work kept me so busy that I did not read much. Thoughts of travel and adventure were in the back of my mind, but that could wait. I was young; I must have money first. My two old, rusty pistols, almost forgotten now, lay neglected in the bottom of my little valise.

Tex had a "run of luck" and raised me to four dollars a week. I collected more bills for the milkman. Some of them he called "bad bills." I kept after them persistently and nearly always got the money. The more hopeless the bill, the greater my commission was. I enjoyed going after them. The Tenderloin women were sure pay; and poor families were good, always had the money ready. I called on a tough saloon man, in a dingy little dive, about ten times to collect a two-dollar bill.

One day when I called he was serving several men at his bar, and when he saw me he said: "No use commin' in here with that bill, kid. I ain't goin' to pay it. If your boss comes up here I'll bust him in the nose. His milk is no good and he's no good."

"Mister," I said, "I know he is no good, but I have to work and want to keep my job. If you knew just how hard my boss is you would feel sorry for me instead of being angry. He is so hard and no good that he told me if I did not collect your bill of two dollars to-day I need not come to work to-morrow, and that's why I'm here."

The customers looked at me. I stood my ground.

"Hell," said the man, "I didn't think he was that bad. Here, take the lousy money."

I hurried back to the milkman. "Here's Mr. Finucane's two dollars."

"How on earth did you ever collect it?"

"Oh, he just got tired and paid me, that's all."

"Well, I'll make you a present of them," said he handing me the money. "You certainly earned them."

The following week I called at Madam Kate Singleton's with my bill. The colored maid who opened the door showed me a seat in the hall and told me to wait. The madam was dressing. I sat there a few minutes and there was a ring at the door. The maid opened it and an excited little man brushed in, followed by two big men who were not a bit excited. As the door was closing I got a glimpse of a policeman in uniform on the steps.

One of the two men spoke to the maid who went upstairs, and in a minute the madam came down. She waved the men into a room off the hall and closed the door. I listened, but they talked too low for me to hear what they were saying. Presently the madam opened the door and called out: "Oh, girls, come downstairs every one of you." Half a dozen girls appeared as if by magic. They were all brought into the room and the door closed again.

Nobody paid any attention to me. Now I heard loud voices in the room, but so many were talking at once that I could make nothing of it. Then one of the big men came out, went to the front door, opened it, and said to the policeman: "Send Mike around to the back; tell him to let nobody out. I'll phone for the wagon. We'll have to take them all to the station. They won't talk."

He disappeared into the room. I got up and opened the front door.

"Where are you goin'?" said the policeman.

"I'm going out, if you please."

"Get back in there, if you please," he snarled, "and stay there."

While the officers were waiting for the wagon one of the big men went upstairs and brought down two "guests." They were about half awake and looked as if they had been on a drunk. They sat down beside me on the settee. One of them fell into a sound sleep and the other sat with his elbows on his knees and his hands on the sides of his head. Neither of them spoke. In a few minutes the wagon arrived. The girls were all ordered to go out and get in it, which they did. Then the two men and I were ordered to do the same. The madam and one of the big men got into a hack that appeared to be waiting and drove away.

The excited little man who had caused all the trouble got into the wagon with the other big man and sat beside him.

When I was being put in the wagon I protested and tried to explain, but the detectives roughly ordered me to shut up. The "harness cop" who had been at the front door went back to his beat. I did not see anything of Mike, who had been ordered to stay at the back door.

The girls laughed and joked on the way to the station and shouted "rubberneck" at everybody that looked in at the back of the open wagon. The police station was on one corner of Market Square, one of the busiest corners in the city. Hundreds of people were there daily, selling their produce. Their time was about evenly divided between serving their customers and watching the patrol wagon spewing its loads of humanity into the city prison. It seemed to me they were all there as we were unloaded and hurried through a solid lane of them into the police station. Madam Singleton was there before us, and with her was a tall, sharp-looking man, gray and about fifty. I never found out who he was, but he looked like a lawyer.

The madam, the tall man, and the two big men, who were plainclothes detectives, went to one side, talking earnestly for a minute or two. The rest of us just stood there and waited. One of the detectives went into an office off the big room we were in, and came out at once with a man in uniform he called "captain." The captain was a big, red-faced, gray-haired, good-natured Irishman. "Well, what's this all about?" he said, smiling. The detective stepped over to the small, nervous man and said to the captain:

"Captain, this man complains that one of the girls in Kate Singleton's place took one hundred dollars, two fifty-dollar bills, from him some time last night or this morning. We went down to her place and saw the girl. She denies that she took it.

"We searched her room and couldn't find it. The balance of them don't know anything, so they say. He wants them all searched. We couldn't do it there, so we pinched everybody in the house and here they are, ten of 'em, seven women and three men."

The captain took the little man in hand. "Who are you?" The little man hesitated.

"Come on, out with it. If you want any help here you've got to come clean."

The little man gave him a name. I could not hear it.

"Where are you from?"

"Emporia, Kansas, is my town."

"What do you do for a living?"

"I'm a hog raiser."

"When did you come to the city?"

"Yesterday morning."

"What did you come here for?"

"Oh, just to look around."

The captain smiled. "How much money did you have when you got off the train here yesterday morning?"

"I had two hundred dollars in paper money and some small change."

"How much have you spent since you arrived here?"

"I spent twenty-five dollars for a suit of clothes and fifteen dollars for an overcoat. I paid a dollar for a room and I spent about five dollars around town."

"Is that all? Are you sure, now? Think again."

"Yes, that's all," said the hog man.

"You're a liar," Madam Singleton said in a cold, level voice.

"You gave Julia ten dollars."

"Now, now, Kate," said the captain, "don't get excited. I'll take care of this thing all right." Then to the hog man:

"Guess you forgot about that ten dollars, hey?"

"Yes, I forgot that," he said meekly.

"All right; now, how much have you in your pockets?"

He took out some bills and counted them. "Forty-five dollars is all I have."

The captain counted them and returned them. "That's correct. Now, which girl took your money?"

The man pointed out the youngest girl of the bunch. She was about twenty or twenty-two, a plump girl with a boyish face and lots of black hair. She was pleasant looking, but not pretty, and she did not look as worn and tired as the others.

She looked straight at him but never opened her mouth. The lawyer-looking man said to her: "Julia, did you take that man's money?"

"No," she answered.

"Take all these women in and have the matron search them. Madam Singleton, you have no objection to being searched, have you?" smiled the captain.

"None at all, captain, only make it short and sweet. I am losing time and money here."

They all trooped off to a room down the hall.

An officer came out from behind the desk and searched me and the two drunks. We had no fiftydollar bills, so he told us to sit on a bench in front of his desk. The lawyer, or bondsman, or fixer, or whatever he was, paced up and down the room nervously. The captain had gone back to his office.

In a few minutes a big, mannish-looking woman with red hands and a tough walk came along.

"Well, what did you find?" said the lawyer.

"Nothing. They didn't have a hundred dollars among them."

The lawyer then hunted up the detective and the hog man. The detective got the captain. The matron made her report and the officer who searched me and the other two did the same.

The captain turned to the hog man.

"All these people have been searched and your money has not been found. What do you want to do now?"

"I want that girl locked up. I know she got my money. I know I had two fifty-dollar bills rolled up with my other bills when I went into that house, and when I got to my room I looked at my money and they were gone."

"How long was it before you got to your room after you left Madam Singleton's?" asked the lawyer.

"Oh, I walked around for an hour or two."

"Oh, you did, eh? Why, you probably had your pocket picked on the street."

The big captain roared out a laugh and said to the lawyer:

"It must have been an Emporia, Kansas, pickpocket. No Missouri dip would take his roll, extract two fifty-dollar bills, and put the rest back in his pocket."

The lawyer appeared to get angry. "You've searched everybody but me."

He turned to the hog man fiercely. "Do you want me searched?"

"No, I don't."

"Well, I want you searched. You are just the kind of a yap that gets up in the middle of the night and hides his money so carefully that he has to have a policeman find it for him in the morning. Go ahead and search him," he said to the detective.

"All right, go ahead," said the hog man.

The detective went through his trousers carefully, placing everything on a counter, then through his vest, then into his inner coat pocket. No money. Then, as an afterthought, just to make a good job of it, he felt in the coat pockets. In the first one was a bag of tobacco, and as he pulled a handkerchief from the last coat pocket two bills fluttered to the floor.

The lawyer stooped, picked up the two bills, looked at them, and handed them to the captain. The hog man's eyes bulged till they looked ready to fall out of his head. He was making a dry noise down in his throat that sounded like the quack of a duck. The captain handed him the bills.

"Is this your money?" he scowled.

After inspecting the bills and recovering his voice, the hog man said: "Yes, I think it is."

The lawyer plucked him by the lapel with one hand, and shook the other in his face. "You dirty little swine, get your property off that counter. Get out of here and back to your hog pastures before I have you locked up."

The dazed and thoroughly crushed victim hastily gathered up his things and went out with them in his hands.

I was pop-eyed with amazement at this swift, smashing reversal of the situation. The two drunks beside me were but mildly interested. Nobody, from the captain down to Julia, the accused, seemed surprised. I could not understand why the whole crowd did not fall on the hog man and tear him to pieces. The captain disappeared into his office. The detective walked out to the sidewalk. The lawyer turned to Kate and the girls, bowing:

"Madam, and ladies, shall we depart?"

"It's about time," said the madam in a positive voice. "I'm hungry enough to eat a raw dog."

They all moved out into the street. I was left on the bench with the two drunks. The detective strolled back in. The desk man pointed to us.

"What will I do with this outfit, Hayes?"

Hayes appeared to be disgusted. "Oh, charge them with drunk."

"The kid's not drunk."

"Vag him then."

"What were you doing in that joint, anyway?" to me.

"I went in there to collect a milk bill, sir, and was waiting for the money when all this happened."

"Where is the bill?"

I produced it.

"Do you work for this man?" he asked, after inspecting it.

"Yes, sir."

"Why in hell didn't you say so at the start?"

"I tried to, sir, but everybody told me to shut up. The policeman would not let me go out."

He turned to the drunks and asked them if they had ten dollars to put up for bail to appear in the morning. They had, and the desk man took them into another room. I saw them no more. When he came back, Hayes said: "Take the kid upstairs: lock him up with George. I'll find out about him."

The women were gone, the drunks were out, and I was the only one detained. It looked all wrong to me. The sergeant took me down to the end of the hall and opened an iron door. It was as if he had opened the door to hell. My blood stopped circulating. We stepped inside and he locked the door behind us. Never since, except perhaps in the half dreams of opium, have I been so frozen with horror. We were standing on a balcony overlooking the half basement that served as the city prison. In front of us was a latticework iron door that opened on an iron stairway leading down into the cell house. The cells were built around the four sides of a cement-floored square, and opened into it. It was supper time and pandemonium was on.

The sergeant rapped on the iron door with his heavy keys, trying to attract the attention of some one below. Failing to make himself heard, he told me to stay there till he could get a "trusty" to take me upstairs. He went out the way we came in, and left me locked in between the two doors on the balcony. The cells below had all been thrown open and there were about fifty prisoners in the open space. They seemed to be about equally divided between negroes and whites, of all ages. The air choked me; it was putrid, heavy, and thick with the stench of foul food, foul clothes, foul bodies, and foul sewers. In the farthest corner of the square a gigantic black was standing guard over a huge smoking caldron.

He was shirtless and barefoot. A leather belt supported his overalls, his only clothing. Sweat glinted on his broad back and chest. He was armed with a long-handled ladle which he dished out the "stew" with, or beat back the stronger and more venturesome prisoners who crowded too closely around the caldron.

I saw no jailers or guards. There was no pretense at order. The younger and stronger men shoved and elbowed their way to the big stew pot, snarling and snapping at each other like a pack of starved dogs. Old men and young boys stood around waiting meekly for the strong to be fed first.

The big negro wielded his ladle, filling the tin pans nearest him. Bread was being served from a large box in another spot, but there appeared to be plenty of it and there was no scramble there. Several new-looking prisoners walked about, making no effort to get food. They were "fresh fish," new arrivals, who had not yet acquired the "chuck horrors," that awful animal craving for food that comes after missing half a dozen meals.

At last the weaker ones were served. The cursing, shouting, and fighting were stilled. The big negro wheeled his stew pot away and the empty bread box disappeared. Some of the prisoners went into their cells to eat; some sat down outside on the floor, while others ate standing. Some had spoons, others ate with their fingers, sopping at the bottom of the pan with a piece of bread.

The meal was quickly over. The tin pans, unwashed, were thrown into the cells. The young negroes began singing and buck dancing. White men who had been tearing at each other ten minutes before around the big pot were now laughing and talking in a friendly fashion, and everybody lit up a smoke. The air was so filled with tobacco smoke and steam from the stew that I could barely distinguish forms below.

It was growing dark and gas jets were lighted but gave no light. I heard a rattling of keys; somewhere some one shouted "Inside." The shadowy forms shuffled into their cells, and there came the tremendous din of iron doors being slammed shut. The prison was locked up for the night.

I do not know how long I had been standing there. Not more than fifteen minutes, but it seemed a lifetime. A trusty prisoner appeared at my side.

"Come on, you."

I followed him up a short stairway where he opened a door and we went into a short hall with cells on either side. It was directly above the city prison. As we passed down the hall I heard women's voices; one of them shouted, "Fresh fish, girls."

Faces appeared at the barred doors. A colored girl, as we passed her cell, said : "Hello, boy, what you-all been doin' ?"

At the end of the hall the trusty stopped at a large room with a barred door. I could look inside. The room was well lighted. Newspapers were lying about. I saw two clean-looking cots, a table on which were books and a box of cigars, and a couple of chairs.

A man was pacing up and down the room, smoking. He wore a comfortable-looking pair of slippers and was in his shirt sleeves. He paid no attention to us till the trusty said: "George, the skipper sent up some company for you."

He turned sharply and came to the door. He was a fine-looking man about forty years of age, well groomed, fresh shaven. He was tall. His hair was gray. His face was pleasant to look at. He might have been a doctor or lawyer. I found myself wondering what he could have done to get locked in a jail. He looked at me carefully for a minute. When he spoke his voice was surprisingly pleasant. There was a suggestion of the South in his drawl.

"I don't want to hurt your feelings, kid, but if you are lousy don't come in here, that's all."

The trusty assured George that I was not lousy, that there was no charge against me and I would be out in an hour or two.

I was locked in.

I had no jail manners then, so I just stood at the door with my hat on, intending to wait there till some one came to let me go. All prisoners do that the first time. Presently my companion told me to take my hat off and sit down, and try to be comfortable.

"You may get out in an hour and you may not. You never can tell. You are beginning young. How old are you?"

"Sixteen."

"What are you pinched for?"

I told him all about it.

"That's everyday business here," he said. "Usually the sucker is a married man and can't squawk. But when he does squawk, like this one, the only thing to do is to blow back his money. Either the lawyer or one of the girls eased it into his coat pocket. That's better than returning it to him and admitting that they tried to rob him.

"The whole thing was a stand-in from the captain down. Everybody's satisfied. The sucker has his money, the girls are all out, Kate will charge Julia fifty dollars for the lawyer's fee, and that ends it.

"You appear to be the only real sucker in the bunch. By God! Those coppers are fierce. They'll leave you here till you rot. I've always said a copper is a copper till you cut his head off."

He got a tin cup and scraped it across the bars of the door. The trusty bounced in. "Go down and get the desk sergeant."

I never saw a prisoner get quicker action. The sergeant came at once.

"It's a rotten shame to keep this kid locked up, Sam. Did you hear his story? Go down and get Hayes and tell him to let him go home. Send a messenger to his boss. I've got plenty of money down there; charge it to me."

The sergeant went out, promising to "look into it right away." Our cell – it was more like a room – was in a small corridor set apart for the women prisoners' quarters. Down the hall I could hear them calling to each other and chatting back and forth from their cells. Somewhere a colored woman was singing a mournful dirge about "That Bad Stackalee." The verses were endless. The point of the song seemed to be that the negro bully, Stackalee, had been killed with "a big forty-four gun over a damned old Stetson hat." In the most harrowing tones at the end of every verse the singer moaned the sad refrain, "That ba-a-d Stackalee."

Later I came to know that this song is a favorite among negroes when in great trouble, such as being locked in jail, being double-crossed by a friend, or parting with their money in a dice game. At such times thirty or forty verses of "Stackalee" invariably restores the laughing good humor and child-like confidence of the wronged one.

We heard a rattling of keys and a door opening. George put the side of his face against the cell door, so he could see down the hall.

"Get your hat, kid; here they are."

The detective came up with my two bosses – the milkman and Tex, the gambler. The trusty opened the door.

"Out you go," said the detective, "and the next time you get jammed up say something before you get thrown in. Holler before you're hurt; that's my motto."

I said good-by to my benefactor, George, and thanked him awkwardly. When I met him years after and had a chance to return his kindness, I learned he was a most distinguished criminal; a man who had stolen fortunes and spent them, who had killed a crooked pal, and served many prison sentences.

"Forget it, kid, and don't let them scare you out of your job. You go right back next week and collect your bills."

Tex and the milkman escorted me to the cigar store. The evening games had not started when we went into the back room, so I told my story again. The milkman sympathized and promised to raise my commission on the bills. Tex was relieved to learn that I had not mentioned his "store" to the police.

Collection day came around again, and I made my rounds without incident till I got to Madam Singleton's, the last place. A colored maid, the only person that escaped arrest the week before, opened the door.

When she saw me she screamed at the top of her voice:

"Oh, Miss Kate, here's the pore milk boy."

"Bring him right up here, Jo, this minute."

The maid led me upstairs, then down a hall and to the madam's room. She was in the midst of dressing for the evening, but when I appeared in the door she stopped, kicked a bunch of clothes to one side, came over and, putting her arm around me, led me into the room.

"Well, you poor boy," she patted my back. "We are ashamed to face you after going off and forgetting you in jail. Julia thought of you about nine o'clock that night, and I sent down word right away about you. They said you were out and gone home. We never expected to see you again. You must have dinner with us. It's ready now, and Julia wants to apologize to you. Not that it was her fault," she added quickly. "It was just something that couldn't be helped. Those men from the country are always – ah – misplacing their money. We are continually having trouble with them."

She was so charming and friendly and natural, so different from the crabby widow at my boarding house, the only woman I had any contact with, that I found myself wondering if George had not been too severe in judging them.

She went on with her dressing, and I looked about the room curiously. I had a dim recollection of my mother's room – a plain bed, a bureau, a big rockingchair, and a rag carpet. I had looked into the widow's room at the boarding house, too. That was plainer than my mother's. It had a cheap, single bed; a packing case covered with a sheet, and a cracked mirror propped against the wall served as a bureau. There was a hard-looking chair at the head of the bed. There was no carpet on the widow's floor.

Madam Singleton's room had carpets an inch thick, and the biggest, softest bed and the fattest pillows you could imagine. Her bureau was half as large as the bed, but seemed too small for the things piled on it – boxes, bottles, brushes, combs, pieces of jewelry, and a hundred other articles I had never seen and could not guess the use of. Mirrors were everywhere; from where I sat I could see my face, my profile, or my back. A huge trunk, as big as a bungalow it looked, was in a corner. Its top was thrown back and the tray was on the floor. It was piled high with letters and cards and photos of men. The trunk was overflowing with stockings, garters, ribbons, feathers, and soft, silky-looking garments. My eyes strayed into the open door of a closet. It was full of coats and cloaks, long and short, some of fur of different colors, and others of expensive cloth. Wide rimmed and feathered hats hung everywhere, and the carpet was half covered with shoes, slippers, sandals, gloves, and silk dresses. Over everything hung the odor of perfume. Years after I heard Madam Singleton described as a very beautiful woman. When she turned from her mirror, I thought she looked as a queen ought to look.

Tall, straight, dark-haired with big, brave black eyes; warm, full of color, glowing; a dominating woman.

I heard a small bell tinkling downstairs.

"That means dinner, young man. Come with me."

FIVE

"GIVE me a name, any name you like," said the madam as we went downstairs "I want you to meet my girls. They'll all be glad to see you again.

I had but one name then, so I gave her that, and was introduced to the girls who were waiting in the dining room, the same six girls that had been arrested. If they noticed my embarrassment they did not show it. Two or three of them nodded, looked at me half curiously, half amused; the others, excepting Julia, did not even glance at me. She came over to where I stood, put her arms about my neck, and kissed me.

"Oh, you poor kid, I never felt so sorry for any thing in my life."

I was seated between the madam and Julia. The dinner was a marvel – fried chicken, hot biscuits, green vegetables. Beer was served, but I did not like it and the maid got me milk. The madam and Julia were the only ones that ate heartily. The others picked at their food, yawned, and looked at each other with low-lidded, feline calculating glances, seldom speaking. They looked and acted tired, worn, old, frustrated, disappointed. A big dark woman opposite me got a bottle from the sideboard and poured herself a drink of something.

"Now, my dear, be careful," said the madam.

"Why didn't you say that a year ago, Miss Kate?"

She took a piece of chicken in her fingers and went into a room across the hall where she played "Annie Rooney" on the piano and sang with her mouth full of food. Two others got up and went out. A blond girl pushed her chair back, lighted a cigarette, and began doing her fingernails. The maid came and whispered to another, who jumped up quickly and disappeared.

Julia had finished the chicken and was crunching the bones between her strong white teeth. The last of the tired-looking girls stood up, put her foot on a chair, and ran her arm, elbow deep, into her stocking. She came up with a small roll of bills which she threw across the table to the madam, sullenly. "Thank the Lord that's over," she said, and went out.

The madam counted the money carefully, bent over, and put both her arms under the table; when she straightened up the money had disappeared.

Julia chattered away and ate everything in sight. She wanted to know if I had ever lived in the country, if I could ride a horse, if I had ever caught a fish, if I could "shoot off a revolver."

The dinner was over and I was thinking about my milk bill. After this wonderful hour I hesitated about presenting it to the madam. She may have seen what was in my mind, for she said, "Julia, you have talked so much to this boy that he has forgotten what he came here for."

"I'm not done talking yet, Miss Kate. You know Sunday is my day out, and I've made up my mind to have a horseback ride in the country. I've been wanting to do that ever since I came here and here is my chance. The kid here can ride, and I'll take him with me. If you'll go," turning to me.

I hesitated.

"Oh, come on. I'll pay for the horses and everything, and see that you get back before dark," she laughed.

"All right, I'll go," I said.

Julia looked at the madam. "Oh I have no objection, Julia. You'll be out of mischief for one day and you're just a couple of kids, anyway."

She took my bill, gave me the money and went out.

Julia was hopping around like a sparrow. "Let's see," she said. "You be here Sunday morning at, oh, ten o'clock. No, not here, that's no good. Be at the drug store down on the corner at ten. I'll meet you there."

I promised to be there and departed. On my way home I passed the police station and pictured in my mind the inferno inside – the big negro swinging his ladle above the snarling, cursing horde of half-starved prisoners in the stinking bowels of the city prison.

At Madam Singleton's my boyish mind had not grasped the greater tragedy. Fresh air, light, meat, drink, and music – that was all I saw there then. But the tired women were prisoners more hopeless than the savage men fighting for food in the jail. The bodily comforts they had at Madam Singleton's but served to tighten their shackles. Life-timers of society, they were slowly sinking without a straw to grasp at.

The time flew till Sunday. I looked over my clothes and wished I had my gray suit and gray hat. I had saved my money but had not enough yet to buy them.

I was apprehensive about meeting Julia. I could picture her coming into the drug store for me in a dashing big hat, rustling silk dress, expensive shoes, all powdered, perfumed, and painted as she was in Madam Singleton's. And me with my pants too short, my coat sleeves way up my wrists, and my shirt open at the collar. I wanted to go, but at times my heart failed me, and when I went to bed the Saturday night before I was

still undecided, hesitating.

Sunday morning I got up early, determined to face the thing. I also settled another matter that had disturbed my mind of late. I got a shave. I walked around till I found an idle barber in his empty shop. He fixed me up with as much ceremony as if I had been an old customer.

At ten I was at the drug store, and Julia was inside, waiting. I had to look twice to be sure of her. She wore a faded blue tailored suit, a wide-rimmed straw sailor hat with a ribbon, and a pair of worn but substantial shoes. No powder or paint, nothing to remind me of Madam Singleton's.

"Don't pay any attention to my clothes." She saw me looking at them. "These are the ones I had on when I went there. I have lots of others, but Miss Kate won't let me wear them when I go out unless I am with her. I owe her so much money she is afraid I'll run away. All the girls owe her. They are always in debt to her; that's the way she keeps them there."

We hunted up a livery stable near by. A big, good-natured fat man was in charge, and we told him we wanted some gentle saddle horses. He looked at Julia. She had a cocky air, and acted more like a boy than a girl.

"Do you want to ride straddle-legged, gal? If you do, I've got some of them bloomer things."

Julia did not blush or stammer. "No, I don't want to ride straddle. What do you think I am anyway? She was angry. "You get me a riding habit and a side saddle and mind your own business."

He went after the horses.

"We'll go down to the river, get the ferry, and go over into the woods. I hope we find some place to eat over there. I am hungry already," she said.

I had been too occupied to think of breakfast and was hungry, too, and suggested that we go across the street and get a bite. When we came back the horses were ready. The fat man boosted Julia up into her saddle, and we dashed off like Indians. Our way to the river led past Miss Kate's. When we were in front of it Julia pulled up her horse, and we stopped.

"They are all dead to the world in there except Jo, the colored girl. They won't get up till four this afternoon. God, what a place! How I hate to go back there!"

The treacherous April showers came on us when we got into the country and drove us into a deserted cabin on an abandoned weed-grown farm. I built a fire in the old fireplace. We found a couple of homemade three-legged stools in a corner and in a box nailed to the wall there was the greasiest pack of cards I ever saw. We got a board that we put on the stools, making a table, and played casino. The roof leaked in a hundred places, the cabin was full of smoke, the rain beat in from all sides, and

Julia won every game. She chattered away through it all, and hoped there would be "a regular cyclone." Discouraged, I threw the cards in the fire. We were half wet and watery eyed from the smoke, the horses pawed restlessly in the leaky shed behind the cabin. Julia laughed at me and accused me of being a bad loser. I couldn't think of anything else, so I said: "Oh, I'm half starved, and there's nothing to eat within miles of here.'

She was just a healthy young animal, always hungry like myself, and the thought of food, especially when it was so far away, started her to raving. Nothing would do but we must head for home. The afternoon was half gone, the rain let up, and the sun shone again. I stamped and beat out the fire.

Julia climbed upon a tree stump in front of the cabin, where she got into her riding habit. I brought her horse around and she leaped to the saddle like an acrobat. The horses, homeward bound, needed no urging. We let them go as fast as they liked, and in the evening pulled up safely in front of the livery stable, where Julia insisted on paying the bill. The fat man reached for the money I proffered, but she snatched it out of my hand and made him take hers.

"This is on me," she said, returning my money, "and so is the dinner. Come on, let's find a good place to eat."

The fat man looked at me slyly, started to say something, but changed his mind. He was afraid of Julia.

Any place is a good place to eat when one is young and hungry, and not burdened with money. We wasted no time looking, but went into the first restaurant we came to. Neither did we haggle over the menu card. Julia found chicken, and there we stopped. She never seemed to get enough of it. The dinner was a long time coming; she popped her head out of the box every minute looking for the busy waiter.

"I wonder what's happened to him. He has either dropped dead or the police came and arrested him," she was saying when he appeared. We fell on the dinner and devoured it like a couple of hired men. She had the waiter bring a cigar. I managed it fairly well.

Her chatter ceased. She sat quietly, elbows on the table, her face covered with her hands, strong-looking, large, capable hands, but white and shapely. I smoked and wondered about her. What a partner she would make for me if she were not a girl! She pushed her hair back, rested her hands in her lap, and looked up at her bedraggled straw hat on a hook. I thought she was ready to go, and got up to get it.

"Don't touch it, I despise it," she burst out. "I hate these shoes." She put her foot up. "And this dress and every stitch of clothes on my back. Do you know why? Because every one of them means a different man.

Do you want me to tell you about it; what a tough time I've had? But you wouldn't understand it. You're only a kid, like I was a couple of years ago."

"Tell me, anyway, Julia."

Her story, new to me then, was as old as man's duplicity and woman's inherent desire to be loved and protected. Betrayed and deserted, fearing to face her family, she stole enough of her father's money to take her to the city and into a hospital where her baby was born. "And," she continued, "I was glad when it died, it was a girl. When I was well enough to leave the hospital they couldn't find my clothes. Cheap as they were, somebody had taken them. A man can go out into the street without a hat and coat, kid, but just let a woman try it, even if she has the nerve, and watch what happens to her. I had no money. The doctor gave me this dress; that is, he sold it to me and I paid for it the first time he got drunk. One of the interns traded me these shoes. He was just a dirty little beast and didn't wait to get drunk. Then the hospital cook got me that hat and some cheap stockings and underclothes. He happened to be a white man," she said bitterly. "I suppose I would have taken them just the same if he had been a negro or a Chinaman. After the drunken doctor I thought of nothing but suicide, anyway. But I had to have enough clothes to get through the street and down to the bridge where I could jump into the river.

"The cook told me he would get me a job in a restaurant downtown and that stopped me from going to the river. He gave me money for a couple of night's lodging, and something to eat, and told me where to go for a room. He came that night to my room. When he left in the morning his last words were: "I'll go right out now and get you the job."

"I waited all day but he never came back. He was a liar; I never saw him again. When the third night came my money was gone. I was starving, and the rent was due. I wanted to go down to the river then, but was so hungry I couldn't bring myself to do it."

She had talked furiously, with a storm of bitter words. Now she stopped and smiled. "Yes, this appetite of mine saved my life. I'll never die hungry if I can help it.

"Anyway," she resumed, "this is the long and the short of it. About nine o'clock that night the woman of the place came up and wanted the rent. I told her I was broke, and asked her to stand me off for a few days till I could get a job or give me something to do so I could earn the rent.

"What do you think she did, kid – the big man-eater! She took me by the arm, dragged me out into the hall and pushed me downstairs. She went back and got my hat, that straw hat hanging up there, and threw it out on the sidewalk after me.

"A policeman was standing there and saw her do it. He came up and asked me what the trouble was about. Here is where I may get help, I thought, so I told him I had just left the hospital, that my money was all spent, and that I had been put out of my room. He asked how old I was. I told him I was eighteen – that's two years ago, I'm twenty now. He asked if I lived here in the city. I told him I lived in the country, but was going to stay in the city and work. He wrote something on a card and gave it to me, saying: "I'll get a hack driver to take you to a hotel. When you get there give that card to the landlady."

"The driver took me a few blocks to a place where he stopped, let me out, and helped me up the steps. He rang the bell and went away. I gave the card to a colored girl who opened the door. She came back in a minute and asked me to come in – and," she finished wearily, "I've been in Miss Kate's ever since, kid.

"Miss Kate took me in and dressed me up. She charged me double for my clothes. I pay her, she pays the milliner. It's the same with all her girls. No girl ever goes into her place unless she is broke and ragged and sick and hungry. I've been there two years, and if I stay there twenty years I will still be in debt to her. The longer I stay the more I owe. Everybody charges us double for what we buy. We have to go to a certain drug store where we get robbed. On our days off, Miss Kate takes us around to her friends in the saloons and restaurants, and they rob us. We go out with her because we can wear our best clothes and look good and she shows us off to her customers.

"Once in a while a girl gets so discouraged that she runs out into the street in her wrapper, but she don't get out of the block. Some other landlady's door is open and she goes in hoping to get fairer treatment and a chance to save part of the money she earns, but it's the same old thing. What the madam don't get goes to the doctors, druggists, hack drivers, and messengers. All we get is enough to eat, enough to wear, and plenty to drink if we're foolish enough to go that route. God only knows what becomes of these girls when they get too old and ugly. They go down and down from one place to another till they finally land in the street, old, worn out, dissipated and diseased. No man will have them. I guess they go to the river or to the hospital.

"Bad as Miss Kate's is, it is better than having to trade yourself for a few shabby rags like I did. Miss Kate won't let drunken men come in and beat us and abuse us. The men we meet don't lie to us or deceive us like they do out in the world. They come in and look us over just like the butcher used to look at my father's fat hogs in the fall. We know what they come for; they know we know. So there's no lying and deception and promising you a job. Of course they will steal your money out of the bureau drawers or your hair brush or a pair of garters or silk stockings, but you soon learn to protect yourself. Sometimes, when they get drunk, they give you a few dollars for yourself, or lose it on the floor and you put your foot on it. Sometimes a girl gets so in debt that she steals a few dollars from the men to spend decently when she can get out by herself."

"Julia,"I asked, "did you take the hog man's money?"

"No,"she snapped, bristling. She lied bravely, and I knew it, and respected her for it, somehow. It was one of those lies you know to be a lie and yet believe. The beauty of her lie was that she just let it go with that plain, short "No!" she did not go into any long explanations or excuses, or blame it on anybody else. It was a perfect lie, any way you look at it.

She lied to me and made me like it. My mind was much disturbed by this terrible story, so new to me, and a hundred plans came into it for helping her, but she seemed so independent, confident, and resourceful that I hesitated.

She struck the table with her fist. "If I ever put my foot out of that place again I'll stay out. I was foolish to go out to-day; it's so much harder to go back now, after all the fun we've had. If I had a change of clothes I would stay away and try to get a job and start over again. I've got to get out of there while I'm young and strong enough to work."

"Don't go back, Julia," I advised. "Take my money, get a room and a few clothes. I'll help you find a job. I know how. I have forty dollars saved up. You take that and we will earn more. It's at my room. You wait here till I get it."

"Sit down," she said. "Sit down. Why, you poor kid, I wouldn't take your money on a bet. I'd rot in Miss Kate's first. Don't you know you are the only human being I've met since I left home that hasn't tried to do me some kind of dirt? I am going to start in saving every nickel this week, and if I can find some way to get a few clothes out of there I'll kiss Miss Kate's good-by forever."

Here was a chance for adventure. "I'll take your clothes out of there, Julia." I could see myself going into Miss Kate's with my two rusty pistols and demanding Julia's clothes. I could see the madam blustering and protesting, the girls all gathered around, myself standing there, adamant.

"No excuses, madam, if you please. I want Julia's clothes and Julia."

Nothing to it, simple!

"How are you going to do it?" Julia asked. "If you went in there and tried to take them they would throw you out."

"Well, how can I do it? Any way you say."

She thought a long time before she answered: "I could tie them in a sheet and throw them out the window into the alley, kid, to you."

This wasn't heroic enough to suit me, but it sounded practical. I wanted to help her, so I consented.

"And how are you going to get away if I get your clothes?"

She thought again. "This week, kid, you hunt up some hack driver you can trust and tell him what you want to do. You can have him in the alley with his hack. I'll throw the clothes out. You put them in the hack. Then I'll come downstairs, go out through the kitchen, and over the back fence into the alley. Nobody will pay any attention to me going out in my parlor wrapper without a hat.

"Next Saturday when you come with your bill I'll see you in the hall and tell you what night to come and what time." Julia was herself again; all animation, chattering like a sparrow. "It can't fail, kid. I can feel myself out of there already. All you have to do is get a hack driver, a big, tough one that won't get scared and run away. That's all settled, and it's time for me to get back to Miss Kate's. It's not so hard to go now."

Again she insisted on paying the bill. I said good night in front of the restaurant. She shook hands with me heartily, boyishly: her hand was hard, firm, and her grip something to inspire confidence. "Saturday" she said, darting away.

I went home with my chest out, my shoulders up in the air, and my head high. I thought of all my heroes. No, I wouldn't trade places with any of them. Here was real work to do. I must find a hack driver, a big, tough one.

Cocky McAllister was tough enough. A lean, hungry pirate with a balky eye, who cruised about my neighborhood with his spavined horses and rickety hack.

I told him what I wanted.

"Never let it be said that I refused to help any young feller get himself a girl and get up in the world," he declared. "Say when. I'll be on the spot an' it won't cost you a dime, either."

Julia was waiting Saturday when I got to Madam Kate's.

"Did you get a driver, kid?"

"Yes."

"Be in the alley to-morrow night at eight."

I promised to be there. That night I found Cocky and readied him up for Sunday evening. He showed up on the minute, and we were in the alley by Madam Kate's early. Julia was waiting at the window and out came the bundle. I threw it into the hack. A minute later Cocky snatched her off the fence, leaving part of her wrapper behind. More of it was streaming out of the hack door as I slammed it and we drove away.

She wiped the powder and rouge off her face. "No more of that stuff," she said.

On the way back to my neighborhood she spotted a "Housekeeping Rooms" sign in the window of a dingy-looking house. She stopped the hack and put some money in my hand. "Dash up there, kid, and hire a room, anything that's vacant."

I secured a room quickly enough, came down, and got her. Cocky followed with the bundle of clothes. I lit the gas, Cocky threw the clothes on the bed.

"This is the dirtiest room I ever saw," said Julia, "but it's better than Miss Kate's, and it's home to me. Good night and many thinks. I'll see you later, kid."

Back at the cigar store I treated Cocky to a good smoke. "Kid," he said, leering at me admiringly, "You've got a gold mine; that dame's a money-getter. She's young and healthy and good for years. Listen, you put her right out on the street. Make her walk the blocks. She's workin' for you then an' not the landladies and landlords. Keep her away from the other women. They'll wise her up an' you'll lose her, or put her against hop an' you'll have a bum on your hands. That's all, now. Are you goin' to start her in to-night? The sooner the better."

"No, Mac," I was anxious to get away from him. "She's tired and nervous. I think I'll let her rest to-night."

The police got Cocky that night. I never saw him again. He never learned of my treason in allowing Julia to stay off the streets.

She came into the cigar store a few days later, beaming, happy. "'I've got a job kid, at the Comique jerking beer. Not so good, but better than Miss Kate's. It will do till I get a better one. Come down and watch me work."

The Comique was an old-time collar-and-elbow variety show long since supplanted by the modern vaudeville show house. A dozen girls sold drinks to the patrons on commission. A girl could live on her commissions but few of them did. I think Julia managed to do it. I went down to see her and found her bouncing with energy.

"I've made three dollars already to-night, kid, and it's all mine."

I waited till she was ready to go home, and walked with her. She had cleaned up the room till it looked halfway decent. "You don't have to go; the place is as much yours as mine," she said when I was leaving. I didn't think about her being a girl; I went home because it was my habit. If she had been a boy I would have done the same.

I was busy all the time learning to gamble at Tex's, collecting bills for the milkman, and taking Julia home after work. There was no mention of her the next time I went to Madam Singleton's. She was forgotten, and they never suspected me.

I was saving my money, hoping some day to get my gray suit, hat, and trunk. I told Julia of my ambition to have the suit and leather trunk.

"I'll buy them for you, kid, as soon as I get a few things myself."

"Never mind that, Julia, I'll pay for them," I said, thinking of Cocky McAllister.

I hung around the Comique every night, waiting for Julia. She knew all the "actors" and told me about them.

The handsome young man who came out in a green suit did a clog dance and sang "Tis a handful of earth" so feelingly worked daytimes in a near-by chophouse. The two girls with skirts almost to their knees that did the buck and wing dance sold beer in the boxes. The comedians that beat and pummeled each other about the stage starved around between engagements at the local theaters. The strong man, my favorite, turned out to be the bartender upstairs; he also served as bouncer.

Julia was ambitious to make more money and every night practiced dancing in hopes that she could some time do a turn at the theater. I served as her audience, sat around till the small hours, and often fell asleep in a chair or on the bed. One night we hurried home ahead of a storm and I was on the bed asleep before she had her supper cooked. She woke me up tugging at me. "Get up, you poor kid; take your clothes off and go to bed if you're that dead for sleep." She helped me take off my shoes and I was soon asleep again. She went to bed without waking me, but as I tossed about in the night I knew she was there and was glad. Once my body touched hers – it was hot and sticky. I pulled the sheet down between us and turned away. The next morning as we were walking to the restaurant for breakfast a heavy hand fell on my shoulder; I turned to face my father.

My father's hand was heavy on my shoulder as he pushed me into a doorway. He looked sad and his stern voice shook. "John, do you know what you are? You are a pimp."

Julia never stopped, never looked back, just kept going which was the right thing. She probably thought I had been taken by the police. No good in her getting arrested, too.

Although for years I kept a sharp eye out, I never saw her again; that is, to know her. Of course the gray-haired old lady that sat next to me in the car this morning might have been Julia. But anyway, if she is alive and this meets her eye, I want her to know I never doubted for a minute that she stayed away from the life she left behind at Madam Singleton's.

Later, when I went to her room, it was vacant. The man in charge told me a strange, bearded man with a policeman called on her – my father, no doubt – after which she packed up and left without a word.

I called at the theater and inquired, but they had forgotten her.

Six

AS WE walked to our boarding house I told my father the whole story of my job in the cigar store, my collecting for the milkman, my arrest, and our rescue of Julia. He listened without comment, and when I was done, said: "Well, John, you'll be what you'll be, and I cannot help or hinder you. Go back to your job in the morning if you like."

Those were his last words to me. They were kind, and I have always remembered them and their ring of fatality. I never saw him again. I learned later that he lived out his life orderly and died decently. He went away the next day, and when he returned I was far away, westbound in search of adventure.

I was tired of Tex and his tribe and their smoky back room and cheap cheating. I was sick of the sight of the crabby widow at the boarding house. It was springtime. Sundown found me miles away on a country road, walking westward. Yes, I was going in the right direction. There was the sun going down away off in front of me. Darkness was coming on, but it did not strike me as unusual that I had no supper or no room for the night.

I came to a bridge and stopped when I heard voices below. I looked over the side and a voice came up "Come on down, kid. Don't be leery, we're only a couple of harmless bindle stiffs."

I picked my way down to the level place beside the small creek where they were. One of them was unrolling a "bindle" of blankets, the other was washing a large tin can in the creek.

"Throw out your feet, kid, and get some wood before it gets too dark. We'll have a fire and a can of Java, anyway."

Wood was plentiful. I soon returned with an armful. The other bum came up with the can from the creek and began breaking up some twigs to start the fire. He barely looked at me. "Take a look around the jungle, kid, and see if you can find a pan," he ordered.

"What in hell do you want a pan for?" asked the one that sent me after wood. "Are you going to fry some water?" The other was on his hands and knees blowing up the weak fire. He stood up and looked at the speaker with a most superior air. "Not so fast, brother, not so fast. I've got a gump in my bindle."

He unrolled his blankets and produced a live chicken, big and fat.

The other bum was humbled. "A gump!" he muttered, "and me carrying a fryin' pan with me for the last week." He dived into his bindle and got the pan.

The owner of the chicken took the pan and held it between his eye and the fire looking for holes in it. "It'll do," he said. "More wood, kid," they both ordered.

We were three strangers well met under the bridge; one had a chicken, one coffee and a stale loaf of bread. I had nimble legs and gathered the firewood.

The gump was picked, cleaned, unjointed, and put in the pan with neatness and despatch that would have done credit to any chef. The coffee boiled fragrantly in the tin can. The owner of the stale loaf hacked it into three equal parts with his strong pocketknife, while the chicken man deftly turned sections of the bird with a sharp-pointed stick.

"This is a pretty snide jungle," he said, "no cans. Throw your feet, kid, and get some cans for the Java."

I scurried around and was lucky to find one small can in the dark. The cook inspected it. "Go down and wash it, bring it back half full of water an' I'll boil it out."

I washed the can and brought it back. The chicken and coffee were cooked and cooling near the fire. The cook scalded out the small can and filled it with coffee. He held out the pan of chicken to the other bum and then to me, helping himself to a piece last. The small can of coffee was now cool enough to drink, and was handed around in the same order. The first bum took several swallows and passed it to me. I handed it to the cook without drinking any. He looked at me for the first time.

"Say, brat, listen. If you was some kind of a rank dingbat you wouldn't have been invited down here. Don't think because you couldn't hustle a can that you ain't entitled to your coffee."

"You're right at that, Jack," said the bum that furnished the coffee. "Go ahead, kid."

I drank my coffee and passed the can along. We ate in silence. The chicken and bread soon disappeared. My companions lit up their pipes and smoked while we finished the coffee.

I was learning fast. I took the frying pan, filled it with water and put it on the fire, without waiting for orders. When the water boiled I washed it at the creek, scrubbed it with sand, and returned it to the owner.

"Where you from, kid?"

"The city," I answered.

"How long you been on the road?"

"This is my first day."

"Got any people?"

"No, they are all dead."

"Where you goin'?"

"Oh, just west, anywhere, everywhere."

"Got any pennies?"

"No pennies. I've got a couple of dollars." I looked from one to the other. "Do you want any of it, either of you?"

"No," from both of them. "But," said the cook, "if we was in the city I'd take fifty cents of it purty pronto and get myself a four-bit micky."

"A what?" I asked, mystified.

"A four-bit micky, a fifty-cent bottle of alcohol – Dr. Hall, white line," he translated in disgust. "If you're goin' west you better learn to talk west."

"Yes," said the other, "and 'pennies' don't mean pennies. It means money, on the road."

They didn't talk much between themselves; they had probably compared notes before I arrived at the bridge. They were both past fifty, wore clean overalls, substantial shoes, and clean-looking blue shirts. A month later I could have classified them correctly as professional bums, too old to ride the trains, satisfied to throw their feet along the "star routes," or country roads, where food was seldom refused, and to sleep in their bindles, or blankets, under the stars.

It was time to "flop." They took off their shoes and coats. The shoes were neatly placed together on a level spot; the coat was folded and placed on top of them making a fair pillow, and at the same time protecting them from theft. Each of them threw me a piece of blanket. I made a pillow of my coat and shoes, rolled up in the blankets, and was soon asleep.

A farmer's team crossing the bridge woke us at daylight. I got up at once, cold and sore from the hard ground, and made a fire. The other two crawled out of their blankets and went down to the creek to wash. I followed them. They both had soap wrapped in paper. One of them gave me his piece. I washed and returned it. He placed it on a rock till it was dry, then wrapped it up and put it in his coat pocket. They also had pocket combs and small round mirrors.

We went back to the fire and discussed breakfast. "Nothing but Java," said the bum that had the coffee.

"I'll go to the farmhouse," I volunteered, "and buy something."

"Nix, nix," said one: "buy nothin'," said the other, "it's you kind of cats that make it tough on us, buyin' chuck. They begin to expect money. You go up to that house," pointing to a place on a small rise, about fifteen minutes' walk, "and tell the woman you and two other kids run away from home in the city three days ago and you ain't had nothin' but a head of cabbage that fell off a farmer's wagon between youse since you left. Tell her you are on your way back home and the other two kids are down by the bridge so hungry they can't walk. On your way up there git a phony name and street number ready in case she asks you questions. She'll give you a sit-down for yourself, chances are, but bring back a 'lump' for us. You're a decent-lookin' kid; she might git worked up about your troubles and ask a lot of dam' fool questions. Cut her off. Tell her you're ashamed to be settin' there wasting time and the other boys starvin' under the bridge."

Before I got to the house a couple of dogs dashed out, barking savagely. A healthy, matronly woman came out and quieted them, looking at me inquiringly. I told her myself and two boy friends, runaways from home, were hungry and I wanted some food, that I would be glad to pay her for anything she could spare, and if she would wrap it up I would hurry down to the bridge with it, where my chums were waiting.

"Yes," she said kindly, "come in. I haven't much here, but maybe I can find enough." She gave me a seat outside near the kitchen door, where I waited and made friends with the dogs. In no time she came out with a large parcel, and refused the money I offered. I thanked her and went down to the bridge with my "lump."

The bums had coffee boiling. We found enough tin cans to drink from and opened the parcel. It contained cold, fried chicken, cold biscuits, and half a pie.

"You're a good connecter, kid; sure you didn't pay for this?" one of them said.

"No, and I didn't have to answer any questions. It was easy except for the dogs."

"Don't let dogs worry you, kid; they're cowards. I ought to know, I've been battlin' 'em twenty years. They'll bite you if you turn your back or run away, or if there's a pack of 'em they'll pull you down. If you get up against a hostile dog rush him and he'll weaken. I never got bit but once an' that was in the town of Pueblo. I was just after gettin' a six months' floater out of Denver an' went down to Pueblo to do a little D.D.ing with lavender for myself. I got myself a bunch of lavender and a ducat."

The other bum laughed, his mouth full of chicken. "You're talkin' Chinook to that kid. What does he know about the D.D. and lavender and ducats."

"You're right," I said. "I don't know what he is talking about." I was anxious to learn, but didn't like to ask questions.

"Well, it's this way," he went on. "I was dummyin' up, see? Imitatin' a deaf an' dumb man. D.D.ing, see? You surely know what lavender is – stuff women put on clothes. You put about a spoonful in a small envelope. You've got a pocketful of the envelopes ready when you go out to make your 'plunge.' Then you get your ducat, see? That's the main thing. I got a bartender to write it for me on the back of a lawyer's card. When the women opens the door you slip her your ducat and she reads:

'I am deaf and dumb. I got hurt by a street car and just came out of the county hospital. I am trying to get seven dollars to pay my fare home to Cheyenne. Please take a parcel of lavender and give what you can. Sometimes they take your lavender an' sometimes they don't, but they generally give up something, an' they can't ask you a lot of questions, and if a copper grabs you you've got an out. You ain't exactly beggin'.

"As I was sayin' about dogs. I was battering the privates, see? Private houses. A woman had just slipped me a dime an' was standin' in the front door watchin' to see that I got off the premises. I'm about halfway to the gate when I heard a dog snarlin', an' comin' up behind me. I'm D.D., see, an' don't want to round on the damn dog an' give myself a bawl-out in front of the woman, so I stand my ground figgern' she'll stop him. The next thing I know he's got half my pants leg ripped off an' a chunk out of one of my shins. Anyway, I run him under the house. The woman took me in an' fixed me up with arnica an' a bandage. Then she gets me a good suit of her old man's clothes, gives me two dollars, and holds the dog under the house till I get out the front gate. That's dogs for you," he finished, "an' women."

I had a question, but the other bum asked it for me. "What do you do if you bump into a natural dummy when you're D.D.ing?"

"Well," said the dog expert, "I never bumped into one, but if I did I suppose I'd do what everybody else does when they're wrong an' get caught at it. I'd get mad an' cuss hell out of 'em."

Breakfast over, the bums shaved. Both had razors. All bums carry razors for shaving, fighting, or cutting through a sleeper's clothing to get into his pocket. One of them had a big silk handkerchief that he stropped his razor on, the other used his belt. They heated water in a tin can, lathered their hands, and rubbed it on their faces. One used his mirror, the other used none. After shaving they dried their blades carefully and secreted them about their persons. Blankets were rolled up, and the bums were ready to take the road. The D.D. man was going into the city for a few days. "So long." He scrambled up the bank to the road.

The other was traveling in my direction and volunteered to direct me to a junction where I could make a westbound train.

"You're welcome to travel with me, kid, if you want to Jungle-up for a month or two," my companion said. "The fruit will be gettin' ripe soon, and there'll be green corn and new spuds and the gumps are fat already. I promise myself some famous mulligans around these parts."

Many boys would have jumped at this chance, but I declined. Maybe it was a dislike for begging, or ambition, or my imagination pulling me westward.

I don't know; but it wasn't the hardships, I'm sure. At the junction we parted.

"So long, kid. May see you out West next fall when I make the poultice route."

"What's that?" I asked.

"That's southern Utah, kid, the land of milk and honey. You're always sure of a big pan of milk and a fresh loaf of home bread – the poultice route, see? So long."

A long, heavy westbound freight train was slowly pulling out when I got to the railroad yards. A car of lumber, clean and white, piled halfway to the roof, the door invitingly open, came along. Nimbly I swung up and in.

Inside the car I looked about for a place to secrete myself. The lumber was about six feet shorter than the car, which left a large space at one end. I dropped down into it, took off my coat, and stretched out on the floor, feeling sure of a long ride. No brakeman would crawl over that pile of lumber even if he knew there was a hiding place at one end.

Along in the afternoon, after one of the many stops, I heard a scrambling above and a young fellow about my own age dropped lightly down beside me. I had been in the car so long that the half light was enough. I saw he was ragged and frightfully dirty, road dirt – coal smoke, cinders, ashes, grease. His coat, too large for the thin frame, was full of holes and its lining hung in tatters. His trousers were greasy and full of hot-cinder holes. His calico shirt was open in front, his skin was dirty. He was sharp-eyed and thin-faced. He eyed me wolfishly.

"How long you been here?"

"All day."

"Where you headin' for?"

"Denver."

"Got a smoke?"

He dug a dirty newspaper out of his back pocket, neatly tore a piece off the border, tearing it downward with the grain, till he had a piece the size of a cigarette paper. A search of his coat pocket yielded a cigar snipe, which he crushed in his hand and then rolled up in the paper he had held in his mouth. "Got a match?"

He looked at me in disgust, dug up one of his own, and lit up. The smell of his cigarette was fierce. He now took off his shoes. One of them was laced with dirty white string. He had no socks, his feet were grimy and smelled. His coat came off next; with it and his shoes he made a pillow and stretched out on the floor.

"Won't the brakeman smell that smoke?" I asked.

"To hell with him an' you," and he spoke no more. Finishing his smoke, he adjusted his pillow and went to sleep. I rolled my coat up, made a pillow, and dozed. I was afraid he would steal my shoes, so I left them on.

Something woke me in the evening. I think it was the lumber shifting. The train was on a down grade, the car creaking and rocking. We were in the front end. Suddenly my companion jumped to his feet. He looked scared, started to crawl up on top of the lumber. He was too late. There was a grinding noise, and a crash. About four feet of the top of the lumber slid forward against the front end of the car and he was crushed, flattened between. I was a prisoner below, unhurt. This shifting of the lumber cut off the light from the open side door, but its weight against the end of the car opened up some cracks and I was soon able to see about me dimly. The boy had died instantly. His body, from the waist up, was flattened between the lumber and front end of the car. His legs dangled below, down where I was imprisoned, with each movement of the car, like the legs of a scarecrow in the wind.

I can't remember that I was shocked or frightened, but I do know that as soon as I found I was imprisoned in that car I got hungry. I hadn't eaten since morning and was hungry before the thing happened. But then I knew I could get out and eat at any stop. Now I couldn't, and my hunger became unbearable.

The place I was in was large as ever, except in height. The shifting of the lumber had reduced that to about three feet. I couldn't stand up. I was in no danger. The lumber could not shift at the bottom, the weight of that above was too heavy. I had a strong pocketknife, and went to work on the side of the car near the end. The boarding was thin, weather-rotten, and old. In a couple of hours I had cut almost through one end of three boards. My hands were blistered. I sat down and waited till I heard the whistle blow for a town.

As the train went into the yards I kicked the boards loose at the top where they were cut, and pulled them away from below where they were nailed. This gave me a hole large enough to crawl out of, which I did, feet first, pulling my coat after, when she stopped. Up on the main street I learned I was in Dodge City, Kansas, a town at that time largely given over to gambling, fighting, and whisky drinking. I wasn't interested in any of those amusements then. I got something to eat and went to a cheap room for the night. Tired out, I slept till noon the next day. Then I went down to the yards to look for another train out. Near the depot I met a character who looked like a bum. He gave me a sharp look.

"Goin' down in the yards, young feller?"

"Yes, why?"

"Better wait till night if you want to make a train. The railroad bull is hostile. They found a bum dead in a car of lumber this morning, and they had to tear the end of the car off to get his body out. He must have been an awful gay cat to get into the end of a carload of planed lumber. It's suicide."

I went back uptown and into a lunch counter. The waiter was idle and talkative.

"Traveling?" he asked.

"Yes."

"Which way?"

"Denver."

"Beating it?"

"Yes."

"Listen here, it'll take you three or four days to make Denver that way. You'll ruin your clothes and maybe get grabbed off a train and handed thirty days at Colorado Springs – big chain gang there – they're cleaning up the streets. If you can dig up five dollars I'll give you a card to a porter on the Overland to-night. Give him the five and he'll do the rest."

"Thanks, I'll try it."

I met the train and the porter who took the card and my five dollars, stowed me away in the linen closet, and locked the door. I was almost suffocated. Once in the night he opened the closet. "How you makin' out, buddy?"

"All right," I said, and the door was locked again.

Next morning he gave me a piece of steak between slices of bread, and a bottle of coffee. After that I felt better and dozed in a cramped, sitting position in a corner.

That afternoon at Denver I was released, happy, hungry, cramped, and tired. I rented a cheap room for a week, went to a barber shop, and had a bath. I thought twenty-five cents for a bath a rank waste of money and decided to find a swimming hole. In a few days I found one.

There was a sort of camp for bums on the river bank under some trees. They had their fires there, and cans for boiling coffee. They used to lie around, washing and boiling their clothes, and swimming. They stole chickens around the neighborhood and anything else they could get.

One afternoon I was in swimming, when suddenly there was an alarm and everybody ran. I didn't pay any attention to it at first; then I got out of the water and ran for my clothes. I had just about got them on when the police arrived and grabbed me.

They put me into the patrol wagon. I was the only one they got. Later they picked up one or two others around in the woods, and took us all down to the jail. I was scared half to death.

They put us all in one big room with a lot of other bums they'd picked up. The police had had a general order to clean up the town.

In the morning they took us all up to court. It was the first time I had been in court. We were all charged with vagrancy. When my name was called, I protested. I said, "Judge, you can't call me a vagrant. I have twenty dollars down in the jail office."

He looked at me as coldly and impersonally as if I had been a dish of parsnips. "Fifteen days on the chain gang. Next case."

SEVEN

I WAS taken downstairs and locked in a cell; I saw no more of the "bull pen" where I spent the night. My cellmate was a handsome, smiling young fellow about twenty-two or twenty-three. He looked like a country boy, rugged, red-cheeked, blue-eyed, sandy-haired. He seemed to be well acquainted in the jail. Some one sang out, "Who's the fresh fish, 'Smiler'?" "Another vag," he answered. "Fifteen days."

I told him about my case at once. I felt outraged. "Forget it, kid. Your fifteen days will be in before your name's dry on the commitment. They won't put you on the gang. You'll get a trusty job. I'm just finishing ten days, haven't been out of this cell, goin' out this afternoon and out of this man's town, too," he smiled. "Let's eat. You've got money in the office. I'll send for a messenger."

"All right," I said, "do it."

A trusty took my name and our orders. Smiler ordered tobacco and papers also. A messenger came in an hour with two meals and the "makings" of smokes. I signed my name on the check and he was paid at the office. After we ate, Smiler sang songs, danced, or stood at the door waiting to be released.

"I'm going West, kid; hope I see you on the road so I can return that feed," he said, when the trusty came to release him.

I liked "The Smiler" and wished I could be with him. In the morning coffee and stale bread were served in the cells. Fifteen minutes later there was a banging of doors. Some one shouted "Chain gang." My door was opened.

"Outside, kid," said a trusty.

I followed other prisoners down the corridor to a big, open room where they washed up in running water at a sink and dried themselves with handkerchiefs. The trusty came with my hat.

"You won't need your coat, kid. I'll look out for it."

An officer opened a door to the street and stood inside; another was outside; the chain gang filed out and climbed into an open wagon with seats on each side facing each other. A crowd of curious men and boys stood around the wagon. When my turn came, instead of getting into the wagon I dashed down the street, instinctively, like a wild animal. The guards didn't chase me for fear the others would escape. The crowd shouted and cheered me on. I was free.

There was nothing in my room. I didn't go near it. I had no money, and hunger seized me at once. I walked out of town, walked all day and till dark, when I found myself exhausted at a bums' camp twenty miles away, on the outskirts of a small town. Confidently I walked up to the fire. I was one of them.

I had escaped; I was hungry; I was ready for anything; I belonged around the fire. I heard an exclamation. A form rose up from the fireside and grabbed me with both hands. It was Smiler.

"That's doin' time, kid, what! Did you beat it? Where's your coat?"

"Yes. My coat's in the jail."

"Take a rest for an hour, and we'll go up to the burg. I'll get you one."

On our way into the town he explained. "There'll be a train through here about ten o'clock, kid; I'll kick in the first private house that looks good. We'll surely find a coat and maybe a few dollars and something to eat if we have time."

He looked about sharply at the houses. Across the street we heard a door slam. A woman and man came out the front gate, the cottage was dark. We walked around the block and back to the cottage. Smiler walked confidently in the front gate, I followed. He rang the doorbell, no answer. We went around to the back where he found a kitchen window open, climbed through, and unlocked the door for me.

"Look around for some chuck, kid, and stay right there till I come back." He disappeared. In a minute or two I could see about me, and explored the pantry. I found bread and meat and tied them in a cloth.

Smiler returned from the front carrying a bundle of clothes, and we went out. I found a coat that fitted passably. We left the balance, and departed unseen.

The train was pulling in and we made a run to the water tank where it had to stop, and by the time we found a car we could get into it was pulling out.

The lunch was spread out on a paper and quickly disappeared. Smiler had some cheap jewelry, an old silver watch, and a few dollars in cash. He divided the money, and after inspecting the other plunder threw it out the car door. "That junk would get us five years, kid, if we got grabbed with it, and it ain't worth two dollars."

This adventure fascinated me. I gave no thought to the burglary. It seemed right that I should have a coat and food. My money was behind in the jail. I couldn't buy them. I had stolen them. Somehow I felt satisfied, as if I had got even with somebody.

"How do you like this racket kid?" Smiler asked as we rolled up our coats for pillows.

"It's great. How long have you been doing it?"

"Oh, a couple of years. Ever since the coppers run me out of my home town, Detroit. That was a snide little caper we cut back there and I wouldn't have touched it only you had to have a coat. How would you like to be a prowler, kid?"

I liked him, always smiling, for his ready help when I needed it and his companionable ways.

"I think I would like it; it's exciting."

"All right, kid. When we get to Salt Lake I'll show you the real thing."

"Good," I said. "How long will it take us to make Salt Lake?"

"About a week at this rate."

"Let's ride the passenger trains," I said, anxious to take my first lessons in burglary.

"We'll get a passenger train out of Cheyenne, kid, if we can duck Jeff Carr," said Smiler. "Never heard of him? He's a railroad bull and he's 'bum simple' – simple-minded on the subject of killing bums. If you run he'll shoot you; if you stand he'll get you six months, and he'd rather have you run."

I learned all about Carr later, and his feud with the bums. They made many efforts to kill him, but never succeeded. He was later put in charge of the railroad's train-robber detail, but he never killed any train robbers and the bums rambled through Cheyenne in peace.

We got a train out without falling foul of the murderous Carr and rode the baggage into a division point where there was a twenty-minute stop for dinner. Looking around for a place to get coffee, we passed a jewelry store. The jeweler was working at his bench in front. When we got to the alley, Smiler said:

"We'll make that tray of watches in the window, kid. You get a handful of rocks, go around to the back, and throw them against the jeweler's door till he opens it. When he does, I'll make the front. Don't throw them too hard and scare him. Easy – just enough to make him curious."

I followed instructions and was preparing to throw the fourth rock when the door opened. The jeweler stepped out and took a good look around. I walked down the alley to the street, and soon caught up with Smiler, who was stepping away briskly.

"We've got to plant this junk, kid. We can't take chances luggin' it around."

We were in the yards now and Smiler was looking at the cars curiously as we passed between them. He stopped beside a car of coal and looked at the card tacked on it. "Billed to Butte, Montana," he said, "this'll do." He tied the watches, which he took from his coat pocket, in a big handkerchief. We climbed up on the car and the parcel was planted in one corner and plenty of coal put back on top of it. On the ground again, Smiler tore off a corner of the destination card. "Don't forget that, kid; in case anything happens to me you'll know this car."

This was all accomplished in less than twenty minutes, and we had plenty of time to catch our passenger train, which we did, leaving our plunder behind but sure to follow.

"He may not miss that junk till he goes to close up, kid, or he may have missed it already. Anyway we'll sure be stuck up and frisked at Evanston. All we have to do is tell the truth, say we rode this rattler out of Cheyenne and never left the yards at Rock Springs. And they won't hold us. They can't figure that we could touch that joint and go out on the same train. We'll stop at Evanston anyway and wait for our coal car. Then, instead of going to Salt Lake, we'll ride the freight over the cut-off to Pocatello and I'll get the coin on that junk in an hour from Mary."

"Who's Mary?" I asked.

"Wait till you see her to-morrow. She'll buy anything from a barrel of whisky to a baby carriage."

It was a warm night, and riding the front end of the baggage was pleasant enough. "If the bulls grab us off, kid, you say nothing; I'll talk and tell them who we are and where we're going. You listen, that's all.

"Say," he said suddenly, "take off that coat and let me look at it." He went over it closely by the light from the engine. It was tailor-made, and he found the owner's name on a piece of white cloth sewed in the inside pocket. He ripped it out, and I put the coat on.

"You never can be too careful, kid. We ought to have looked at that before. If Jeff Carr had picked us up at Cheyenne you might have been charged with that lousy burglary by now."

How could a boy help admiring such wisdom? I was flattered to be taken up by one so experienced, so confident and active about his work, and withal, so carefree, happy, and smiling.

We were not molested at Evanston, where we got off and waited for our freight train. It came along next day, and that night we dropped off it at Pocatello, Idaho.

Pocatello, at that time, was just a small railroad town. A famous stopping-off place for the bums bound East, West, North and South. There was a grand jungle by a small, clean river where they boiled up their vermined clothes, or "rags" as they are always called, cooked their mulligans, or, if enough bums got together, held a "convention." These conventions, like many others, were merely an excuse for a big drunk. Sometimes they would end in a killing, or some drunken bum would fall in the fire and get burned to death, after which they would silently steal away. Oftener, the convention lasted till there was no more money for alcohol, the bums' favorite drink. The bums then began "pestering the natives" by begging and stealing till the whole town got sore.

The town marshal would then appear with a posse armed with "saps," which is short for saplings, young trees. He stood guard with a shotgun, while the posse fell upon the convention and "sapped up" on those therein assembled and ran them down the railroad track and out of town.

We found our junk without trouble, and hastened to "Mary's."

If I knew more of composition and writing and talking I might do justice to Mary, the fence, and friend of bums and thieves.

It's an injustice to the memory of Mary, or, as she was lovingly called by the bums, "Salt Chunk Mary," to try to crowd her into a few paragraphs or even a chapter. She should have a book.

"Did you eat yet?" was the first thing you heard after entering her house. "I have a pot of beans on the stove and a fine chunk of salt pork in them." She invariably produced the beans and "fine chunk of salt pork" and always ate as heartily of them as any of her famished guests.

Her principal business was selling wine, women, and song to the railroad men and gamblers. She ruled her half dozen "girls" with a heavy hand. Her house on the outskirts of the town was a dingy, old two-story frame building with a couple of rooms added to one side of it where she lived and received her friends from the road.

Smiler knew her and we were welcome. The feed of beans and salt pork was spread for us. She locked the door and, while we ate, this most unusual woman estimated the value of our loot, spread out on one end of the oilcloth-covered kitchen table where we sat.

Salt Chunk Mary put no acids on the watches, nor pried into the works. She "hefted" the yellow ones with a practiced hand and glanced but once at the white ones.

I surveyed her as I ate. She was about forty years of age, hard-faced and heavy-handed. Her hair was the color of a sunburned brick, and her small blue eyes glinted like ice under a March sun. She could say "no" quicker than any woman I ever knew, and none of them ever meant "yes."

She went into the adjoining room and returned with a roll of bills. "Four hundred dollars, Smiler."

"Good! Give us small bills, Mary."

He divided the money equally between us and we got up to go.

"Let's go in and buy a few bottles of beer for the girls, kid, just by the way of no harm."

"No, don't drag that kid in there – and here's something else, listen," said this plain, blunt woman to Smiler. "I guess that kid is all right or he wouldn't be with you. If I'm grabbed with this junk I'll rot in jail before I put the finger on you, and if either of you gets grabbed (she was looking at me), and thinks he can get a light jolt by turning me in, he's wrong. I'll throw it in the river, and he can rot in jail."

We got a room to rest up, and before going to sleep decided that Salt Lake was too small for us. San Francisco was better. Smiler had never been there, and was as anxious to see it as I. Buying tickets was throwing money away. So we "beat it" down to Ogden and over the Southern Pacific, riding the front end of passenger trains at night, making long jumps, avoiding bums' camps, paying for our meals, and stealing nothing. We got into Sacramento without mishap, rested up a couple of days, and journeyed along toward "the city." We got "ditched" off our train at Port Costa, and crawled into a hay car for the night. There were a couple of bums in the car already, and more came in later and flopped.

Early next morning we were aroused by a pounding on the side of the car. "Come on out of there!" shouted a man with his head in the door, "yez are all pinched." We hit the ground, eight of us in all, young and old, large and small. Two men were outside, carrying shortened billiard cues.

"March!" one of them ordered.

One of the bums started to march and the rest followed. He seemed to know just what to do and where to go. A short walk across the tracks brought us up in front of a big barnlike house with a hotel sign and broad steps in front. The bum led us straight up the steps and into a barroom, where he stood up against the wall opposite the bar. We did the same. A stout, grayish, red-faced man with a very positive air was busy serving drinks. He paused and spoke to one of our captors:

"What have you there, Mike?"

"Eight bums, judge."

He served another round of drinks and turned to us again.

"Are you guilty or not guilty?"

The big bum that led us in immediately answered:

"We're all guilty, judge, an' hungry."

The judge – and he was no less person than Judge Casey, famous and celebrated in song and story for his speedy trials and the human quality of his justice – waved a short, hairy, muscular arm toward the dining room.

"Feed them first, Mike."

We followed our leader into the dining room and all sat at one big table where we had a substantial breakfast. When the last bum had his fill, we marched back to the barroom and lined up against the wall again.

"All ready, judge," said Mike.

The judge stopped dealing drinks and pronounced sentence. His voice sounded tired, weary; there was a note of kindness in it.

"Oh, well, Mike, leave the big bums take ten days, and the little bums five."

He turned to his work. The big bum now led us out and to a near-by box car that served as a calaboose. One side door was nailed up and both end doors fastened outside. We crawled in and the other side door was shut and padlocked on the outside.

Smiler sat down in the car and laughed. "What's next, I wonder, kid?"

Someone answered out of the darkness: "They'll hook this box car on to the first freight and haul us over to Martinez, the county seat, an' slough us in the county jail."

I had told Smiler about cutting myself out of the car when my companion was killed.

"Better get busy with your 'shive,' kid." I started cutting on the side opposite the boarding house. The bum that pleaded guilty for all of us saw what I was doing and protested. "Hey. kid, lay off o' that. You want to get us all six months, destroyin' railroad property?"

Smiler was on him like a tiger and cuffed him around till he whined. "Go over in that corner and lie down, you greasy, big gay cat, or I'll cut your tail off." The bum sat down and stayed quiet. In an hour we kicked the boards out.

"You first, kid."

I dropped out and Smiler followed. As we dodged across the yards I looked back. Two more bums had wriggled out. The other four elected to stay in the car, too lazy to run away.

We hid all day under a warehouse and at dark rode a freight into Oakland where we got the ferry. We bought new clothes, rented a room, and got cleaned up. San Francisco fascinated us. We spent days on the water front watching the ships and sailors, or at the Cliff House where I first saw the ocean, and in the park. Our nights were spent about the "Coast," Broadway and Pacific Street, at Bottle Koenig's or the Bella

Union or downtown at Pete Dorsey's and other dance halls.

Gambling was open everywhere; we experimented and lost. We wasted our money around the shows, dance halls, and hop joints, which were open and unmolested by the police. In a month we were almost broke, and ready for the road. Salt Lake was decided upon where Smiler had something special in view.

An uneventful week on the road put us into Salt Lake City.

Then swiftly came the tragic night that separated us forever – I to jail and the kindly, lovable Smiler to his grave.

EIGHT

THERE was a legend on the road that the Mormon Tabernacle in Salt Lake City was a veritable storehouse of gold, silver, and precious stones and it was this that lured Smiler back to that city. At that time a high adobe wall surrounded the block on which stood the Tabernacle and the then unfinished Mormon Temple. We looked it over for several days and nights but could get nothing tangible to work on. Sunday we attended services and the plate was to be seen, silver and gold; more than we could carry away if we got it. At last we decided to go over the wall and give the place a good reconnaissance. If it looked feasible we could get a couple of other idle burglars and give it a thorough looting.

On top of the wall we pulled up our light ladder and placed it inside. Smiler went down first. I barely had my feet off the ladder when a dozen men rose up out of the shrubbery armed with shotguns, and surrounded us. We stood still by the wall. One of them spoke, sternly, evenly: "Go back over that wall."

Little we knew the Mormons. We went up the ladder, pulled it up, and went down and away.

When Smiler's good humor returned he held up his hand. "Kid, I'll never try to rob another Mormon. I'll go to work first."

The next day we went into a small gambling house where we hung out to read the papers. We sat at a table near the big safe in a corner of the room. A man in overalls was taking the lock apart. The place had changed hands a few days before and the new proprietors were having the numbers of the combination changed. When the mechanic finished his work he wrote some numbers on two slips of paper. These he threw on the floor beside his tools and went back to the bar for a drink. Smiler stooped, picked up the slips, looked at them closely, and threw them back on the floor.

Outside, he said: "We've got the combination of that box, kid. Those two pieces of paper are for the new proprietors, their new combination."

Neither one of us knew enough about safes to feel sure of opening one even when we had the numbers. Smiler knew a chap doing time in the penitentiary who knew all about safes. The "stir" was only a mile out of the city and we decided to go up and get some expert advice.

Next day we visited the expert at the "stir," who gladly gave us instructions and declared himself in with any money we got.

That night Smiler opened the box as easily as if it belonged to him and locked it again. We got but a few hundred dollars where we expected several thousands. The new owners had no bankroll, just opened up on a shoestring, hoping to get off lucky and win. The next morning they accused each other of the theft, almost fought with pistols, and dissolved partnership, calling each other thieves.

The money was split three ways. The expert at the "stir" took his bit with bad grace, intimating that we got more than we were dividing, and that we were thieves. As we were leaving, Smiler said: "Goodby, 'Shorty.' Everything's all right now, ain't it?"

"Oh, sure," he grouched. "Everything's all right – just like Denmark."

"Kid, we'll go up to that joint and give them a chance to win their money back," said Smiler. "I feel lucky."

We went up, but they were closed and we had to go elsewhere to gamble. The habit had fastened on him. He became a fiend for gambling. When his money was gone I let him play mine in, and he kept us broke. In a few days the money from our last venture was gone, and we were sparring about for more.

The oldest and commonest system of the house burglar in locating money and jewelry is to stand about theaters, cafes, and the better shops, watching their patrons and following them home if they display wealth. Smiler and I followed a woman and man to their home one night from the theater. The woman wore enough diamonds to stun any thief or pawnbroker. They went into a well-kept, two-story house, back in a big yard full of trees and shrubs, only a dozen blocks from the main street. They let themselves in with a key and appeared to be the only occupants of the place.

We looked the spot over for several days and evenings. There was a servant girl about the place, but no children and no dogs. This was good. Children, particularly young ones, often need attention in the night, which interferes with the prowler. Dogs, young or old, are the bane of the burglar's life. A dog inside a house where people are sleeping prohibits burglary, and the smaller he is, the louder he prohibits. So far as we could see, the place looked made to order for us. House burglars customarily work single-handed. Two men prowling about in a house in the dark are apt to get confused if any one wakes up, and shoot each other. It has happened.

"I wish this stool-pigeon moon wasn't so bright tonight, kid," said

Smiler as we waited in the shrubbery for our people to put out lights and retire. At eleven o'clock the house was in darkness. "About three hours more, kid, and we'll get busy."

We had been in the yard since nine o'clock, tense, watching, listening. Six hours lying on the damp grass and wet from the heavy dew. And still the burglar wonders how he catches those terrible colds that hang on and on and finally develop into T. B.

It was agreed that I should stay outside and lend a hand in case anything went wrong in the house with Smiler. Inside the house, inexperienced as I was, I would be in the way. Smiler looked at his watch for the hundredth time.

He removed his shoes, putting one in each hip pocket as far as it would go, buttoned his coat tightly, and pulled his hat far down over his eyes. Always clean, handsome, smiling, he wasn't good to look at now. We stepped toward the house, keeping out of the moonlight when possible. On the rear porch Smiler tried the door and windows – all fastened. He motioned me to stay where I was, and disappeared around the side of the house in search of an unlatched window. No burglar uses force till he is sure there is no window or door unfastened.

He was gone so long that I was getting worried when he silently appeared from the other side; he had gone around the house. I left the porch and joined him beside a window he had found unfastened. He pointed to some vines near by, where I took my stand to wait till he rejoined me. I watched him intently, a pupil, apt at learning. The bottom of the window was about even with his shoulder. He stood with arms upraised, hands against the window sash, slowly, silently pushing it up. I listened, but he made no sound. The night was calm, still, dead.

Then came a blinding flash of fire and the deadly roar of a rifle. Broken glass, falling, tinkled, and a woman shrieked once hysterically.

My eyes had never left Smiler. He staggered back from the window clutching his throat with both hands; his legs trembled like a spent fighter's, as he sank slowly to his knees.

For a moment I shrank with fear and shock, cold and helpless, into the vines beside the house. The flash and deafening explosion coming out of the still night when my nerves were at their highest tension petrified me on the spot. Then my legs ran away with me and I found myself at the back gate to the alley, the way we came in, fumbling at the latch. My mind was clearing up now. The gate was open. I was wondering whether to run up or down the alley, into the city or out of it. I expected to hear more shots. Then I thought of Smiler, and looked back.

He was there in front of the window in the moonlight, on his hands and knees now, shaking his head from side to side slowly.

There was no alarm yet. The night was calm and still again. There was the smell of burnt powder in the air.

This was my first desperate experience. I didn't know what to do. I wanted to run on and save myself and I wanted to help Smiler. Something – I don't know what it was, but I don't think it was courage or bravery – turned me around and I ran back through the shrubbery to a spot opposite the window from which the shot had been fired. In the clear moonlight I could see that it was raised about six inches and one of its lower panes was shattered.

The house was still in darkness. There was no sound inside. I must have been in a panic still. No sane-thinking human would have done what I did next. I ran out in front of the window to Smiler, and standing over him, put my arms under his, lifting him slowly to his feet. Blood was streaming out of his mouth. He slowly and weakly put one arm around my neck. I held it there, grasping the hand that hung limply over my shoulder, and with my other arm around his waist slowly dragged him to the gate and out into the alley where he collapsed. His dead weight was too much for me. I let his body slip gently to the ground. A twitching shudder ran through him. He straightened out on his back and threw his arms wide. He was dead.

Still no sound came from the house. Next door I now heard a window thrown up and voices calling, a light appeared. It seemed an age since the shot was fired, yet it wasn't three minutes. Smiler was beyond my help. I must be off. I was drenched with the blood that spurted from a wound in his neck. It was on my face and hands. My shirt front was saturated with it. My coat was dripping blood. I thought of our room downtown – no chance to make it in that condition.

Smiler's watch chain glistened in the moonlight. I tore at his pockets and found his money. I went through them all, took everything, and ran for blocks and blocks through the alley toward the outskirts of the city. The dawn was coming fast. I must hide. I turned out of the alley into a street and walked on wondering what to do, where to go.

A "For Rent" sign on a large, neglected-looking residence halted me. Not a soul was in sight on the street. I dodged into the yard, around to the back, and found the kitchen door unlocked. Inside, I went into what had been the dining room and sat down on the floor exhausted, nervous, and covered with blood.

When it became light enough I explored the old house, finding nothing but rags and old papers. There was no water in it and washing was out of the question. I gathered up an armful of the rags and papers, making a pallet of them by a window upstairs in a front room, where I could look out on the street. I sat down on the pallet and began to think things over. It was the first good chance since I had left my father. I heartily wished myself back with him. If this was adventure I wanted no more of it. I was done with it. It had brought me to this. Tired, hungry, bloody, afraid to go to sleep even if I could, lest I should be found and dragged off to jail and surely convicted. Smiler was dead. I had no ties to bind me to the road.

Yes, I would get out of this mess somehow and go back to my father. I was sorry for poor Smiler and would have stayed with him on the road, but now it was different. I felt no remorse for any of the things we had done. I wasn't sorry. I didn't even think they were wrong. That phase of it never entered my mind.

Then I fell to thinking of Smiler's tragic end; trying to puzzle it out: Why the woman shrieked, why the house remained so dark and silent, and why I wasn't shot when I went to his assistance. There was no answer to it all. I felt easier in my mind now that I had decided to quit the road and go home, and longed for the night to come when I could leave my hiding place and wash the blood off my hands and face and get fresh clothes.

As the day wore on, feeling more secure, I stretched out on my bed of rags and paper and tried to sleep, but it wouldn't come to me. Later, in the afternoon, I removed my coat and shoes and managed to doze fitfully till evening. When it was dark enough to walk through the streets safely I left the house and made my way to a hot sulphur spring that gushed out of a hillside a mile away. There I stripped and scrubbed myself as best I could in the dark, and without soap. My clothes were stiff with dried blood. I threw the shirt and underwear away, put my handkerchief about my neck, and, buttoning my coat, started off in search of a store where I could get a new outfit.

Since the night Smiler stole the coat for me we had never allowed ourselves to get flat broke. With all his passion for gambling he would hold on to a few dollars. With the money I found on him and my own, I counted up thirty dollars. His watch wasn't worth two dollars, a cheap one he bought in San Francisco. I kept it as a memento. There was nothing else of value in his pockets.

In a few minutes I found one of the many little general stores that flourished in Salt Lake at that time, and purchased a suit, the cheapest one there, for twelve dollars, and a fifty-cent shirt. I went back to the spring with my bundle, where I donned the cheap bullswool suit and threw my good one away. Tired and hungry, I crawled aboard a street car citybound from the sulphur springs.

In the car I looked closely at my hands and saw there was still some blood around my finger nails; there were dark spots on my shoes, too. Hungry as I was, I first went into a barber shop, had a bath, and scrubbed my shoes. Then to a restaurant, and while eating I decided to go to our room and have a good sleep and get a suit of underclothes and a few other things that I would need on my way home. I turned the whole thing over in my mind and was sure there was no danger in going to the room.

I was sitting at the table nearest the kitchen, finishing my meal, when a policeman came in and sat opposite me. The waiter brought a steak which was ready and waiting for him.

"Did they identify the dead burglar yet?" the waiter asked.

"No, not a thing on him."

"How did it happen anyway?"

"Just like the morning paper says. The woman's husband was called away unexpectedly. The hired girl had the night out and she was alone in the house, sleeplessly walking around the rooms when this bird appeared at the window. Scared half to death she got her husband's rifle and fired at him; then she fell in a faint. When she revived, the neighbors were called and they got the police. The bird ran as far as the alley, and dropped dead. The bullet cut an artery in his neck."

From the restaurant I went directly to our room and to bed, where I slept the sleep of exhaustion till some time next forenoon, when I was roused by heavy knocking at my door. When I opened it, two big, red-faced men shouldered in, told me I was under arrest, and ordered me to put on my clothes. I washed and dressed. One of them put handcuffs on me and made me sit in a chair while they searched the room without finding anything that interested them.

The other then produced a bloodstained piece of paper, and, holding it out before my eyes, said:

"Did you ever see that before?"

I looked at it. It was the landlord's receipt for our room rent. They had found it in a corner of one of Smiler's pockets. Smiler had continually drummed it into me never to answer any questions in case we were arrested.

"Just clam up, kid. Tell them you'd rather not say anything till you get a lawyer. They might slug you, but don't talk; that's your only salvation."

I remembered his advice and said to them as respectfully as I knew how:

"You gentlemen have arrested me for something, I don't know what. But I would rather not make any statement till I can see an attorney and get his advice."

The landlord now came to the room.

"Was this young man in this room night before last?"

"The bed wasn't slept in," he replied.

"That's good, we'll lock him up. Maybe he'll talk then. You come along with us, too. We want you to identify the dead one."

The city jail was but a few blocks away and all four of us walked there together. They took me inside and unlocked the handcuffs. A man at a desk asked my name and age. I was then taken out the back door, and across a yard into the jail building and locked in a cell with a solid iron door, in a remote corner of the building. They didn't threaten to beat me up, and asked no more questions. A jailer came at noon with a trusty, who put a pan of very good stew, a tin cup of coffee, and half a loaf of bread in the cell.

I said to the jailer: "Mister, could I see a lawyer?"

He shut the door and locked it without answering me. The door wasn't opened again till midnight. I was lying awake on a bunk fighting bedbugs in the dark. It seemed they were trying to eat me alive.

"Step out here, young man."

I stepped out in my stocking feet.

"Put your shoes on, and come with us."

They were the same two men that arrested me. They took me out and up the streets into the next block where we stopped at an undertaker's. They led me to a back room and up beside a table on which a figure was lying, covered by a long, sheetlike, white cloth. I stood there beside the table between the two officers for a moment. Then, suddenly, one of them snatched the sheet away from the upper part of the figure. The other shook me violently and shouted:

"Did you ever see that man before?"

I knew Smiler was there before he snatched the sheet off. When we went into the undertaker's I felt they were going to show me his body, but I couldn't understand why. I learned later that some people are unnerved at the sudden sight of a gruesome corpse, and, weakening, talk.

It hurt me to look at Smiler, his smile forever gone, changed to a hideous, snarl-like grin, and a gaping hole in his throat.

I couldn't think of anything else, so I said : "I want to see an attorney, please."

"You'll get a lawyer when we get done with you. You were with that fellow when he was shot and we are going to charge you with an attempt to commit burglary if you don't tell us where you were night before last."

I was locked up again.

The following day the two officers took me out to the booking desk where I was formally charged, and on the morning of the third day I went into the police court for my hearing. One of the shyster lawyers, or "stir steerers," as the bums call them, came over to me.

"They tell me you want a lawyer," pointing to the officers.

"Yes, I do."

"Got any money, or friends ?"

"I've got fifteen dollars in the office – and no friends."

"Give me an order for the money, and I'll look after you," he said.

I gave him the order, he spoke to the two officers for a minute, and then asked the judge for a continuance of twenty-four hours. This was granted, and I was led back to the bedbugs in the dark cell.

The next day when my case was called, the lawyer stood up and started talking.

"Sit down!" roared the judge.

He obeyed.

A woman wearing a thick veil was called. I could not distinguish her features. In a few words she told of shooting a man at her window. She saw but one man, the one she shot. She was excused and hastily left the courtroom.

My landlord was called, and testified that I was the roommate of the dead burglar; that I was not in the room the night he was killed, and when I appeared the following night I had on a different, a new suit.

The officers testified that they arrested me in the room and that I had refused to make any statement. The prosecutor stood up.

"Officer, when you accused this defendant of being an accomplice of the dead man, did he deny it?"

"No, sir, he did not."

The prosecutor looked wise and sat down with a satisfied air – as if I had been found guilty.

"Anything more?" asked the judge.

The prosecutor got up again. "It's as plain as the nose on your face, Your Honor. The dead man and this chap went out to rob that house. When the other fellow was shot, this chap tried to help him away, but he was too far gone. Then, what did he do?

"Your Honor," he said, ominously pointing a finger at me, "he robbed his dead companion. The dead man's pockets were turned inside out. But in his haste this man overlooked this – this telltale blood-soaked receipt," and he waved it about with great effect.

The judge frowned at me. The courtroom chair warmers craned necks in my direction.

"What about that new suit he has on?" continued the prosecutor. "He either bought it or stole it since the shooting. Why? Because the suit he wore that night had blood on it. Blood, Your Honor, blood," he finished hoarsely.

I looked down at my shoes, wondering if the wizard was going to point out the dark spots on them that I hadn't succeeded in scrubbing off entirely.

"Anything for the defense?" inquired the judge.

"We waive our defense," said the "stir-steerer." He left the room, and luckily I never saw him.

"Defendant held to await the action of the grand jury."

I was led away.

It was a relief to get into the county jail, away from the bedbugs. It was clean. I was put in a cell with a fine old Mormon farmer, charged with polygamy – unlawful cohabitation, to use the legal phrase. He was well supplied with tobacco and food, from friends outside, which he shared with me. We were confined to the cells all the time, and I made no acquaintances while there. I did not try. I was much discouraged at this turn of things against me, but was still hopeful of getting out and returning to my father.

"You've been indicted by the grand jury," said the jailer one morning, some three weeks later, "and to-day you go up to the 'big house'."

Utah then was a territory and all persons indicted were at once transferred to the custody of the United States marshal who, in addition to his other duties, acted as warden of the territorial penitentiary. An hour later I was taken out of my cell and turned over to a big, rawboned man with a worn pistol swinging from a holster on his belt.

"Young feller, I don't put irons on none of 'em," he said to me, tapping his gun. "Ef you want ter run, that's yore business."

In an hour I was at the penitentiary, where I made friends and incurred obligations that turned my thoughts away from home and sent me back on the road.

NINE

TO SAY I was shocked, stunned, or humiliated on entering the penitentiary would not be the truth. It would not be true in nine cases out of any ten. It would be true if a man were picked up on the street and taken directly to a penitentiary, but that isn't done. He is first thrown into a dirty, lousy, foul-smelling cell in some city prison, sometimes with an awful beating in the bargain, and after two or three days of that nothing in the world can shock, stun, or humiliate him. He is actually happy to get removed to a county jail where he can perhaps get rid of the vermin and wash his body. By the time he is tried, convicted, and sentenced, he has learned from other prisoners just what the penitentiary is like and just what to do and what to expect. You start doing time the minute the handcuffs are on your wrists. The first day you are locked up is the hardest, and the last day is the easiest. There comes a feeling of helplessness when the prison gates swallow you up – cut you off from the sunshine and flowers out in the world – but that feeling soon wears away if you have guts. Some men despair. I am sure I did not.

Inside the prison I was brought before a convict clerk who took my name, age, and nativity. I lied about them all. I couldn't cheat the scales or a measuring machine, and they got my correct weight and height. I did screw my face up a little when I was photographed, and felt good about it. My clothes were not taken, nor was my hair cut. I had a bath and was turned loose in the yard where there were about one hundred prisoners, some, like myself, in outside clothes awaiting trial, and others in convict stripes doing time. The penitentiary was small then. There was no work except farming and gardening, which was all done by "cohabs," Mormons convicted of unlawful cohabitation, and a very decent lot of men they were, never complaining of persecution, always ready to help their fellow prisoners, and freely dividing the food, money, and tobacco with which they were well supplied by friends and relatives.

The other prisoners played poker all day in the yard on blankets, and occasionally a game of baseball, when they could get up enough ambition. The food was fair. There was no discipline. Prisoners were expected to appear at their cells at evening to be locked in, and to stay in them till they were let out in the morning. They didn't always do that. In prison parlance, the place was a "playhouse."

The first man to speak to me in the yard was Shorty, the safe expert we had visited. He came directly up to me and put out his hand. "Kid, that was tough about Smiler. I wanted to see you both and apologize. I thought you put me in the hole for some coin, but I found out that the people lost just what you both said. I couldn't imagine a gambling house with a six-hundred-dollar bankroll."

Shorty was one of the patricians of the prison, a "box man" doing time for bank burglary. "I'll put you in with the right people, kid. You're folks yourself or you wouldn't have been with Smiler."

I had no friends in the place. But the fact that I had been with Smiler, that I had kept my mouth shut, and that Shorty had come forward to help me, gave me a certain fixed status in the prison that nothing could shake but some act of my own. I was naturally pleased to find myself taken up by the "best people," as Shorty and his friends called themselves, and accepted as one of them.

Shorty now took me into the prison where we found the head trusty who was one of the "best people" himself, a thoroughgoing bum from the road. The term "bum" is not used here in any cheap or disparaging sense. In those days it meant any kind of a traveling thief. It has long since fallen into disuse. The yegg of to-day was the bum of twenty years ago.

"This party," said Shorty, "is one of the 'Johnson family.' " (The bums called themselves "Johnsons" probably because they were so numerous.) "He's good people and I want to get him fixed up for a cell with the right folks."

"Why don't you go out and see George and his outfit? There's an empty bunk in their cell."

We hunted up "George and his outfit." They knew all about me apparently, for George said, "Sure, put him in with us. If you don't they'll only stick some gay cat in there and we'd have to throw him out in the middle of the night."

"What have they got on you, kid?" asked George. I sat down with them all and went over the whole thing from the shooting of Smiler to my arrival at the prison.

"And you've made no statement yet?"

"No".

"Not even to the shyster?" George inquired.

"Not even to the shyster," I replied.

George turned to the others. "He'll beat that case."

"Sure, he will," they all said.

"Judge Powers can beat that case before lunch any day," said Shorty.

"How's he going to get the judge to defend him? He hasn't a dime, and you're talking about the best lawyer in the state," George wanted to know. It was Shorty's time to get superior now. "Where did I get that two hundred dollars that's out in the office? Didn't him and Smiler bring it up here to me for my end of that chippy gambling house's bankroll. The judge will take this case for a hundred; it's only an hour's work for him."

George smiled. "Shorty, I knew damned well you'd do that," and to me, "Kid, that's what comes of bein' on the square. If you'd burnt Shorty for his end of that coin, you'd have been here just the same and you'd have got a beatin' instead of a lawyer and a lot of good advice from real people."

My case was disposed of right there. I had an attorney. But the bums had already tried me and I was found not guilty. All I had to do was wait for the day to come and I would be free. I was very grateful to them all, and tried to tell them. "Aw, forget it," they said.

"You can pay me the money when you get out and are lucky," said Shorty. "I'll send for Judge Powers in the morning."

At supper time I fell in line with my new friends and ate at the same table, after which we marched to our cells and were locked in. These scheming yeggs had managed to get possession of the most desirable cell in the prison, probably by bribing the trusty prisoner whose duty it was to look after the cell house. On each side of the cell was a framework ingeniously made of angle iron that contained two bunks, one above the other. The mattresses were filled with clean straw, the blankets were new and clean. George gave me a small feather pillow. In the center of our cell at the upper end was a table on which stood a fine Rochester oil lamp that gave plenty of light. Newspapers were produced, and the "best people" settled themselves for the evening.

George, who by reason of his age and experience was "captain of the outfit," explained to me that, being the last man in the cell, it was my duty to empty the slop bucket in the morning and sweep out.

I must stop to describe briefly my three cellmates, all persistent and professional criminals, because of their influence on my after life.

A name on a prison register doesn't usually mean anything. Although I knew George well later, I never learned from him his family name or birthplace. To ask about those things in the underworld is to invite suspicion. All criminals conceal them carefully and resent questions. George was known on the road and to the police as "Foot-and-a-half George" because of an injury to one of his feet that cost him a couple of toes and caused a slight limp. It happened in this way, as he told me one night when we were waiting to open up the powder house at a rock quarry and get a supply of fresh dynamite, caps and fuse.

"I always crush into these powder shacks for my 'puff' for two reasons; first, it's always in good condition; second, if you buy it you've got to leave your mug with the storekeeper. He's always suspicious of anybody buying explosives and is apt to remember you and cause trouble later in case of a pinch.

"I got this bum foot," he said, sticking it out, pointing to the shoe with its bent-up toe, "through buying a roll of rotten fuse at an out-of-the-way general store in Montana. I was goin' against 'P.O.'s' then. I always favored post offices because in the small country ones the postmaster has to furnish the box himself and gets the cheapest one he can find. He don't care because the government stands the loss if it's a plain burglary from the outside.

"Besides that, you're a cinch to get some coin and a bundle of stickers out of every 'P.O.' You can peddle the stamps anywhere at sixty or eighty per cent and they can't be identified. Then again, if you do fall, the government don't hang a lot of prior convictions on you and bury you. The limit for a 'P.O.' is five years and you never get that if you use a little judgment. Yes, I'm strong for the government," mused the veteran, reflectively.

"This caper I'm tellin' you about was a third-class 'P.O.' outside of Butte, Montana. It was soft, and good for a few hundred dollars so I decided to go against it alone. No use takin' a bunch of thirsty bums along and stealin' money for them to slop up in some saloon the next day. Anyway, I had a hole in the old box an 'a shot in it in half an hour. I strung the fuse to a window and touched it off from the outside. It spluttered along the floor and up to the door of the box, but nothing happened. After a few minutes I went back inside to put on a fresh piece of fuse. Just as I got in front of the box there was a roar, the door came off, and knocked me flat. The edge of it caught my foot on the floor and smashed all the toes"

"Did you get the coin?"

"You're damn right, I did.

"After my wind came back I got the coin and stickers, limped outside where I had an old 'swift' tied to a hitching rack. I had no saddle and it was a tough ride into Silver Bow Junction. But I got there before daylight and grabbed a rattler into Pocatello where 'Salt Chunk Mary' put me away, got a doctor, and got rid of my 'stickers.' That's why I'm so particular about my fuse," he concluded.

This grizzled old yegg was a by-product of our Civil War. Apprentice to a village blacksmith, he was drafted into the army, where he learned the disruptive force of powder, and many other things useful to him in his profession of safe breaking. His rough war service, his knowledge of mechanics and explosives combined to equip him for what he became – one of the pioneers of safe breaking. From black powder he turned to dynamite and afterward was one of the first to "thrash out the soup" – a process used by the bums and yeggs for extracting the explosive oil, nitro glycerine, from sticks of "dan" or dynamite. He boasted that he had never done a day's work outside of prison since he was mustered out of the army, except one year in a safe factory in the East where he went deliberately and worked for starvation wages to learn something of the construction of a very much used make of safe and its lock. Fortified with this knowledge, he followed that particular make of safe to many parts of the world, and, as he said, "knocked 'em open like ripe watermelons."

George inherited a very ordinary set of features to start with. His war scars and rough bouts on the road and in prison hadn't served to add anything to them in the way of refinement. His head rose to a point from all four sides. The "Sanctimonious Kid," one of my cellmates, once said of George: "If you were to put a dime on the top of George's head and start it sliding down the back it would fall inside his shirt collar; if you started it down his forehead it would wind up in his mouth, his lower jaw sticks out so far." His eyes were small and cunning. They looked as if they had been taken out, fried in oil, and put back. Dead, pale blue and expressionless, they gave no hint of the cunning, always-busy brain behind them. His nose wasn't worth looking at, just a small knob of soft red flesh, long since collapsed and hanging like a pendant from between his eyes. He was of medium height, broad, heavy and rugged. With all his ill-favored appearance and his rolling, limping walk that seemed to start at his shoulders and work its way down into his legs, he had a heart of gold and oak, and knowing him one readily forgave him ungovernable temper and violent outbursts of rage. He was square. His life was stormy and his death sudden and violent as "Smiler's." But that has another place in this story.

The "Sanctimonious Kid" was, in point of years and experience, second to George, and naturally second in say in the cell. All matters of importance were submitted to George first, then to "Sanc" and lastly to "Soldier Johnnie," the third man. Nothing was submitted to me. I had no say about anything. All I had to do was to keep my mouth shut and listen all I wanted to.

"Sanc" had everything that George lacked. Tall, six feet, slender and soft stepping, more active than most men half his size, you would not suspect him of two hundred pounds, solid flesh and bone. Straight without stiffness, natural, like an Indian. Dark hair, eyes and skin. Handsome, intelligent. Years after, I saw him in the dock of a crowded court room in a big city. His head was the finest, his face the handsomest, and his poise the surest of any there, from the judge down to the alternate juror. His nose, eyes and forehead might have been those of a minister or divinity student. But there was a hard look about his mouth, and something in his jaw that suggested the butcher. He was educated and a constant reader. Whether it was his appearance or his careful manner of speech that got him his monoger, "The Sanctimonious Kid," I never knew. He was serving a short sentence for house burglary, at which he was an expert.

We traveled together for several years after he was released, and I found him one of the squarest and most resourceful thieves I ever knew. At last, after one of the cleverest prison escapes on record, he went to Australia where he was hanged for the murder of a police constable.

"Soldier Johnnie," who had served a term in the army, was the youngest of the three. He was an industrious and trustworthy yegg who made his living serving as "target" or outside man, for the yegg mobs that preyed on country banks. The "target" is the most reliable man in the mob. To him is given the job of sticking up the town bull if he appears while the others are inside. He is the first one to get shot at and the last. It's his job to carry the heavy artillery and stand off the natives while the others get the coin, and then to cover the get-away.

He was born lucky. His face and figure were neutral. A hard man to pick up on his description. Medium size and weight. After one look at him you couldn't say whether his hair was brown or black, whether his eyes were gray or blue. Quiet, unobtrusive, soft-spoken, a copper would hesitate before halting him on the street.

Such were my companions, guides, friends and philosophers, day and night, till the day of my trial, which soon came.

Shorty's letter to Judge Powers brought one of his office men out to see me the next day, who got the points in my case and went away with one hundred dollars of Shorty's money. I felt better after his visit, he was so fresh, vigorous, confident. "Nothing to it, young man," he said breezily, "I'll be in court when you appear to plead and have a day set for your trial; that is, if they want to waste their time trying you."

I went back into the prison yard with his card in my hand and gave it to Shorty. He passed it to George and then to "Sanc."

"I know him," Sanc said. "He is in Powers' firm. Powers will tell him what to do. You are all right. True, he is but a second-class man, but that's not so bad. These second-class lawyers can skin a first-class bunko man any day in the week. I see no reason why he cannot skin a third-class judge in a territorial court."

I soon saw that these three cellmates of mine practically controlled the inside of the prison. They had brains and character backed by courage and the valuable background of a reputation for doing things outside.

I say they had character because, while they did wrong things, they always tried to do them in the right way and at the right time. The thief who goes out and steals money to pay back room rent rather than swindle his poor landlady has character. The one who runs away without paying her has no character. The thief who holds out a lady's watch on his pal to give to his girl has no character.

In the underworld one has good or bad character as in any other layer of society. The thief who pays off borrowed money, debts, or grudges has a good character among his fellows; and the thief who does the reverse has a bad character. Thieves strive for good character and make as great sacrifices to keep it as men do anywhere else. A burglar can have friends, but he has to pay his room rent or he will lose them, and they will despise him.

Because of this quality these three men had money in the prison office, sent them by friends at liberty.

They had visitors frequently, who kept them well supplied with books and magazines. The evening mail brought newspapers from many cities. They kept well informed, particularly about criminal and legal doings. The papers were carefully read at night, and the next morning "routed" throughout the prison till, torn and read ragged, they found their way into the hands of the lowliest "bindle stiff" in the farthest corner of the yard.

There were fat times when we didn't go into the dining room for a week. A half-gallon bucket of milk was left at the cell every evening. Loaves of fresh, hot bread were smuggled up from the bakeshop, and juicy steaks from the guards' quarters. These creature comforts helped to take the curse off the place, and mitigate the prison pangs. Our light was put out, not when the nine o'clock bell rang, but when George, or Sanc, or Johnnie felt like going to sleep. The guards looked the other way when they went by in their felt-soled shoes, on their night rounds through the prison.

In the prison yard there was a deep well from which water for bathing and other uses was pumped to a large tank on the prison roof. The pump was manned by four prisoners who had to work in one-hour shifts. A gang of eight men were detailed each week for this work, which was not hard – nothing more than exercise – and no one ever complained. My name was called one Saturday evening and I was instructed to report at the pump the following Monday morning. I thought nothing of it and would have pumped cheerfully. But that night "Soldier Johnnie," who was something of a jail lawyer and agitator for his and his friends' rights remarked that they were wrong in forcing me to work because I had not been convicted of any crime and that I ought to refuse to do it. The other two took the matter up and it was argued pro and con. They were pretty technical about it, and the weight of opinion was that it would be establishing a dangerous precedent for an unconvicted man to do any work of any kind in the prison and a test case should be made of it

I was willing enough, and, looking back at it now, I believe I was glad of the chance to do something to raise myself in the estimation of these distinguished characters.

Monday morning I refused to work, explaining to the officer in charge that I was not lazy, but felt they had no right to order me to work before I was convicted. He appeared surprised and took me to the office of the prison captain. He heard me out, and turning to the guard, said "Throw this fresh kid in the cooler and leave him there till he gets ready to work."

I was given an old pair of overalls and a cotton shirt to wear in the "cooler," where my outside clothes would have been ruined. The cooler or dark cell was the same as other cells, except that there was nothing in it and the door was solid. admitting no light. The floor and walls were of thin steel and very cold. I slept on the floor without any kind of bedding or cover. There was but one fixture in the cell, a sheet-metal bucket smelling strongly of chloride of lime. My sentence carried the further punishment of bread and water, one thick slice a day and about a quart of water.

A guard opened the cell in the afternoon the first day and put in a quart tin cup of water but no bread. As he was closing the cell, he said, not unkindly:

"You're a damned fool, kid. You'd better weaken and promise to go on the pump. I'll tell the captain now, if you want, and you won't have to freeze in here to-night."

"No, I won't weaken," I declared.

"All right, but if you change your mind just rap on the door with that tin cup."

My teeth were chattering before nine o'clock that night, it was so cold. I could not sleep on the cold steel floor and walked up and down in my stocking feet all night. The next morning it became warmer and I slept in fits till noon when the guard came with my bread and a fresh cup of water. The bread was about half eaten when something got between my teeth that made me stop chewing, hungry as I was.

I examined it, lying on my belly at the bottom of the door, where there was a crack of light. It was a piece of chicken quill about an inch long. I couldn't imagine how it got into the bread, and out of curiosity and having nothing else to do, I broke it apart. There was a tightly rolled piece of paper inside, on which was written: "Stick. We'll feed you tonight." There was no name, no explanation. I knew it was from my cellmates, and put in the balance of the day trying to figure how they would manage to get food into that tight cell in plain view of a guard all day and night.

The cell above me was part of the prison proper, and was occupied by two prisoners doing time. That afternoon I heard unusual noises in it, and they indicated that someone was moving out or in. Immediately after "lockup" in the evening there was another new noise. Prisoners in dungeons rely almost entirely on sounds to tell them what is going on about them. Every sound has its meaning. No sound escapes them, and any new or unusual sound must be thought out and classified at once.

The sound that attracted my attention was a low, grinding rasping that seemed to come from the floor of the cell above, which was the roof of my cell. One person above walked back and forth with his shoes on, making considerable noise. Something very unusual. The rasping became more distinct, and after an hour's thought I concluded that somebody up above was boring a hole through the thin steel floor and that the walking was to cover the noise of drilling and to keep watch for the guard. Before nine o'clock there was an inch hole in the floor, and strips of tender meat, long pieces of bread, toasted to hold them together, cigarettes, and matches were being lowered into my cell. After them came a long, thin piece of rubber hose, from which I sucked about a quart of strong coffee.

I spent about three weeks in the cooler and never missed my evening meal. My cellmates bribed the night guard to give me a blanket at night which he took away from me before he went off watch in the morning, to protect himself. All in all, I didn't fare so badly and was getting pretty well settled down to life in the dark cell when they took me out one evening and sent me back to my cell with instructions to be ready in the morning to go to court. I found my clothes in good shape and a clean shirt had been procured for me by my cellmates.

They seemed to think they owed me an apology for not being able to get food into the dark cell until the second night, explaining in great detail how they had to get two gay cats moved out of the cell above me and have two members of the "Johnson family" put in it, who would attend to the matter. I was instructed by them to ask for an immediate trial; the captain had declared that he would keep me in the cooler till I either got acquitted or went to work pumping.

The next morning the man from Judge Powers' office was in court and told me to plead not guilty. When this formality was done with, he asked for a trial on the earliest possible date, saying that it would not take more than two hours to try the case.

"Two hours," said the judge, looking over his calendar, "how would the day after to-morrow do?"

There was no objection from either side. The case was set for trial. I went back to the prison and into the cooler. That evening my rations came down as usual. The guard gave me my blanket, but I couldn't sleep. Everybody was confident I would be acquitted, but I was afraid. I remembered my experience in Denver when the judge gave me fifteen days without giving us a hearing, and at Port Costa when Casey gave us ten days. I imagined the procedure would be about the same in this case and was very uneasy.

The next evening I was sent back to my cell. I found plenty to eat waiting me, and after a good supper my case was tried by my cellmate lawyers. They threshed it out from every conceivable angle, and declared that if I got convicted I would have to do it myself on the witness stand. They were so sure I wouldn't come back that George gave me a ten dollar bill.

"Take that, Kid, you'll need it. You can send it back when you feel able."

I promised to write them, and we agreed on a fictitious name for me to use. They all shook hands, bade me good-by, and sent me away in high hopes.

Judge Powers himself was in court the next morning. A fine, tall, gray, elderly gentleman, he patted me on the back in a fatherly manner.

"Young man, I am going to put you on the witness stand and ask you one question: 'Are you guilty or not guilty of this charge?' You answer 'No,' and don't answer any other questions from anybody unless I tell you to."

The jury was drawn in ten minutes. The witnesses that testified at the police court came on in the same order and gave the same testimony. Judge Powers asked the veiled woman we were preparing to rob if she had seen me at her house on the night in question or on any other night. She answered that she saw but one man, the one she shot. The detectives confined themselves to the truth. Powers looked at his watch with the air of a busy man being detained over a trifling matter, and dismissed them without cross-examination. He waved the landlord off the stand without questioning him. When the prosecutor said: "That's our case, Your

Honor," Powers looked at him, and then to the jury.

"Is that all?" he asked, frowning.

I was put on the witness stand and answered "No" very positively to his question. The prosecutor hadn't anything to cross-examine me about. He started a few questions, but was stopped and gave up. My attorney made some motion and was overruled. He then offered to let the case go without argument from either side, but the prosecutor wanted to talk and the judge told him to go ahead.

He argued about the same as the prosecutor in the police court, waved the bloody room-rent receipt and harped about the change of clothes and my absence from the room, and my refusal to make any statement. He dingdonged away till the judge ordered him to stop.

Judge Powers went over the case in five minutes, the jury was instructed in five more, and went away to the jury room. I was nervous. I thought my attorney had not asked enough questions, hadn't argued enough. The judge went into his chambers. Judge Powers followed him in for a visit. A few courtroom hangers got up and went out. Nobody paid any attention to me. The bailiff who had me in charge strolled about the room, gossiping. There was no dock in the courtroom. I was sitting outside the railed-off enclosure at the attorneys' table. The jury hadn't been out fifteen minutes, but I was so nervous I couldn't sit still, and got up to stretch my legs. The bailiff was busy talking to a man who came in from the street. His back was turned to me as I walked a few steps up the aisle in the direction of the door, and then back.

The next time I walked farther toward the door before turning, and still he never looked at me. The third time I went to the door and out, and oozed down the broad, single flight of stairs into the main street. Dodging between two hacks at the curb I crossed to the opposite side of the street and looked back up the stairway to the courtroom – no alarm yet. Directly in front of me was a basement restaurant. I went downstairs, straight through the dining room to the kitchen, into the back yard, and then to the alley without being molested. When I got out of the alley I turned every corner I came to for fifteen minutes and finished in the railroad yards, instinctively.

The whistles were blowing for twelve o'clock, noon. I saw no signs of any outgoing trains and decided to plant myself somewhere nearby till night, when I could get a train or walk out of town in safety. I found an old deserted barn and hid up in the loft, hungry and thirsty, till dark.

A passenger train was due out on the Rio Grande at eight. With much caution I made my way along between lines of box cars till I got near enough to the depot to get aboard the blind end of a baggage car. I held the train all night, carefully dodging about at every stop.

At daylight, as the train slowed down for a stop, a man climbed up beside me. "You're arrested," he shouted, tapping a big gun in its holster.

I was discouraged. After all my hiding and dodging and starving, I must now go back to Salt Lake. He took me off the train and held my arm as the train pulled out. I was scared and desperate. I could see the penitentiary opening up for me again, and the dungeon. As the last coach was even with us, I gave the constable, that's who he was, a vicious push and he fell into a ditch beside the track.

The train was moving fast now but with a tremendous effort I clutched one of the handbars and the momentum threw me up on the rear steps. Just as I landed, one of the trainmen opened the rear door and saw me. He had his mouth open to say something when he saw the constable crawling out of the ditch, firing his pistol in the air and making signs to him. He pulled the bell cord.

As the train slowed down two more trainmen appeared and the three began kicking me. I jumped off and fell into the hands of the constable, who came up reinforced by some natives from the depot. They all fell on me and gave me an unmerciful skull dragging. After they got done scruffing me around, two of them took me by each arm and the constable fastened both hands in my coat collar from behind. The ones that couldn't find a place to lay hold on me surrounded us, a tribe of small boys appeared from nowhere, and I was dragged, pushed, and bumped across the fields to the village and thrown into the jail.

When I was safely locked in, the constable mopped his forehead with his sleeve, and, shaking his fist at me, said: "Sure as God made little apples I'll see that you get ten days." They all went away then except the small boys. They lingered around all afternoon peeping in at the windows.

It was a mail-order jail – two steel cells on a concrete foundation. A cheap wooden shack had been built around the cells to keep the weather out. The door of the shack was always open and there was plenty of light. The cell they put me in was clean, and there was a roll of new blankets in it. I was the only prisoner.

I unrolled the blankets and, stretching out on the floor, tried to figure out what had happened. I couldn't understand the constable's threat to get me ten days, and concluded he was so excited that he said ten days when he meant ten years.

He turned out to be a very decent fellow. He was postmaster, section boss, and constable. He appeared at the jail in the evenings with a big dishpan full of food – bread, meat, butter, a fruit jar full of fresh milk, and half a pie. He apologized for having lost his temper and treating me so roughly, asked me if I wanted tobacco, and made a special trip back to his house for some old magazines.

I was surprised to learn that I had been arrested for trespass or stealing a ride. He explained that the bums had burned a string of box cars farther up the road and the "company" had sent out orders to arrest them on sight and give them ten days.

"It's a wonder somebody along the road didn't tell you about it." he said. "You're the first one I've seen for a month. The bums are all going over the Union Pacific now instead of the Rio Grande. It's too bad. You'll get ten days sure in the morning. Company's orders. Good night."

I put in most of the night trying to think up a talk for the judge next morning. After bringing my breakfast the constable went after him, and about nine o'clock they appeared, a few town loungers following them. They didn't even take me out of the cell for my "trial."

The judge asked my name, read the law from a code he brought along, listened patiently to my talk, and solemnly sentenced me to ten days in the jail. I asked him to take my ten-dollar bill and let me go, but he refused it.

"Sorry, young man. Can't do it. Company's orders, ten days."

One of the loungers threw me a Salt Lake newspaper, another gave me a sack of tobacco, cigarette papers, and matches. When they had gone I opened the paper and found the story of my escape from the courtroom. The reporter treated it humorously, and made fun of everybody connected with my trial. I didn't know what he saw about it that was so funny till I got to the end of it, where he said the jury came in with their verdict of "not guilty" before I was out of the block.

This took a big load off my mind; nothing to fear now. I could go back to Salt Lake and wait for my friends to come out of prison. The Sanctimonious Kid had but two weeks more to do, Soldier Johnnie but a month. George had almost a year yet to do.

All thought of going home was gone. I owed money to Shorty and George. That must be paid. All worry was off my mind now and I began planning to get some money when I got out. My head was full of schemes I had absorbed during my month in the penitentiary. George's tales of fat post offices and country general stores came back to me. Idle all day in my cell, my eyes and thoughts turned to the big general store directly across the street from the jail.

The constable often talked to me in the evening while I ate supper. I learned from him that all the money in the town was in the big safe in the store, his post office money and stamps included. The store owner, as was often the case in small towns, did a banking business and had acquired about all the money in the place.

It was a puzzle to me how to get out of the town when my time was up without spending my ten dollars for fare. This was not to be thought of. The constable solved it by volunteering to put me on a freight train that stopped there in the daytime and fix it with the crew to let me ride back to Salt Lake, where I could start east over the Union Pacific.

The morning my ten days expired I went over to the store, bought some tobacco, and waited around till time for the train. I got the make of the big safe, its location in the store, and any other information I could, without asking questions, and decided to report the matter to my friends at Salt Lake. The constable fixed me for a ride, as he promised, but instead of stopping at Salt Lake I went on to Ogden and wrote a letter to Sanc, telling him where I would be when he came out. I was careful with my ten dollars and had half of it when he appeared at Ogden.

I at once told him of my ten-day sentence and about the fat general store. He had promised to wait for Soldier Johnnie, who was due in three weeks, and offered to pay my expenses till then, when something might be done about my store.

Johnnie was discharged in due time and arrived at Ogden. He was pretty well supplied with money and there was no rush about doing anything. We talked over the general store, but Johnnie didn't like the looks of it. The night trains didn't stop at the town, and it was so far from Salt Lake that horses were out of the question.

"No getaway," he said. "I can beat the box all right, but we can't get out of there if we do get the money." Sanc agreed.

During my ten-day stay in the town I had turned over in my mind a hundred plans, but only one of them seemed feasible, and I was almost afraid to broach that to them. At last, when I saw they were going to give it up as a bad job, I said to them:

"Can't you both go over there, get yourselves ten days like I did, make a key for the cell, and go out at night and get the box? You could plant the money and lock yourselves up again. Then when your time is up you can go away and come back for the coin when the thing cools off."

They looked at me and laughed. An hour later Sanc said to Johnnie, "Say, there might be something in that, after all. We would have a perfect alibi."

The bizarre appealed to Sanc.

After some discussion they decided to "look into it."

TEN

AN apprentice to a mob of yeggs has to do the rough unskilled work just as if he were learning a trade from any craftsman. I was sent out to get dynamite, caps, and fuse at a railroad construction camp, and returned with them safely. My next job was to go out and buy a number of twist drills. Johnnie hired a horse, bought a couple of blankets and a pair of overalls, and set off to look over the general store. The dynamite and drills were to be left near the store so they would be available in case they decided to "crush" into the jail and beat the box while serving their time.

He returned in a week, very enthusiastic. The box looked good. There were guns and ammunition in the store. The jail was empty. There was a blacksmith shop where other necessary tools could be had, the town was dead at night. He had fitted keys to the padlocks on both the jail cells (all this would have been my work if I had not been known in the town), and had planted his "dan," caps, and fuse safely near the jail. He had picked out another spot near the jail where the money was to be planted.

Their plan was to buy tickets to the town nearest the one where I was arrested, on the same passenger train, then to get out and on the baggage, where the hostile constable would find them. I was given enough money to supply my wants till the business was over. They secreted the jail keys carefully in their shoes. The cautious Johnnie had also planted in the empty jail files and blank keys to be used in case they lost those they were carrying.

"The only danger is," said Sanc, "that some other bums may be picked up and thrown into this jail with us."

"In that case," Johnnie replied, "we'll have to do our ten days and crush right back in again and stay there till we can get the jail all to ourselves."

"Kid," said Sanc, as they were leaving, "watch the papers. If it goes all right we'll be back in about two weeks. If it goes wrong, and you never can tell, you will know from the papers what happened. Then send somebody up to the 'stir' to see George and he will tell you what to do."

Ten days later the burglary was reported in the papers. Four thousand dollars had been taken from the general store and the man hunt was on.

The burglars had worked quietly. The theft was not discovered till opening-up time the next morning. The thieves were evidently experts, and left behind them the most complete set of safe-breaking tools seen in years, etc., etc. They had escaped by taking a hand car from the section house. It was found wrecked several miles down the railroad track.

Johnnie and Sanc had strengthened their alibi and strangled any suspicion that might fall on them by taking the "John O'Brien" – the bums' term for hand car, so called because every other section boss in those days was named O'Brien – and starting it down the railroad. There was a slight grade and it traveled several miles before jumping the track into the ditch, where it was found wrecked, "abandoned by the burglars."

The hunt started from there. Blanket stiffs looking for work were brought in, questioned locked up for a day or two, and let go. The trains were searched up and down the line. Bums were brought in, got their ten days, but the burglars escaped and in a week the hue and cry was over. It was almost three weeks before the burglars showed up at Ogden. They were nervous and irritable, complaining that the jail had got uncomfortably filled up the last few days they were there. They got lousy from the blanket stiffs. The constable was sore about the burglary and wouldn't square them for a ride into Salt Lake as he had done for me, and they had to pay their fare out of the town. Their money was almost gone, and there, in that little burg, was four thousand dollars that couldn't be touched for at least a month, and somebody was liable to "steal" it on them. I got nervous, too.

We decided to go up to Pocatello and kill the month around Salt Chunk Mary's, where we would be safe and welcome, and where they could borrow enough money to live on until the time came to go after the four thousand. After a night's ride we were welcomed by Mary, who spread the customary feed of beans and salt pork before us. She inquired anxiously about Foot-and-a-half George. She seemed to know every bum on the road of any consequence.

Johnnie put in his time down in the jungle drinking with the bums. Sanc and I either watched the fine six-foot Indians that stalked about the town looking scornfully at their white inferiors, or the tinhorn gamblers who skinned the railroad men on pay days and each other afterward.

Pay day was coming on and the town took on a busy aspect. Small-money gamblers appeared with their women companions. "Brass peddlers," bums who sold imitation gold jewelry, principally rings, appeared on the streets with their ninety-cents-a-dozen gold "hoops" made in Wichita, Kansas, and "dropped" them to the Indian squaws and railroad laborers for any price from one dollar up. Other bums had bundles of pants and shoes planted in the jungle, the proceeds of a boxcar burglary on the Oregon Short Line. These articles were peddled openly about the railroad shops and to trainmen in the yards. A band of yeggs on their way to Great Falls and then to the "Canadian side" stopped off to thresh out their "soup" in the jungle.

The "Johnson family" became so numerous that a "convention" must be held. In any well-ordered convention all persons of suspicious or doubtful intentions are thrown out at the start. When a bums' "convention" is to be held, the jungle is first cleared of all outsiders such as "gay cats," "dingbats," "whangs," "bindle stiffs","jungle buzzards", and "scissors bills." Conventions are not so popular in these droughty days. Formerly kegs of beer were rolled into the jungle and the "punks," young bums, were sent for "mickies," bottles of alcohol. "Mulligans" of chicken or beef were put to cooking on big fires. There was a general boiling up of clothes and there was shaving and sometimes haircutting.

The yeggs threshed out their "soup" and prepared for the road. The "brass peddlers" compared notes and devised new stunts for "dropping" their wares. Traveling beggars, crippled in every conceivable manner, discussed the best "spots" for profitable begging. Beggars of this type are always welcomed at a "convention" or any other place where thieves or bums congregate.

This may seem strange, but it's a fact. The underworld beggars are the most reliable and trustworthy, the most self-sacrificing and the quickest to help of any class of people outside the pale of society. Crippled, wounded thieves, fugitives and escaping prisoners, if they know what they are about, always turn to the beggars for aid and are never refused. They are sheltered in the beggar's humble "flop," his small "plunge" (money he begs) is divided with them, and he carries messages any distance to their friends and relatives. The beggar minds his own business, settles his own feuds, and I cannot recall ever seeing one of them in court testifying against anybody for anything.

This convention at Pocatello ended in a most unusual way. Nobody was killed, none of them fell in the fire. There was no fighting. When their "pennies" were all "slopped up," and the food eaten, the bums folded their tents and stole silently away to their different activities.

Sanc and Johnnie borrowed money from Mary and we went back to Ogden, where they prepared for their journey, horseback, after our coin.

"Are you both going?" I asked.

"Yes," they answered without looking at each other. I wondered if each mistrusted the other, and if I would ever see either of them again, or any of the money.

My fear of never seeing Sanc or Johnnie was groundless and a wrong to them. They returned within a week to the cheap lodging house where we quartered at Ogden. The four thousand was split in three equal parts. I was sent out with about seventy-five dollars in silver coin to lay off for paper or gold. They looked at me curiously as I stowed away my bit.

"Top dough for you, isn't it, kid?" said Sanc.

"Yes, two hundred was the most I ever had. I didn't expect to get one-third of this money. I doubt if I earned it. I took no chances. You two did all the work."

"We talked that over," he replied, "and decided you were entitled to an even cut. It was your caper, you located it. You had the nerve to propose what we first thought was a bughouse caper. We are clean so far as the coppers are concerned. If we ever do any time for this we'll have to plead guilty to it. The constable of that town would be our best witness if we got picked up on it. He would never admit that we could screw (key) out of his jail, beat that box, plant the coin, throw the jail screws in the creek, and go back and lock ourselves up. He might admit that it could happen to some other jail, but he will swear it couldn't be done to his, see?

"But here's the main reason we gave you an even cut of the coin. From the way you stepped in Smiler's case, and the way you took your jolt in the cooler at the 'big house' we know you are 'right.' If anything had gone wrong with this caper and we had to take a pinch, we figured you would have been a big help on the outside. That's why you are declared 'in and in' with the works.

"And now that we can lay off for a while, where will we go?" turning to Johnnie.

"First," said Johnnie, "we'll go back to Pocatello and pay Mary. She told me she was going to Salt Lake soon to visit George at the 'big house.' I want to send a few dollars to some people there. The kid here wants to pay the hundred to Shorty that went to Judge Powers and the ten George gave him. You'll probably want to send something, too. We can give it all to Mary and she'll deliver it. While we're there I'll have her buy me a pair of 'smoke wagons.' No telling how soon I'll be broke, an if I have a couple of guns I won't be helpless. Then I'm going home for the winter, if nothing happens. When I got this last jolt I wrote and told my people I was going to Alaska for two years and they wouldn't hear from me till I got back.

"I go home now and then when I have a decent piece of money. My old people are both living, and I've got seven brothers and sisters. I bring them all something nice for presents, not that they need anything, but just to rub it into them. I am the youngest and always had to take the leavings. The first lock I ever busted was on the pantry in the kitchen of my old New Hampshire home so far away.

"Where are you going kid?"

"I'd like to stay with you people, but if you are going to split out, I'll go to San Francisco for a while."

"You can go with me," cut in Sanc. "I'm going to San Francisco for the winter. No New Hampshire winter for me."

I think the two of them were looking forward to a few months of quiet peace, and maybe dissipation. My thoughts were running ahead to future burglaries. No thought of going home, even when Johnnie was telling of his home life. When I was hiding in the empty house covered with Smiler's blood, I wanted to go home, because I was in a tough hole. Now I was safe, independent, the life fascinated me. No thought of home now.

"What shall I do with the balance of the dynamite and drills?" I asked. "Somebody might step on the bundle and blow the house down. It's planted out in the back."

"I'm going to meet George here in the spring when he gets out," said Sanc. "It would save us the trouble of stealing more if we could plant it." He was thoughtful for a minute.

"Kid, in the morning you go up to the bank and rent a safety box for a year – it's about four dollars. Arrange with them to let any one into it that brings a key. Tell them there will be nothing of value there, just papers, and that you may want to send some one else after them and to let any one open it who comes with the key better get two keys. After you get the box arranged for, come down, get the 'dan' and 'stems' (drills) and put them safely away in the box. When you get the receipt for the box rent tear it up, throw the pieces away, and bring me the keys. I'll plant them here in this joint somewhere where I can find them when I return."

Johnnie laughed. "Sanc, are you going to plant that stuff in the 'jug'?"

"Certainly, the bank will take good care of it and it won't deteriorate. I'm not going to carry the box key around on my watch chain and put the receipt carefully away in my pocket. If I get snared by the bulls they won't know I've got a safety box unless I snitch on myself, and if I were going to stay in this town my money would be in that box, too."

When the bank opened next morning I rented the box and was given two keys and a password, and was told that anybody bringing a key and the password would have access to the box. "Even if it's a Chinaman," said the attendant.

The receipt was destroyed, and the stuff, in a neat parcel, put in the box. Sanc took the keys, planted them somewhere about the premises, and buried the password in his fertile mind.

"Go down to the depot, kid, and get three tickets to Pocatello. We'll all stay uptown till the train is ready to pull out. No good hanging around that depot, it's lousy with bulls."

Johnnie was a typical knight of the road. He believed that beds were for sick people in hospitals, that room rent was wild extravagance, and paying fare on the railroad nothing but ostentatious spending. He protested.

"Sanc, you're not going to start paying fare?"

"Yes, I am, and I'll buy you a ticket to California if you'll come. Just look at the pleasure you would have beating your way from there back to your home town in New Hampshire."

"That's the funny part of it," said Johnnie. "My home town is twenty miles off the railroad and I always have to pay fare on the stage going in and out."

Back at Pocatello we paid Mary the borrowed money, and spent some in her place for interest. She gladly undertook to deliver the money we wanted to go to our friends at the prison, and we gave it to her, capable woman that she was, feeling as sure they would get it as if we were doing it ourselves.

Mary bought or sold anything crooked. Johnnie paid her for a couple of guns and gave her an address in Chicago to express them to. He could have bought them cheaper there, but in the matter of buying guns he was careful. Mary was square and no matter what happened, she would not talk.

"Be sure and get thirty-eight caliber, Mary," he cautioned. "I won't have any off calibers or strange make of guns. I want the kind that everybody else has. I don't want to shoot anybody, but if I do they won't dig a forty-one caliber slug out of him and find a forty-one caliber gun on me.

We parted at Pocatello, agreeing to "weigh in" (meet) at Ogden in the spring; Johnnie starting home, where he never arrived, and we to the Coast.

Eleven

WE arrived in San Francisco safely and without incident. The first thing was to get rooms. My experience in the matter of Smiler inclined me toward a room by myself. Sanc, always cautious, decided it would be safest to have separate rooms. I found a nice, quiet German hotel in the Mission where I located, and Sanc found himself a place downtown. After getting settled, Sanc took our paper money to a bank and got gold for it.

At that time storekeepers hesitated about taking paper. Many of them did not know good from bad paper, there was so little of it in circulation, and they had been loaded up with Confederate bills till they were suspicious of any paper and sometimes called in a copper to inspect it and the person who proffered it. We didn't want any of this thing, and got gold at once.

"Now for another safety box," said Sanc. "I would prefer the bank, straight, but there's too many formalities about putting it in and getting it out, and besides that you can do a lot of locating if you have a safety box. You can go in two or more times a day and you will always see people going and coming to their boxes with money or jewelry. Many women have all their jewelry in safety boxes and only take it out when they want to display it at a theater or party. They lift it on the afternoon of the evening they want to wear it, and put it back the next morning, but they have to keep it at home that night. Simplest thing in the world to tail them home from the bank.

"The safety box is also used," he continued to illuminate me, "by race-horse men, gamblers, and the moneyed macquereau, and I don't mind telling you that I'd rather "prowl" one of them than any business man. It's a joy to hear one of them squawk, and most of them would put the old index finger on you or me in a minute, just by the way of alibi.

"There is one bad objection to a safety box for a thief. The coppers are beginning to get wise that they are the greatest receptacles of loot in the world. They are loaded with stolen money, jewelry, bonds; and the larger boxes are often used to store smuggled opium and other contraband drugs. The coppers hang around them, doing a little locating themselves, and if I were known in the town I wouldn't think of having anything crooked in one of them. I will pay for the box, and tell them I play poker and may want to get money before or after banking hours, and that you are to have access to it at any time."

He got two keys and gave me one. "You can carry the key with you if you want, kid. There's nothing crooked in the box yet, but if there is later on, and I hope there will be, you must plant it till you need it. And here goes the receipt," he said, tearing it to bits and giving them to the wind.

"To-morrow, Kid, while we have plenty of coin, I want you to get a couple of guns. Thirty-eights," and he named a certain standard make. "No other kind, remember. You heard what Soldier Johnnie said, and he knew what he was doing. I suppose you'll go to the first hardware store for them, eh?" he said rather severely.

Those were the good, or bad, old days when any wild-eyed maniac could rush into a hardware store or pawnshop with money enough and buy a gun, guaranteed to kill a man a block away. They would take the number of it, to be sure, in order to get witness fees if the gun worked properly. To-day it's a little more difficult to buy a gun in California. The better stores will not sell them unless the purchaser has a permit. The other stores, and they are quite numerous, take your money to-day for the gun, and to-morrow you go to the store and get it.

"Oh, I don't know, I might look around a bit," I said. "How about getting them in a hockshop?"

"That would be just the place, kid, if you were going to shoot a burglar or stick-up man, but in this instance there's a difference. I've been carrying a gun around for ten years. Every time I fired it I was in the wrong, legally speaking, see? I've been lucky enough so far not to have killed anybody, and hope I never do, but you have to be careful just the same. The hardware store has the number of every gun. The hockshop man not only notes the number, but in most cases puts a mark on it for future reference. Your hockshop man, kid, is the hangman's handmaiden.

"You will get those guns in Chinatown at different places, one to-morrow morning and one in the evening. You have plenty of time, and the best way to spend it is in taking precautions against trouble. The Chinks are safe to do any kind of business with, buying or selling. They don't talk. I'll show you the kind of place to go this evening. The guns you will buy are probably stolen from some pig-iron dump (hardware store) outside of the state, and come into the Chinks' hands by such devious routes that the numbers are long since lost track of."

The guns and cartridges were duly bought and put away in the safety box with most of our money. The keys we planted about the places where we lived. Our clothes were few and in bad shape. Sanc proposed going to a tailor.

"Yes," I said. "Here's where one of my ambitions comes to a head. I'm going to have a nice gray suit, gray hat, and a fine leather trunk," my mind going back to the gray man and his traveled trunk that I worshipped on the depot platform in my little town. It seemed an age since then.

"If you dress yourself that way, Kid, we part. Where did you gather that insane notion? A gray suit, gray hat, leather trunk! I suppose you'd have stickers on the trunk so the coppers wouldn't have to ask you where you were from."

I was silent, ashamed to tell him where I got the notion.

"It's just as I said about the guns; you might wear that rig if you were out hunting burglars, but you wouldn't get many. Even the 'dicks' have too much sense to dress that way. Do you want everybody to look at you? Do you want every body that looks at you to remember you? You do not. You want as few people to look at you as possible, and you want those few to forget you as soon as possible," he continued, with emphasis.

"What you want is clothes that will not detain the eye for a second. Expensive as you like, and well fitting, but not loud or striking. You want clothes that a man or woman could not describe as blue, brown, or black five minutes after looking at you. You want neutral clothes. Be as positive yourself as you like, but no positive clothes. You've got to watch yourself, kid. You know that old maxim, 'eternal vigilance.' You'll have enough trouble come to you naturally and unavoidably – accidents that you cannot foresee – without advertising for it with a loud suit of rags. Ninety-nine men out of a hundred are picked up through some peculiarity of dress and identified by the same. You don't want any funny hats, either, or loud ties.

"You know when you are doing things to people you depend largely on the element of surprise. They do not look at you carefully and memorize your features. They get a fleeting, frightened glance, and you are off. But a red tie, Kid, a glance is enough, and no matter how surprised your party may be he remembers your gray suit, gray hat, or red tie."

The Sanctimonious Kid was a sober, careful character. He did not gamble and keep us broke as poor Smiler had. We went along easily and got some good out of our money. I spent days along the water front and in the park and at the beach, and evenings at shows or in the dance halls, watching the sailors, whalers, miners, lumbermen, spending their winter money in a night.

The night life fascinated me. Grant Avenue, now filled with the best shops, was a part of the Tenderloin, and all the narrow streets or alleys off it were crowded with cribs and small saloons with a dance floor in the back room. Many of them had only the short, swinging doors, and never closed from one year's end to another. The Tenderloin was saturated with opium. The fumes of it, streaming out of the Baltimore House at the corner of Bush and Grant, struck the nostrils blocks away. Every room in it was tenanted by hop smokers. The police did not molest them. The landlord asked only that they pay their rent promptly. If it was not paid on the hour, he took the door of the room off its hinges and put it behind the counter, leaving the occupant's "things" at the mercy of his fellow lodgers.

Dupont Street, now Grant Avenue, began at Bush and carried the Tenderloin over into Chinatown, where old St. Mary Church rose from the heart of it, brooding over it all. It was a colorful Tenderloin – loud, drunken, odorous, and stupid from hop. Its bad wine, ill women, and worse song have gone to join the Indian, the buffalo, the roulette wheel, and the faro box. Deeply and securely dug in, it yielded slowly, inch by inch, and with scant grace, to the sledgehammer blows of the militant Father Caraher.

I made a few acquaintances around the dance halls and found my way into the hop joints. Curiosity was my only excuse for my "first smoke." It made me very sick, and although I became a "smoker" after, it was years before I touched the pipe again.

Sanc spent his time in his own way, and there were times when I wouldn't see him for a week. One night when he appeared at our eating place, he handed me a sheet of paper.

"Here's some work for you, kid. There are the names and addresses of about fifty people here and in Oakland who carry burglary insurance. It cost me one hundred dollars. The lawyer who got it for me probably gave the clerk who got it for him ten dollars. It's cheap though, at that, for it will save me a lot of footwork, guesswork, and uncertainty. A glance at that list tells you where they live, it tells you they have valuables because they are insured, and it tells me that they are careless because they are insured. It also tells me that in case of a show-down they will give up their valuables without a murmur because they are insured. It further tells me that some of them are going to collect insurance shortly, providing you get out and do your part of it, and that's this.

"I want you to look over some of those shacks. To-morrow you copy off about three names and plant that list somewhere around your hotel; then go out and look over the places. Later I'll look at any you think are possible of approach. I want to know about dogs, kids, servants, sick people – everything. The house, the porch, the basement, the yard, the alley.

"You've read a lot of books about criminals, but forget it all. Don't scrape acquaintance with the nurse girl to ask questions. Don't ask a question in the neighborhood. Just walk by and look, or get a book or paper and read where you get a good view of the house and its occupants. Look at the porches especially. This is about the time of the year for a good 'supper sneak'; it's dark when they are at dinner now.

"Take your time, and when you see one that looks tough, forget it. There ought to be a few soft ones on that list. One good one would do."

There was nothing of the Bill Sikes about Sanc. He ordered me to do things as a plumber would an apprentice. I took orders and obeyed them as any apprentice should, cheerfully. I worked faithfully day after day, reporting several places to Sanc, who took a look at them and said, "Keep on going, Kid."

At last I found a house that seemed to interest him. He looked at it and told me to quit my search and turn my attention to the place for a few evenings. It was built to be burglarized. Big yard, trees, shrubs. House of about ten rooms, two stories, porch in front and around one side. It was on a corner lot and from the side street the family could be seen, assembled at dinner.

We looked at it together for several evenings, and Sanc decided it would do. "Ordinarily," said he, "I would get this alone, but to-morrow night you will come along. That old porch may not bear my weight. If it won't, you will have to go up."

The next evening we were in the yard when they gathered round the dinner table. The upstairs was lighted as usual. Sanc left me in the shrubbery, and stepped to the side porch and upon the railing. When he grasped the upper part to lift himself, the whole structure groaned and creaked and rocked. He tried another place and it was worse. He beckoned me. "Up you go, Kid. It won't hold me. The front rooms first, remember. Take your time; we have half an hour. I'll protect you."

I went up with ease and he back to the sheltering shrubs. The nearest window was unfastened. I doubt if one of them was locked. I was nervous. My heart was pounding with the suspense till I could hear it. Sanc had instructed me well. I was fortunate enough to get the long end of what was there. It was on top of a dressing table. No money. The other rooms were bare of valuables.

I was hanging from the top of the porch, feeling for a foothold on the railing, when a pair of arms encircled me, and, thinking it was Sanc helping me down, I said softly, preparing to let go my handholds, "Have you got me?"

The arms tightened around my waist like iron bands, pinning me to the porch post, helpless.

"Yes, damn you, I've got you good!" said a strange voice. "Oh, Clarence, come out here. I've got a burglar, red-handed."

Captured red-handed, as I was, my mind turned to Sanc. I could not believe he had deserted me. Another man joined my captor in response to his call and they began tugging and hauling me, trying to break my hold on the porch roof. I could see myself being beaten, mauled, despoiled of my loot, and thrown into the patrol wagon by the two outraged and angry citizens.

Just when I was ready to let go all holds and fall into their arms, I felt the iron clasp of the one that had me around the body slacken slowly. One of them exclaimed: "Look out!" Then I heard Sanc's voice. It was not clear and soft as usual. There seemed to be a slight impediment or obstruction in his speech, which was positive enough but so different that I doubted for a minute if it was he. His precise and careful English was gone, too.

"Hey, youse, let go uh that guy or I'll tear your heads off. Want to git yourselves plugged over a bunch of junk dat's insured? Git inside an' stay there or I'll smoke the both of youse off."

My confidence came back, and I found a foothold on the porch rail. My captors were backing slowly, silently toward the door they came out of. Sanc, a fearsome object, his coat collar up, hat down over his ears and eyes, stood in the shadow of a large bush six feet away. waving some shiny thing at them. "Don't try any funny business," he said to them as I jumped to the ground. "You might get us to-morrow but not to-night. Phone your head off if you want, but don't poke it out of the house while we're in the block."

"Did you connect, Kid?" he asked when we were on the street.

"Yes, a coat pocket full," I said, brushing the cobwebs and dust off my clothes; "but why did you tell them to phone?"

"I'll explain all that to you later. You've got to outthink them. You have to have something besides guts at this racket. I sent them to the phone so they wouldn't follow us out. I couldn't have stood them off on the street with this bottle. I had to keep waving it about wildly for fear they would see it wasn't a gun. I found it right at my hand on the porch, and it served the purpose," he said, throwing it into a yard.

"I seldom carry a gun at this evening work because I can flatten the average man with a punch. However, I think I shall put a small 'rod' in my coat pocket hereafter."

We walked away briskly without attracting attention; it was early evening and there were people in every block. At a corner I started to turn toward downtown. He stopped me. "No, no; we must assume that they phoned because they did not follow us. That way you might meet the coppers on their way out."

A short walk brought us to a car line. "Take this car, Kid, and go straight to your room. I'll be on the next one; and don't lock your door when you go in. It looks and sounds suspicious at seven o'clock in the evening in a decent, quiet hotel."

He came in ten minutes after me, without knocking, and locked the door softly. "Now, kid," he said in his best manner, "we will proceed to estimate the intrinsic value of our takings in dollars and cents. That amount, divided by four, will give us an idea of what we have earned this evening."

"Why divide it by four, Sanc?"

"Because it's crooked and no fence will give you more. It's a great game, Kid. The fence divides it by four, taking seventy-five per cent of the value to pay him for the chances he takes. The loser, reporting to the insurance company, multiplies it by four to pay himself for the extrinsic value of his junk, and the annoyance caused by his burglar."

He turned to the stuff I threw on the bed. "Better brush your clothes off carefully, Kid. There are still some smudges on your coat." He looked at me critically. "And a button gone." He pointed to where there should have been a button. "Take that suit off. Put on your old one. That button is around that porch and it's enough to bury us both in Quentin. Tear the tailor's tags out of those clothes, wrap them up, go out, and throw them in a lot somewhere, not too close to this place. To-morrow you can order a new suit. That one is poison. While you're out, I'll take these stones out of their 'harness.'"

It broke my heart to throw away a new suit of clothes, but I was a good apprentice and obeyed. When I returned he had finished "unharnessing" the stones. There was a fistful of broken gold settings, and some small articles of little value. "Wrap that junk up, kid, take it out and throw it in a lot and not the same lot you left the clothes in, either," said the master.

I tore a sheet from a newspaper, and, wrapping the junk up, started out again. He stopped me. "Wouldn't it be just as well to take the balance of that paper and throw it away, Kid? Why leave it in the room? It fits the piece you have in your pocket. And be sure to throw that junk away. Don't plant it somewhere against a rainy day. Throw it away," he finished emphatically.

Again I obeyed. When I got back he had planted the stones, a very small parcel now, in the hotel wash room. On our way out he said, "One more thing now, and I will feel safe. We will get a new hat each."

We left the old ones in the store, "to be called for."

"Now, Kid, something to eat, and I will sum up for you the doings of this evening." Seated in a quiet restaurant with decent dinners before us, Sanc began.

"You probably thought when you were seized coming down the porch that I had abandoned you."

I protested, "No, no."

"Well, that's what I would have thought if I had been in your place. You see, I saw the party coming toward the door just as you were dropping off the porch roof. I was afraid if I started anything then you would go back up and get trapped inside the house. So I let things go along naturally till I thought they had gone far enough."

"You did the right thing," I said gratefully, "but why did you tell them they might get us to-morrow?"

"Ha, that's the psychology of the situation, Kid. I mentioned also that he was insured. That reminds him that he is not losing anything, and it also saves his face with the family. He went inside and said to them and the other chap, after they had looked about the house and phoned the police, 'Oh, well, we're insured. Of course if we hadn't been I would have given that other burglar a battle, tough as he was.' Then the other chap cuts in and says, 'You did the sensible thing, Tom. The police will pick them up to-morrow at some pawnshop.'

"You see, kid," Sanc continued, "those people are excited and frightened. You have to think for them and for yourself, too. When I told them they might get us to-morrow I gave them another out; they say to themselves, 'Why, of course the police will get them. How foolish of us to endanger ourselves and family over a few things that are insured and will be recovered in the pawnshops when the burglars are arrested.'

"Then I send them to the phone, and we depart."

I listened, spellbound. "You did something to your voice. I hardly recognized it."

"Simplest thing in the world. Put a fifty-cent piece or any little object in your mouth and see what a difference it makes in your voice. I venture to say that the loss of one tooth would cause a change that might be detected with certain instruments for analyzing sound. It's just as well to take such precautions. Some people have uncanny memories for voices. And now we come to the last phase of the evening's work. It hurt you to throw away your new suit. Don't worry, it's not wasted. Somebody will find it and wear it, and maybe get arrested. But this is no time for speculating about that. Suppose that button were found on that porch or maybe in one of the rooms. You might have lost it going in the window upstairs. It don't belong in the house. The presumption is that you lost it in the struggle or climbing up the porch.

"Old Captain Lees (you've heard of him) would give that button to one of his smart young 'dicks' and stand him on the Richelieu corner, Geary and Market.

"He would stand there from four in the afternoon till midnight waiting for you to come along, which you do every evening. Just think what might happen to us then. He wouldn't pinch you there. He would tail you to your room, then to my room, then to the safety box, and when they got ready in we would go. Think that over.

"If the case were big enough Lees would go through every tailor shop in town fishing for a line on you, and he might stumble on it.

"The gold mountings you threw away could have been melted at the expense of a fifteen-cent crucible and a dime's worth of borax, and would have brought us maybe ten dollars as old gold at any jeweler's. But think of the chances you take in selling it, jeopardizing the stones we have and our liberty for ten dollars – bad business.

"And that newspaper I made you throw out. Here's the reason. We might be in jail to-morrow on suspicion. We figure to get picked up any time because, well, because we're what we are. Everything in your room, if they find your room, is taken down and held and examined. Suppose that happened to-morrow and while you're locked up the parcel of junk is found in the lot wrapped in the missing part of the paper found in your room. No lawyer in California could beat that case. That proves possession and that's all they need to convict you of burglary. And here's something else about house burglary. You seldom get money. Everything has to be sold. And that's where your danger and troubles begin in earnest. Not one house burglar in a hundred is caught in the act. It's always when he is trying to sell his plunder.

"I could steal, take, and carry away," he continued, smiling, "fifty thousand dollars' worth of plunder – rugs, furs, paintings, statuary, and such junk in thirty days, if I wanted to make a pack horse of myself. But just imagine trying to dispose of it. There's where you 'sup with sorrow' as the poet says, Kid. Take nothing you can't put in your coat pocket. You've got to watch yourself like a fat man on a diet.

The smallest trifle will upset you, and you'll have leisure to repent your carelessness. When you get your new suit from the tailor's, take all the tags out of it, and when you buy a hat don't let the hatter stamp your name on the sweatband. You don't know what house you might lose it in.

"I know thieves so conceited and foolish that they have their names in their hats and monogrammed pocket handkerchiefs, and neat little notebooks with all their friends' addresses and phone numbers carefully noted. That's the type of thief that calls the police 'a bunch of chumps,' and goes to jail crying, 'Somebody snitched.'

"The police are not chumps, kid; they are just lazy, that's all. If they worked as thoroughly at their business as I do at mine, I don't know what would happen. They are human, and take the easy way. Somebody whispers to a dick. He whispers to me, and we go down to the jail, where he locks me up 'on suspicion.' The next morning he and his partner come to my cell, knock me down, walk up and down on my wishbone for a few minutes, and ask me if I am ready to snitch on myself and all my friends. If I decline to help them, they let me out. That's the lazy coppers' notion of doing police duty."

Our dinner finished, he said: "And now, after all this talk, what do you think we should do with the stones we have?"

"Why not spend a hundred dollars for fare to Pocatello and back?" I asked. "Mary's safe."

"You are learning, Kid. That's precisely what I intended doing. Mary is safe, and moreover she'll give me more than I could get around here. The expense of going to her is money spent insuring ourselves against trouble. If I try to drop the stones here, I have to take what the first man offers me or I make a dangerous enemy right there. If I refuse to be robbed and turn down half a dozen offers, I make that many bad friends, and they whisper me into jail. I could give them to some crooked saloon man, who would sell them in an hour and pay me at the rate of five or ten dollars a day, in the hope that before I got all the money I would get pinched for something else, and put away where I couldn't collect the balance. If I get insistent and demand it all at once, he throws a scare into me thus: 'Say, now, what're you trying to do, crowd somebody? If I wanted to be wrong I could turn you in to the coppers and get a favor of them some time. But I'm right. Nevertheless, don't try to crowd me, see?'

"So I am for Salt Chunk Mary's in the morning. She's righter than a golden guinea and is entitled to make the profit on the junk. I'll be back in ten days.

"While I'm away take it easy and don't go around the residence district at all. You can make the safety box about ten o'clock in the morning and four in the afternoon every day. You might locate something from there. Here's something else you can do.

"Every afternoon go into some good hotel and pay for a room for the night. Register from out of town. When you get the key, go out to your own room and make a duplicate of it. Mark your duplicate so you can identify it, and plant it somewhere. Most of the best places are using these spring locks now and you can't do anything without a key when there's a sleeper in the room. In a week you'll have keys to half a dozen good transient rooms in the best hotels, and I might get some real money out of them.

"Go back to the hotel in the evening, tell the clerk you are called out of town and ask for your money back. He will usually give it to you."

I bade Sanc good night and good-by, resolving to have something good located for him on his return from Salt Chunk Mary's.

TWELVE

DURING Sanc's absence I worked industriously, bettering his instructions by renting two rooms a day and making the duplicate keys. In most instances the clerks returned my money when I told them I was called away and could not occupy the rooms. My days were well filled with work, renting two rooms, making two keys, trying to get my room money refunded and visiting the safety box twice a day, sometimes following a depositor out and around the streets to see what he did with his money.

My evenings were my own and I spent them on the Barbary Coast or the water front. With an old suit on and a dollar or two in silver I loved to go to the sailors' boarding houses where seafaring men, brawny, brown, and tattooed, speaking all languages, ate, drank, fought, sang their strange sea songs, and told tales of hardship and adventure on all the seas. Here I learned to beware the crafty shanghaier with his knockout drops, lying in wait for strong young fellows from the country. The cowardly and unscrupulous thieves who later used chloral so indiscriminately and murderously learned its stupefying effects from the busy shanghaier on San Francisco's water front.

The wine dumps, where wine bums or "winos" hung out, interested me. Long, dark, dirty rooms with rows of rickety tables and a long bar behind which were barrels of the deadly "foot juice" or "red ink," as the winos called it. Sometimes the dump was equipped with a small lunch counter in the back where the winos could buy for a nickel a big plate of something that looked like stew, and a hunk of stale bread. The stew was served from a big pot that was always boiling. Several times a day the porter, who was also cook and waiter and wino as well, threw a box of mixed vegetables, discarded from the commission houses, unwashed and unpeeled, into the pot. Then followed a box of bones, pieces of tallow, scraps of meat trimmings, odds and ends of meat covered with sawdust from the floor of the market near by.

The patrons of the wine dumps were recruited from every walk of life. Scholars, quoting Greek and Latin poets, lawyers dissecting Blackstone, writers with greasy rolls of manuscript fraternized with broken bums from the road, sailors too old for the sea, and scrapped mechanics from the factories – all under the lash of alcohol. They sat in groups at the tables drinking the wine, alcohol in its cheapest and deadliest form, from every conceivable kind of vessel: tin cans, pewter mugs, beer glasses, stems, and cracked soup bowls – anything unbreakable that the boss could buy from a junkman. They talked volubly. They seldom laughed and never fought – too far gone for laughing or fighting. When they could drink no more or buy no more, they staggered or crawled to a bare space on the floor in the back of the room where they lay on their backs in a row with their heads to the wall, each with his hat over his hideous, bloated, purple face. The porter-cook-wino watched the sleepers carefully. When he thought they had "slept it off" enough to stand up, he roughly kicked them to their feet and herded them out into the streets to beg, borrow, or steal enough small silver for another bout. Too often they failed to respond to his kicks; he would lift the battered hat, take one look at the purple-blue face, and ring for the morgue wagon.

This pitiful crew, gathered from the four corners of the earth and from every stratum of society, whipped beyond resistance by that mysterious and irresistible craving for alcohol, drank themselves purple in the wine dumps and died on the floors or under the city sidewalks. The wine dumps are gone; can any man regret their passing? And so are the winos gone. In their places have appeared the Jamaica ginger fiend, the canned heat and wood alcohol drinker. It is difficult to study and classify them; their lives are too short.

The most disreputable wine dump in the city was in Clay Street, below Kearny, and I never failed to visit it when in the neighborhood. I had no more than stepped into the place one night when a wino at the door shouted, "Here comes the wagon, " and dashed out wildly. Some of the soberest ran out the back and disappeared. I started to the front door, but the cops were coming in. I was the first one they got, and as the cop threw me into the wagon, in the middle of my explanation, he said: "Oh, tell the judge about it, I'm no court. I'm a hundred-dollar-a-month cop, and it serves me right for being one if I get lousy throwing all you wine bums in and out of the wagon." He seemed discouraged.

I had got calloused about getting locked up and didn't worry, knowing they couldn't do much to me. But going over in the wagon my mind turned to the burglary of the week before. I felt uncomfortable and thought of my room and was thankful that it was "clean," and of the safety box and the keys I had made, and every other crooked transaction in my short life of outlawry. "No danger," I thought as the wagon rattled over the blocks, "if I cover myself up. My name is William Brown, I am nineteen years old. I was born in Pocatello, Idaho. My parents died when I was fourteen. I have supported myself since, selling papers, washing dishes, and working on farms. I came to this city this morning and am going to get a job. I went into that place out of curiosity."

I just had this short biography put together when we got to the city prison. It was in the basement of a building that stood where the Hall of Justice now is, and it was the foulest I ever saw, worse than the first one at home. There was a busy spot, that corridor in the city prison! Officers hurrying in and out, lawyers haggling at the desk about releases for prisoners, "fixers," hawk-eyed and rapacious, lurked about, cheap bail bondsmen coining misery, ignorance, and crime into thick nickels and thin dimes, and on the long bench by the wall sat a thin, wrinkled, poorly dressed woman of fifty holding a boy's hand in hers. He sat beside her, silent and stubborn. She was crying.

Ten of us from the wine dump were lined up at the desk. The officer in charge said to the man at the desk. "We'll vag the chronics and charge the new ones with drunk." The chronic winos gave their names, etc., and were hurried away down the corridor. Another chap and I were the only "new ones. " We answered all questions without angering anybody and getting knocked down. I protested that I wasn't drunk. The desk man said: "Oh, that's all right, you can go out in the morning at five o'clock on the broom." They searched me, but took nothing except a pocketknife.

We were put in a large cell about twenty feet on each side, directly across the corridor from the desk where prisoners were received and registered. The front of this cell was of upright iron bars and admitted plenty of light from the corridor. The cell was foul smelling from a fixture in one corner that seemed to connect directly with a sewer. A broken water faucet leaked continually, with a hissing sound. About ten men were there, some sleeping on the damp asphalt floor, some on the benches that lined the wall; some stood expectantly at the front waiting to be released, others squatted on their haunches in the corners, staring vacantly at the floor.

I sat on the bench and wondered about "going out on the broom" in the morning. I could have asked my cellmates. I looked for the other new one that came with me from the wine dump; he was asleep on the floor. I decided not to ask, but to wait till morning and find out for myself. Even at that age I had stumbled upon one truth, and that is, 'The best way to get misinformed is to ask a lot of questions.'

Nearly all my life has been spent in the company of unfortunate people, and while I never looked upon myself as an unfortunate, I was always accepted as one of them. Whatever knowledge I have of them was gleaned by looking and listening, and it is much more accurate than any

I could have got by asking impertinent and close-up questions. Your best friend would give you a surly answer if you were to ask him the time of day an hour after his watch had been stolen. Ask any one-legged stranger how he lost his limb and you will get something like this : "Well you see, it was this way – I got run over by a ferryboat."

Of all the many friends I have made since I gave up my larcenous life, "Shorty" is one of the most respected and highly prized. His friends are legion, and in every state in the Union; not that Shorty has traveled there and made friends of them, but that they have traveled here and made a friend of him.

Shorty's news stand is on a busy corner in the shadow of a skyscraper owned by ex-Senator Phelan, one of California's most distinguished men, and there, under his patronage and protection, he stands on his stumps ("cut-down legs" he calls them), early and late, serving thousands with papers and periodicals. He hobnobs with doctors, lawyers, business men, and politicians. He finds lost children and dogs, and returns them to their owners. Shopgirls and strangers ask him which is the best show of the week. Men around town consult him about the chances of a horse in to-morrows race. He can borrow more money on his I. O. U. than many business men in his block and pays on the minute. He is no stranger at the banks on the opposite corners. His reputation for truth and veracity is such that if he were to tell me the water had all disappeared from the bay I wouldn't go down to look.

Traveling in search of adventure when young, he lost his legs under a train but instead of despairing and sinking under this terrible misfortune, he braced himself and, picking out a bare corner on the street, built up day by day, year by year, a business that has made him independent and respected. I stopped one day at his stand, and, looking at his massive chest, broad shoulders, and fine head, I saw him in fancy a splendid figure of a man towering ruggedly above his fellows.

"Shorty," I asked, how tall were you before you lost your legs?"

He flashed me a savage look: then remembering we were friends his eyes fell to his stumps and he said with a laugh, "Oh I was taller by two feet."

That's all one gets by asking questions that wake painful memories.

From my position on the bench I could see every prisoner brought to the desk. About ten o'clock there was a stir in the hall and several policemen came in with Chinamen from a gambling-house raid. This was before they had cut off their queues, and instead of handcuffing their prisoners the cops came in driving the silent, stolid Chinese before them like charioteers. Each cop had the tails of three Chinamen's queues in each hand. Ahead of the procession walked a white man with a heavy bag of gold in his hand which he put on the desk, and waited till the names of the prisoners had been taken. Then they all went back up the corridor out of my sight – the Chinamen back to Chinatown to their gambling and the bag of gold into the bond-and-warrant clerk's office to insure their appearance in court.

Several times during the night men were brought in, questioned at great length, searched thoroughly, and led away to another part of the prison – felony cases. About midnight two young fellows about my age were brought in by a copper and stood up before the desk.

"Vag these two 'hypos,' said the cop to the desk man. He searched them most carefully, finding a small package in the torn lining of one's coat. The boy begged for it piteously. "I'll croak, officer, if you take it away from me." The cop gave him to the waiting trusty. "Throw him in." He was put in with us. Nothing was found on the other hypo, and he was "thrown in" too.

They immediately began comparing notes and taking stock, walking up and down the center of the cell nervously. They were in rags and unwashed, their shoes were broken and had no laces, and the tops flapped open showing their bare ankles. They seemed utterly unconscious of their sad condition and walked and talked as briskly as two brokers on Montgomery Street discussing the markets.

"He got my plant, Georgie," said the first one, "but you saved yours, didn't you, Georgie? Gee, Georgie, but you're a fox." His tones were honey.

"Never mind that," the other replied; "you don't have to 'Georgie' me. You're in with what 'gow' I've got. Let's bang it up before they come in and take it away from us. See if you can hustle some matches."

The match seeker glanced sharply around him. When his eye fell on me I produced some matches. "Got any smokes ?" I handed him a pack of cigarettes. He took two, gave one to his partner, Georgie, and returned the pack. His mind seemed detached from the cell. He took the matches and cigarettes from me without a word, as if he had reached up to a mantel and taken them off it. Georgie fished about the front of his trousers and brought up a tobacco sack that had been hanging suspended from a button. The sack contained his "plant," an eye dropper with a hypodermic needle soldered to it with sealing wax, and a small paper of morphine in a little tin box.

They went to a back corner of the cell and prepared their shot. About a spoonful of water and some of their meager store of "morph" were put in the tin box and matches were burned under it till it boiled, completely dissolving the morphine. It was then drawn up into the eye dropper, and Georgie injected his portion into his arm. The other boy did the same with his portion. Their outfit was carefully put away in the tobacco bag and suspended again from a button down inside the front of Georgie's trousers. Nobody paid any attention to them. They took their shot as coolly as if they had been in their room, or under a sidewalk. They seemed a little more interested in their surroundings in a few minutes. The one I gave the cigarettes to came over to me rubbing his hands briskly, smiling.

"Give us a couple more of them smokes, young fellow."

"I'd like to buy some, I said, "if I could."

"Got money?"

"Yes a couple of dollars."

"I'll fix it for you," he said most condescendingly. He went over to the bars and shouted, "Hey, Finnerty!"

In a minute the head trusty, a thin, weazened, rateyed, undersized character, came up.

"Cigarettes, matches? Sure. Anything else?"

I produced a dollar.

"What's the matter with a can of coffee and some snails?" said the hypo.

"Get whatever you can," I said, giving him the dollar.

Finnerty disappeared, and in a surprisingly short time came back with cigarettes, a gallon fruit tin half full of splendid coffee, and a bag of snails. The two young fellows took charge of the coffee and snails, spread a newspaper on the floor, and very cordially invited me to help myself.

While we were having our lunch the talk was diplomatically turned to dope and the shortage that menaced my two hypo friends and the sufferings they would undergo when there was no more and the "habit" came on, and the necessity for a shot in the morning as a bracer for them when they faced the judge. They grew so despondent over their plight that when we were done eating they decided to "shoot up" the small portion of white stuff they had left. They brightened up after this operation was over, and things looked rosier.

Just think, Georgie," said the talkative one, looking at me, "what a four-bit piece would do for us. What a life-saver ! We'll both get a 'sixer' in the morning if we go in front of the judge with our teeth rattlin' so we can't put up a talk. If I had a decent shot for the morning I could talk him out of it.

"And that rat, Finnerty, the trusty," the talker spoke to me now, "has got a ton of it out there to sell, but he wouldn't give us a jolt if we had the horrors."

"Can you buy it from Finnerty?" I asked him, interested.

"Can you? Why, that guy Finnerty would peddle you a six-shooter and a road map if you had the coin, and then snitch on you to the desk sergeant, the rat," he finished.

At that time morphine and opium were almost as cheap as tobacco. Fifty cents' worth would last them a day. I hastily dug up a half dollar and gave it to him. In answer to his call Finnerty appeared, took the half dollar, and from his shirt pocket drew a bundle of neatly folded packets of morphine. In plain sight of the desk sergeant he counted out the required number of parcels and put them into the purchaser's hand extended through the bars. They were divided at once.

Georgie said to his partner. "I think we'd better cook up a shot just to see if the stuff is all right. That Finnerty would peddle you chloride of lime if he happened to run out of 'morph.'" This seemed to be a very rational reason for taking another shot, and they did.

Given a sufficient quantity of hop, no fiend is ever at a loss for a sound reason for taking a jolt of it. If he is feeling bad he takes a jolt so he will feel good. If he is feeling good, he takes one to make him feel better, and if he is feeling neither very bad nor very good he takes a jolt "just to get himself straightened around."

Along about two in the morning a young chap about twenty was brought in to the desk. While he was being searched the two hypos had their eyes glued on him. "He ain't got a dime," said Georgie to his partner when the searching was done. The desk man gave the young fellow his cigarettes and he was locked in with us. He was neat, well dressed, and very wise looking. He sniffed at the hypos, gave me half a glance, adjusted his tie, and polished his shoes by rubbing each foot on the back of the opposite leg. He hung a cigarette on his lower lip and felt about for matches, but found none.

"Hey you," snapping his fingers at Georgie, gimme a match." Georgie gave him a few. "I'll be out of here in an hour," said the newcomer, inhaling his smoke. "I'll send you in anything you want. I'm a quick connector. I can get a ten-dollar piece before I get out of the block – sucker born every minute, you know."

"Yes, I know," Georgie replied. "I'm sorry for them poor suckers. They're all asleep down in the Palace Hotel and you're up here in the can begging matches. There's one born every minute, all right, but there's two wise guys going to jail every minute, an' beggin' matches."

The wise guy said no more, but stood by the door waiting to go out. He was standing there when I left in the morning.

Georgie turned to his companion. "That last shot didn't hit me right; we'd better cook up another an' begin to get straightened up for court."

Having bought the stuff for them, I took the liberty to sit by while they took their shot which they did without seeming to notice me. Their bony arms were gray, like pieces of petrified wood. The skin was pocked with marks, mottled and scarred from the repeated, hourly stabbing of the needle. Their shirt sleeves were encrusted with dried blood from the many punctures. And yet they appeared oblivious to it all.

"Have a little shot, young fellow?" Georgie asked cordially.

I declined. "What would happen to me if I did?" I asked.

"Why, nothing; you'd lie down on the bench and sleep like a baby till time to go out in the morning, that's all."

"Yes! And what would happen to the balance of my silver while I am sleeping like a baby?"

Georgie's partner cut in like a flash: "This is what would happen. Me and Georgie would stick right here by you and see that nobody frisked you for it."

I laughed so loud that the desk officer thinking some one had gone hysterical, stood up sleepily and peered over his desk into the cell. The other bums stirred uneasily in their sleep. Mine was the only laugh there that night. I could laugh then; I didn't know anything about hop.

My companions didn't seem hurt or offended because of my intimation that they had designs on my last four-bit piece. They fell to discussing their case and preparing a talk for the judge in the morning. Georgie was for pleading guilty, and his chum wanted "to talk the judge out of it." They couldn't agree, and looked at me. I ventured to ask what they had done.

"We've got two tough raps," said Georgie. "In the first place a hypo ain't supposed to be found within a block of police headquarters, an we' re grabbed right alongside of the building. In the second place, a hypo ain't allowed to leave Chinatown. Of course the cops know we sneak out. That ain't so bad. Our racket is peddling kindling wood to the Chinks an we've got to go out of Chinatown to get it. Last night we ducks out and down Jackson Street to the commission houses and gather up a couple of fine bindles of wood. They are pretty heavy and we're on short rations of gow and don't feel any too strong, so we decide to dash up Washington Street, the shortest route into Chinatown. We're bang up against the city prison when a big, flatfooted, harness bull steps out an' yaffles us – an here we are."

Their case looked so tough that I could think of no solution. "I wouldn't plead guilty to anything if I were you," I advised him.

"Me, neither," said his partner. "If I get six months they'll have to hang them on me. I ain't going to reach out an' grab them."

They fell into a fresh argument and their words became so personal and threatening that I feared they would do each other some great violence. I took a chance in the role of peacemaker and suggested that they take another shot and talk it over peaceably and quietly. They quit their wrangling instantly and in a minute they were on their knees in the corner of the cell with their heads together, amicably preparing another shot. Somewhere down the corridor I heard a clatter, and a singsong voice droned, "Get ready for the broom. Get ready for the broom."

I was going out. I went over to my friends in the corner with the fifty-cent piece I had left. "Here," I said, "take this." One of them, still on his knees waiting for his shot, held out his hand; his fingers closed on the half dollar. He neither looked up nor spoke to me – his eyes were on the little tin can where the morphine was dissolving in the boiling water.

The door was opened and my name called.

I stood by the door till a trusty prisoner opened it and let me out. My partner from the wine dump was also taken out and we joined four or five others in the corridor. A trusty came with an armful of brooms and gave each of us one. A husky young fellow, half awake, reached for one of the newest brooms. "No, you don't," said the trusty, "the last time you were here I gave you a good new broom and you beat it up to Chinktown and peddled it for a dime. An old broom for you."

We were detailed in pairs to sweep the sidewalks clean all around the block the prison stood on. My space was from the prison door down to Montgomery Street. An old man had the sidewalk across the street from me. Two or three assistant trusties nosed around like bird dogs to see that we swept clean and didn't run away with the brooms. When my task was done I helped the old man finish his, and he carried my broom back to the prison. The trusty dismissed me with a wave of his arm and I went up Montgomery Street in search of a restaurant where I could get some coffee with a dime I had saved from the rapacious and cunning hypos in the prison. I decided to keep away from the wine dumps in future, and out of the hands of the police vag detail that rounded up the riffraff when they got too numerous and pesty.

In a few days Sanc was back, quite satisfied with his trip to Salt Chunk Mary's. The money was split and put in our box in separate parcels. We had more than $1,000 each now, but he had no notion of taking a rest or vacation. He wanted to know right away what I had done in his absence. I reported everything including my night in jail. He asked me what I told the police at the station. I told him. "Not bad," he said, "but be careful."

I gave him the hotel room keys I had made, and he complimented me on my work and put them away for future use.

THIRTEEN

I PAUSED before a jewelry-store window in Oakland one evening, just at closing time. The clerks were clearing it out for the night. In the center of the display stood a slim, polished wood pedestal, on top of which, in a velvet cup, reposed an enormous ruby, the size of my thumb nail, set in a ring. A placard announced that this pigeon-blood ruby, valued at three thousand dollars, was to be awarded by some organization, the name of which I don't recall, to the winner of a contest they were holding.

The window was cleaned up, the display put away for the night, but the ruby was left on its pedestal when the store was closed. I got the next boat across and found Sanc. We went back to Oakland and got to the store about eleven o'clock.

"I don't know anything about rubies, kid, but if it's left there all night it's phony."

Just then two men came along, entered the store, and, locking the door behind them, went to the window and got the stone. They disappeared toward the back of the store.

"It must be genuine, kid. They are putting it away in the 'box.'".

As we walked away, Sanc said: "The window has a burglar alarm. You can see the tape around the edges. If I could devise some way to put an inch hole through the glass without cracking it clear across to the tape, the alarm would not sound and I could take the stone out with a stiff wire. To-morrow night I'll try something I have long thought of."

The next day he bought at a second-hand store a small machinist's hammer, weighing about a pound. One face of it was thick, heavy, and flat, the other was rounded to a nose about the size of a boy's marble. He bought a whipstock of tough, springy wood and made a handle about eighteen inches long, which he fitted into the hammer.

For several nights we went around to new buildings and into deserted streets where there were plate-glass windows of a weight corresponding with the one in Oakland. Sanc used his hammer like a whip, snapping the noselike face of it against windows till he became so expert he could make a hole as clean as if it had been done by a bullet, and without cracking the glass for more than six inches from it.

"Vandalism, they will call it," he said after destroying probably five hundred dollars' worth of glass, "but in reality it is a scientific experiment and a success." The impact of the hammer sounded very much like the breaking of a piece of kindling wood under foot. At last we were ready, and Sanc, as usual, gave me final instructions.

"Oakland is a tough town to take a pinch in, kid. You can't fix your case, and you'll get the limit if convicted. I'll take a gun along. You needn't. There isn't much you can do. When the bull is out of the block and pedestrians are a couple of doors away I will do the best I can. You stand near by and if anybody gets wise to me, you shout to him: "Look out, he's got a gun. Let's get a policeman!"

At nine o'clock we passed the window. A crowd was admiring the ring. At ten the pedestrians had thinned out, and half an hour later Sanc's chance came.

The store was in the middle of a block. The patrolman was at the corner going farther away. Everything was exactly right. A passing electric car swallowed the noise of the breaking glass. Sanc disengaged the hammer's nose from the hole carefully with a rasping noise. The hammer went into his coat pocket, and the wire came from beneath his coat. The top of the pedestal where the ruby rested was higher than the hole in the window, and when Sanc lifted the ring on his wire it slid slowly down and out into his hand. He threw the wire into the street and walked away. I followed behind and overtook him at the corner. A few blocks farther away he tossed the hammer into a lot. We sat apart on the train to the ferry and on the boat across to the city.

In my room Sanc removed the ruby from its setting, which I immediately took out and threw into a near-by sewer opening. When I returned he was admiring the stone. "There's a stone, kid, that, as Shakespeare says, 'A Jew would kiss and an Infidel adore'."

The Sanctimonious Kid's face wore a serious look the next evening when we met to go to dinner. "Kid" he said, "the more I think of this wonderful pigeon-blood ruby the less I think of it, if you understand what I mean. It is possible that we put too much faith in the integrity of the business firm that displayed it so carelessly. I was out to the park today and gave the thing a careful inspection in the sunlight, and there is a cold, clammy suspicion in my mind that we have been swindled – in short, I am afraid the thing is a rank phony.

"And the worst of it is there's not one person in five thousand who knows a real ruby when he sees it. There are probably three men in San Francisco who would know, but they are all square business men and we can't submit it to any of them. The next nearest man is the buyer for the big Mormon store, Zion's cooperative Mercantile Institution, at Salt Lake

City. I will take a run back there with it and get some one to have him give an opinion on it. If it's genuine I can get a thousand dollars on it. I'll be gone about two weeks, and this is what I want you to do while I am away.

"Put on your best clothes, keep clean and neat, and spend your evenings around the Diamond Palace in Montgomery Street. Go through the whole block on both sides of the street. Look into every hallway, basement, empty store, and saloon. Try to locate some place that we can go through and out into an alley or another street. The getaway's the thing, and it you can find one in the block we'll chance the Diamond Palace some evening, maybe Christmas Eve."

He left next morning after giving me strict orders to keep away from the wine dumps and attend to business. I worked faithfully and soon found half a dozen places that would serve. My time was now my own, and once more I began exploring the byways of the city.

The hypos I spent the night with in the city prison had aroused my curiosity about Chinatown. I put in many nights prowling through the alleys watching these mysterious people gambling, smoking opium, and trafficking in their women slaves. There were rumors of strange, mysterious underground passages below the streets and under the buildings, but I never saw them and I have since come to doubt whether they ever existed.

The spots most favored in Chinatown by the hypos and small beggars were the "cook ovens," places built in back of Chinese lodging houses where the occupants did their cooking on the community plan. There were warm places around the ovens to sleep in, and always a bite to eat for the asking – no Chinaman refuses to feed a hungry man.

In my experience with the Chinese I have found them charitable, frugal, thrifty, moral, and honest.

In speaking of the cook ovens I may say that it was there the word "yegg" originated. It has not yet been locked in the dictionary, but it has a place in our language and it's about time its derivation was settled once and for all. It is a corruption of "yekk," a word from one of the many dialects spoken in Chinatown, and it means beggar. When a hypo or beggar approached a Chinaman to ask for something to eat, he was greeted with the exclamation, "yekk man, yekk man."

The underworld is quick to seize upon strange words, and the bums and hypos in Chinatown were calling themselves yeggmen years before the term was taken out on the road and given currency by eastbound beggars. In no time it had a verb hung on it, and to yegg meant to beg.

The late William A. Pinkerton was responsible for its changed meaning. His business consisted largely of asking questions and necessarily he acquired much misinformation. A burglar with some humor fell into Pinkerton's hands and when asked who was breaking open the country "jugs" he whispered to the detective that it was the yeggs. Investigation convinced Pinkerton that there were a lot of men drifting about the country who called themselves yeggs. The word went into a series of magazine articles Pinkerton was writing at the time and was fastened upon the "box" men. Its meaning has since widened until now the term "yegg" includes all criminals whose work is "heavy."

Sanc returned in a very hostile frame of mind. "We've been bilked, kid. It was a French imitation. Been on the market ten years. I sold it to Tom Dennison, who runs the Wasatch gambling house in 'The Lake,' for a hundred and fifty dollars, just enough to pay expenses. If you locate a few more capers like that you'll put us in the poorhouse."

I reported my findings in Montgomery Street, and Sanc after looking them over carefully pronounced two of the getaways feasible.

"Kid," he said, "I read in the papers some time ago that a man named Charlie Rice, in New York City, put on a cheap, black alpaca coat, put his cap in his pocket, and with a pencil on his ear walked into a bank and behind the counter where there were twenty clerks at work. Unnoticed, he picked up twenty-five thousand dollars in bank notes and walked out.

"That suggested to me that I can walk into this jewelry store some evening before Christmas when they will have an extra force of clerks employed, and go behind the counter if I am dressed like a clerk. If I can get behind a counter you can surely get in front of it. I will put a tray of stones out for your inspection, and you will walk out with it. We will go over it carefully now.

"I will walk into the place about seven o'clock some evening, dressed in a black suit, white shirt, high collar, and black tie. You will go in directly behind me. You will carry a harmless-looking parcel that looks like a box of handkerchiefs neatly wrapped and tied. There will be no bottom in it. I will walk to the back of the store where there are two or three settees for patrons and visitors. You will stroll about near by. I will leave my derby hat and overcoat on a settee and try, mind you, try to get behind the main counter. I am depending upon the fact that the place will be full of visitors and customers and that there will be a number of strange clerks and that no one clerk will know all the others.

"You will follow my movements closely. When I get behind the counter I will take out the best tray I can get and set it on the show case in front of you. You will put your bottomless package over the tray, pick it up, put it under your arm, and walk out. We have two weeks to get ready. We will go down there separately and look the place over for a week. When you go in, you rehearse the thing in your mind and don't think of anything else for the next ten days."

We thought and talked of the Diamond Palace only for days and days. "Kid," said Sanc, "I heard 'Rebel George' who invented the gold-brick swindle say: 'The way to sell a brass brick is to bunko yourself first into the belief that your brick is solid gold – the rest is easy. The most successful bunko man is the one who bunkoes himself before he goes after a sucker.'"

"I am going to hypnotize myself into the belief that I am a clerk in that store from the minute I take my hat off till I put it on. You are a visitor from the minute you go in till you get your hands on the stones; then, presto, you are what you are. If we can get one of the larger trays of stones we can get enough money on them to go to Salt Lake or Denver, and open a small gambling house where, while we can't be entirely respectable, we can at least be secure. I am at a stage where I would like to quit. I don't feel like going to work as a laborer at two dollars a day, or as a clerk for fifteen a week. I'm not speaking disparagingly of them, mind you – fact is, they have more real courage than we have, working for such wages. But this life of ours breeds expensive habits of loose, careless spending that are hard to overcome, and even if I could swallow my objections to being exploited I would still find it impossible to survive on the pay.

"I didn't jump into this life I'm leading as I jump into bed, and I can't get out of it in one jump. I drifted in by slow degrees, and if I get out I'll have to ease out of it by slow stages. A gambling joint would be the first step away. Then maybe something better after that. This can all be threshed out later; we must not let our minds stray from the Diamond Palace."

Sanc's philosophy stood up under our bad luck with the near-ruby. "Kid," he said later, "this is the season of peace on earth and good will to men. Who gives to the poor lends to the Lord, but when I give anything to the poor I am going to have a better motive. However, we are not givers; we are takers, and our taking should be reasoned out rationally. We will reverse this 'giving and lending.' We will rob the rich and discomfit the devil; thereby perhaps, finding favor in the sight of the Lord. And this brings us to the front door of the Diamond Palace. It's one of the city's show places and visitors are always welcome. We will visit it."

And we did. Separately, we made several visits in the evening to familiarize ourselves with the inside, and to locate the trays of stones. At night in my room Sanc drew diagrams of the interior and the show cases.

We rehearsed the thing in detail night after night. He made a neat dummy parcel and drilled me in placing it over an imitation tray of diamonds; showed me how to place it under my arm securely yet carelessly and walk out of the store with entire nonchalance.

He bought his black suit, white shirt, and black tie, put them on and rehearsed his part. We put our rooms in order, cleaning out everything that might look suspicious, protecting ourselves against a possible "pinch." The hotel keys I had made were put away carefully against a rainy day – or night. Our money was taken from the safety box, changed into bank notes, and secreted in our clothes.

I asked him about the guns. "No gun for you, Kid. You might get nervous. Leave yours somewhere. I'll take mine along."

Christmas was ten days away. Every evening we dressed for our parts, got barbered, shined, and slicked up, and walked about the block prepared to go into the store when it looked right. We made sure every day that the getaways I had located were still open.

"I could make it now," said Sanc as we stood across the street the third evening, "but I'll wait; it's getting better every day."

His last instructions were "Now, don't get nervous. If you get your hands on the 'junk' walk out quietly and away. If they 'tumble' me up before I get the tray out you fade away. I'll do the best I can alone. If there's a 'tumble' after you get the tray and you are chased, hang on to it and get into one of the spots you have picked out and when you get on the other street don't run; walk briskly direct to the room. If I'm not there five minutes after you, I'll be in jail. I don't like to think of that, but the pitcher can go to the well once too often, and it's better to know beforehand what you are going to do when it breaks. If I don't appear you put the stones away safely and wait till I send you word. Don't try to connect with me."

The next evening as I stood looking at the window display Sanc came by, glanced inside sharply, and snapped his fingers, which was the "office" to me that he was going in. I went in about three steps behind him. All I saw was a fine-looking, elderly man in a policeman's uniform walking up the center of the store, active, alert. When I passed him my heart was pounding so with suspense that I was afraid he would hear it.

Sanc walked straight to the back of the big room and sat on a settee. I strolled about looking at, but not seeing, the wonderful display of baubles. The place was fairly filled with Christmas shoppers and sightseers. Beautifully gowned women and distinguished-looking men stood at the counters inspecting rare stones and costly ornaments. Visitors idled around and clerks stepped about briskly. Parties of shoppers were coming in, the place was filling up with people laughing and chatting.

There was a little pucker between Sanc's eyes as he held his seat, and I knew something was wrong. Looking closer I saw, facing him and but a few feet away, an attaché of the place conversing with a party of women. Sanc was stuck and couldn't transform himself into a clerk under the man's eyes. At last he moved away. Sanc took off his hat, put it on the settee, stood up, and stepped smartly toward the front, a clerk now, and I right behind him with my dummy parcel.

Sanc's unavoidable delay in transforming himself into a clerk was fatal to our plan. One glance along the show cases that contained the most valuable stones showed us that they were all out and under inspection by patrons who came in after we did. Time was precious, worth more than money. He dared not hesitate. Turning quickly, he crossed the room and stepped behind the long line of show cases, passed two busy clerks, and stopped at a case that held a number of trays of small stones.

"Now, here's something, sir," he said to me as he reached in and brought out a tray holding one dozen rings, the best in sight that he could get at. My parcel was on the show case and he did not wait for me to act; he placed it on top of the tray and turned away toward the rear of the store. Shaking with suspense I managed to pick it up and place it properly under my arm, holding it closely to my side.

On the sidewalk I wanted to run, expecting to hear a hue and cry from the store. In turning the first corner I looked back. Sanc wasn't more than twenty feet behind me. I slowed up for him and we went straight to the room.

"Another bunch of rotten luck, kid," he said, peeling off his black suit. "This town has me hoodooed. I'm gone from it to-night, and you had better come along. Wrap up that suit and throw it away along with the shirt and tie. I'll unharness these 'rocks.' We're lucky if Mary gives us two thousand dollars on them."

In an hour he had them out of their settings, which I threw away as before. He went to his room for his few belongings. I threw mine in a bag and we met at the ferry where we got a boat to Oakland, leaving nothing behind us but the hotel keys I had made with such pains and trouble.

The theft was not reported in the papers. There may be a record of it in the police archives, for all I know. "I can't explain their silence," said Sanc. "This much is certain, and it's the worst part of this business of ours. Some innocent party is going to ride the blame. They will never figure that as an outside caper."

The next day we got an eastbound train and in due time found ourselves in the town of Pocatello, the stronghold of Salt Chunk Mary. Our knock at her door was answered by a young and pretty Swedish girl, blue-eyed and fair-haired. In answer to our call for Mary she laughed and her big, innocent blue eyes danced. "Aye tank you have bad luck. Miss Mary she bane on big yamboree."

We went downtown and rented a room. In Pocatello, as in every other Western town in those days, it was the correct custom and usage for sporting people to go on a big jamboree once or twice a year. A jamboree was usually preceded by a run of good or bad luck. If the celebrant got hold of a bunch of easy money he or she "went on a tear" to celebrate the good luck. If the luck got too bad, the way to change it was to go out and get drunk. The length of these celebrations was determined by the size of the party's bankroll or the strength of his constitution.

Salt Chunk Mary's bankroll had no bottom, and her constitution was flawless. So it followed that her periods of relaxation were somewhat extended. Being a very positive-minded person, inclining to action rather than words, her procedure at these times differed greatly from the ordinary. When she "went on a toot" the town marshal went fishing or hunting, and her more timid business rivals closed their places and remained in a state of siege like storekeepers in Chinatown when a tong war was declared. It was her custom to visit her friends' places first, where friendships were renewed and emphasized by much spending and drinking, and where obligations were acknowledged and discharged promptly. She poured liquor into the bums, beggars, ragtags, and bobtails that hung around the saloons till they were legless drunk, and unable to follow her triumphal march through the town. She never let up for the want of money, nor because of inability to "carry her licker." Her jamboree closed when she had "made" the last place in town and that was always the joint of some one she held a grudge against.

Sanc and I were fortunate enough to witness the wind-up of one of her most memorable celebrations. Leaving her hack at the curb, she walked into her victim's saloon and ordered all hands to drink. When the drinks were disposed of and paid for, she put both hands on the inner edge of the bar and pulled it over on the floor. Out of the wreckage she gathered an armful of bottles. One of them was accurately hurled into the mirror, and the remainder at anybody in sight. The boss, bartender, and saloon bums disappeared out the back way and Mary stalked out the front. On the sidewalk she threw away her hat, tore up what money she had left, and crawled into her waiting hack. Inside she kicked all the glass out, lay down on the back seat, and, with her feet out through the broken window, was driven home in state while the town stood mute.

We allowed her a couple of days to recuperate before calling. When we appeared she welcomed us as usual with an invitation to eat from the bottomless bean pot. Sanc threw her the small parcel of stones which she examined carefully with practiced eye, and a high-powered glass. Commercial white diamonds were sixty dollars a carat, wholesale, then, and when she offered us eighteen hundred dollars we took them, satisfied.

We jumped to Denver, where Sanc got the dice-game concession in the "Chicken Coop," a small gambling house. We had three thousand dollars between us. Two thousand went into the bankroll and we opened up bravely. "Soapy Smith," gambler and bunko man, noted for his high plays and big winnings and losings, won our two thousand in three successive plays. Sanc wanted to continue with the balance of our money, but I refused and stubbornly held on to my last five hundred. We had to quit.

Sanc was a hard loser and followed "Soapy" around town for a week trying to "elevate" him. He never got away from the bright lights, and Sanc gave up the notion of sticking him up.

We located a big poker game in a soft spot and decided to "line up" the players. The biggest gamblers in town sat there nightly and there were thousands of dollars in sight. After many nights of careful checking, we were ready to go against it.

Robbery has none of the complications of burglary. It is simple as one, two, three. You get it or you don't.

Sanc with a gun in his hand opened the door softly. I was behind him. The players, six of them, were in the midst of a "big play." None looked up. At the opposite side of the table, facing us, scrutinizing his cards, sat Bat Masterson, the last of the real bad men, the fastest man alive with a gun, and with a record of twenty killings while marshal of Dodge City, Kansas.

Sanc closed the door on the absorbed poker players as softly as he had opened it, and "officed" me to follow him out. "What's wrong?" I asked.

"Nothing but this, Kid. Bat Masterson is sitting in the game. He has a reputation as a killer and he earned it. When he was marshal of Dodge City bad men rode from the Texas Panhandle and from Deadwood, Dakota, to shoot it out with him, and he dropped them all. Nobody knows how many; he probably don't know himself. He beat them all to the 'pull' and even now, when he is not exactly young, he is the fastest human being with a gun. All he has left is his reputation, and he would die rather than lose it to a couple of 'stick-ups.' If I had him in a dark street I wouldn't hesitate to throw him up' and he would 'go up' too, but he would never stand for it with others looking on. I could have put the gun on him, said: 'Masterson, I know you; I'll kill you if you bat an eye,' and you could have started to gather up their coin. So far, so good; but if the brim of your hat or the tip of your shoulder had got between Mr. Masterson and my eye he would have 'pulled' on us and I would have had to let go at him. If I didn't kill or disable him with the first shot, he'd have slaughtered the pair of us.

"I'm not afraid of him, but I am not knowingly going to put myself in the position of killing anybody for his money. When Masterson sits in a game, he lays a gun on his lap. His life is forfeit to any ambitious young bad man looking for a reputation. Anybody but a 'stick-up' could kill him and get away with it, if he were fast enough or dirty enough to shoot him in the back. He has the right to sit with a gun on his lap and besides, it gives him just a slight psychological edge on the other players.

"In short, Kid, I don't want any of Mr. Batterson Masterson's money by the stick-up route. There are a lot of bad men here getting by on gall, but he has guts and I flatter myself that I've been around enough to know the difference. That's my philosophy, Kid; you can take it or leave it," he concluded.

That was the tribute Sanc, who killed one man and was hanged, paid Bat Masterson, who killed twenty and died peacefully in his bed at a ripe and respected old age.

Then came a night when the Sanctimonious Kid failed to show up at the room. I was worried and made the rounds of the gambling houses, joints and hangouts but failed to find him or anybody who had seen him. My fears were put to rest later when Soapy Smith, who won our bankroll, appeared in the "Missouri House" and told with the good grace of a man who had lost fortunes how he had been "taken" by a "stick-up" man for fifteen hundred dollars.

"It was the first time in a year I had been off Larimer Street, and it serves me right," he laughed. "Anyway, I know him and told him so and I'm going to kill him on sight."

"Soapy" Jefferson Smith was a colorful character of the West, the educated, refined, renegade son of a distinguished Southern family who turned his wits to crooked ways. When his luck at the faro tables switched and left him broke, he mounted his box on a corner and sold nickel bars of soap for fifty cents and one dollar. The fifty-cent bars were guaranteed to contain a five dollar bill and the dollar ones a ten. The bills were wrapped with the soap in plain view of the prospective purchasers. and when he finished his "spiel" the rush was on.

His "cappers," "boosters," and "shills" fought with the yokels for a chance to get something for nothing and always beat them to the pieces of soap containing the money.

As a sleight-of-hand man Soapy had no equal off the stage. When the Gentiles wrested the Salt Lake City government from the Mormons, Soapy was brought out from Denver and sat as an election judge in the busiest polling booth in the city. Equipped with a poker players "sleeve holdout" he "went out" with enough Mormon ballots to swing a close election in favor of a "clean city administration."

Always a pioneer, he joined the gold rush to the Klondike. He was killed at Skagway, later, by a bully in the pay of the "Vigilance Committee."

After the robbery Sanc disappeared, and it was long till I saw him again. I decided to leave Denver. I owed them fifteen days on the chain gang, and had no wish to pay by shoveling snow in the streets. I bought a ticket to Butte, Montana, regretting the money but not caring to "hit the road" in the dead of winter across half a dozen of the coldest states in the Union. I did it in after years but it was from necessity – not choice.

Butte was never a "Wild West" town in the accepted sense. Cowboys were seldom seen. Miners and gamblers ruled the town. The miners were orderly, hard workers, deep drinkers, and fair fighters. They had none of the cheap, shouldering swagger of the "gold-rush" miner. Nearly everybody owned a gun, but the bullying, gun-toting, would-be bad men and killers never flourished in Butte. When one of them got peeved and started to lug out his "cannon" some hard-fisted miner beefed him like an ox with a fast one to the jaw, and kicked his "gat" out into the street where small boys scrambled for it.

The mines were worked by Irishmen and "Cousin Jacks" (Cornishmen), who settled their differences with good, solid blows and despised the use of weapons. Gambling flourished and was licensed in Montana by an act of legislature. The possession of any crooked gambling device was a felony. Consequently the cheap cheaters and tinhorn, shoestring gamblers never got a footing there. Many of the faro dealers never made a bet of their own money, and many professional players were married men, who looked after their families faithfully, feeding and educating their children with money honestly and systematically won over the faro layouts. Everybody gambled. Messenger boys stopped to make a bet. The copper on the beat would walk in and bet "two and a half to win breakfast money." If he won his "two and a half" he went out satisfied. If he lost it, he got "stuck," forgot all about his beat, sat down, and "played in" his bankroll.

The town boasted of an all-night barber shop and a clothing store that never closed, for the convenience of late-at-night winners who couldn't hold on to their winnings till morning.

As I watched a game my first night in Butte, a seedy, torn-out looking chap stepped up to the layout and made a bet. He won it, and, expertly shifting his checks about, won a dozen more bets before the deal closed. "Gimme money," he said to the dealer, pushing his checks in, "I'm going to get dressed up this time." He took off his rusty derby hat and tore the crown out of it. Putting his hands behind him, he grasped the tails of his frock coat and with a jerk ripped it up the back clear to the collar. Money in hand he sought the all-night store, and came back in an hour, spick and span from head to heel.

I experimented and soon laid a solid foundation for the faro-bank habit which fastened on me later and kept me broke for years.

Another night a player at the table who had lost steadily for an hour placed his last stack of checks on a card, saying to the dealer, "Turn the cards, Sam, that's the last button on Gabe's coat." The cards were turned and the player lost.

As he was leaving, I looked at him closer, and was sure I knew him. I got up and stuck my hand out to him. He took it curiously. "You are George," I said, "the gentleman who made my fight in the Kansas City jail the night of my first 'pinch.'"

Fourteen

GEORGE smiled and took a better grip on my hand. "Yes, I remember you, young fellow. You've grown some. Have you gathered any wisdom?"

"I've gathered enough to know that you are entitled to any part of this," I said, producing my small bankroll.

"This is payable to-morrow night," he said, taking twenty dollars.

The money was returned promptly and a bond of friendship and confidence was formed that remains unbroken. I came to know him as "Rebel George," prince of bunko men, the man who developed and perfected the "gold-brick" swindle. After stealing a fortune and losing it at faro bank, he quit in answer to the prayers of his faithful wife, who had for years shared his vicissitudes in and out of prison. At the age of sixty, prison bent and money broke, he started life on the level and when last I heard of him he was in a fair way to succeed in his small business.

From Butte I journeyed to Spokane, Washington, and then to Seattle. I marvel now that I did not stop in one of those spots of golden opportunity and go to work. With the money I would have saved in a couple of years I could have bought land or lots that would have made me independent in ten years. I think land hunger is inherited. I had no desire then, nor have I now, to own land. The desire to possess land, whether inherent or acquired, appears to me to be a sure safeguard against a wasted, dissolute, harmful life.

I had now become so saturated with the underworld atmosphere that no thought of any kind of honest endeavor entered my mind. Fully realizing their value I passed by many splendid opportunities in the booming Western towns; not that I was lazy or indolent, but that business and the hoarding of money had no attraction. I will leave it to the scientists and investigators to explain why Johnnie Jones lands in a pulpit, and his chum next door with equal opportunity, lands in a penitentiary. It's too deep for me. I know I never had any money sense and never will have, and I know that had I been blessed, or cursed, with land hunger and money sense I would to-day have more honest dollars than I ever had crooked dimes.

Twenty years of moderate application to his business will make most any man independent. In twenty years a journeyman mechanic will handle more money than a first-class burglar, and at the end of that time he will have a home and a family and a little money in the bank, while the most persistent, sober, and industrious burglar is lucky to have his liberty. He is too old to learn a trade, too old and broken from doing time to tackle hard labor. Nobody will give him work. He has the prison horrors and turns to cheap larcenies and spends the balance of his life doing short sentences in small jails.

In rare instances the broken thief finds friends, sympathetic, understanding, and ready to help him. Strong and kindly hands at his elbows ease him over the hard spots and direct him to some useful place in the world. Some understand such kindness and respond by breasting the current and battling upstream with their best strokes; others do not, or can not understand, and, like dead fish, float down and away forever.

My apprenticeship under the Sanctimonious Kid was all that could be desired by either of us, yet my education was far from finished. At Seattle, almost broke, and doubtful about being able to do anything worth while by myself, I cast about for a "sidekicker." Seattle was rebuilding after her big fire. Money was plentiful, and I never saw such an aggregation of beggars, tramps, thieves, and yeggs as were gathered there. Gambling, prostitution, and the smuggling of opium flourished unmolested. The thieves hung out in Clancey's gambling house, and were protected and exploited by him. They thought Clancey was a little "Hinky Dink" in a little Chicago.

Every time a thief showed up with a hundred dollars he was "pinched," but Clancey took him out in an hour – for the hundred. When it was too late they found out that it was he who had them "pinched." Clancey died broke.

In Clancey's I found "St. Louis Frank," a product of Kerry Patch, a poor quarter of St. Louis, Missouri. I knew him from the bums' "convention" at Pocatello, where I met him first. He was clean looking and healthy and I liked him. About my own age, he was an honest, industrious, intelligent thief.

One night as we were looking around one of the smaller gambling houses, all the lights went out suddenly, but before we could get our hands on any of the money, they came on again. This started us to figuring a way to put them out at a given time when one of us could stand near a table and grab the bankroll. We found where the wires entered the building, and Frank volunteered to cut them if I would stand inside by the faro game and snatch the bankroll which was lying exposed in an open drawer beside the dealer. It looked so good that we enlisted two other "Johnsons," one to plant himself by the dice game, and the other by the roulette wheel. All three of us were to be in readiness to make a grab when the lights went out and make our way out of the building in the darkness.

Saturday night, when the biggest play was on, Frank made his way to the roof and we took up our posts inside.

I took a position by the faro game. The drawer that held the bankroll was so situated that a right-handed man would be handicapped in reaching for the money. Being left-handed, the spot fell to me. The drawer was open and the big leather pocketbook containing the money was lying in the bottom of it in plain sight, and not two feet from where I stood. The second man, in charge of the game, the "lookout," sat in a high chair at the dealer's right. One of his feet was resting on the edge of the open drawer, and I saw at a glance that if he jammed the drawer shut with his foot when the lights went out he would trap my hand.

While I was thinking that over, Frank cut the wires and everybody in the big room did just what we expected; they remained perfectly still for a second waiting for the light to come on.

My hand was on the big fat "poke." I heard a jingle of gold coins across the room, and somebody shouted: "Thieves! Thieves !" The drawer was jammed shut on my hand.

Reaching down with my right hand I got the poke and tore my left hand out of its trap, leaving a piece of skin the size of a half dollar behind. There were three exits and we all got out safely in the scramble, and "weighed in" at my room.

Frank was there ahead of us. My grab yielded two thousand dollars in bills. The chap at the dice game put his hand on a stack of twenty twenty-dollar gold pieces, but it was too heavy and he fumbled it, getting only half. Our assistant at the roulette wheel got a couple of stacks of silver only.

The money was split at once, and our friends departed. Frank took most of our money out and left it with a saloon man we knew. I stayed in my room a couple of days waiting for my hand to heal.

One great failing of the thief is that when he gets money he immediately makes tracks for some hangout where he throws a few dollars on the bar just to "give the house a tumble" and let them guess where he "scored" and how much he got.

He looks wise, says nothing, spends a few dollars, and goes out. Then the guessing begins and it's surprising what good guessers some poor thieves are.

Frank insisted that we go downtown a few nights later. I took the bandage off my hand and went along. We dropped into "Billy, the

Mug's," bought a few drinks, and departed. Half a block away we were pounced on by a couple of "dicks." One of them jerked my left hand out of my coat pocket where I had been keeping it to conceal the skinned place. "That's enough," he said, looking at it. They marched us down to the gambling house and showed us to the game keepers. They got no satisfaction there, the gamblers either could not or would not identify us. We were then taken down to the city "can," where they searched us thoroughly, finding nothing but a few dollars in silver. We were questioned separately and together, but refused to talk – a guilty man's only refuge. The officers ordered the man on the desk to put us on the "small book," meaning to hold us as suspicious characters. "Maybe Corbett can get something out of you," one of them said to us as they were leaving.

John Corbett was the officer in charge of the city jail. He was feared and hated from one end of the country to the other because of his brutality to prisoners. I doubt if a more brutal, bloodthirsty jailer ever flourished anywhere. He did not limit his beatings to underworld people. He beat up rich men, poor men, beggarmen, and thieves impartially. Anybody that didn't crawl for Corbett got a good "tamping." He was repeatedly brought before the commission for his cruelty to unfortunates falling into his hands, but for years mustered enough influence to hold his job. Corbett's treatment of prisoners was the shame and scandal of Seattle, and he kept it up until the women of that city got the right to vote. Then their clubs, in a body, went to the mayor and demanded Corbett's removal. He was removed.

Corbett appeared and took me downstairs where the cells were, in a moldy, damp, dark half basement. He was a powerful man, not tall, but thick and broad. He was black-browed, brutal-faced, heavyjawed. He opened a cell door and I started to step in but he detained me. I sensed something wrong. His brownish-red eyes gleamed like a fanatic's. "You'd better tell me all about that robbery, young man." His voice was cold, level, and passionless.

"I know nothing about it, sir," I answered very decently; I was afraid. Like a flash one of his hands went to my throat. He pinned me to the wall, choking me, and brought something down on my head with the other hand that turned everything yellow and made my knees weaken. Still holding me by the throat he lifted me clear of the floor and threw me into the cell like a bundle of rags. There was about a half inch of water on the cell floor. I lay there in it, and looked about me by the dim light of a gas jet out in the corridor. There was nothing in the cell but a wooden bench.

After a few minutes I crawled over to it, and, pulling myself up, stretched out, more dead than alive. If people can be corrected by cruelty I would have left that cell a saint.

St. Louis Frank, in another part of the jail, got a worse beating than I did.

Our friends outside were busy. At ten o'clock next morning James Hamilton Lewis, affectionately called "Jim Ham," later United States senator from Illinois, then an ambitious fighting young lawyer who never "laid down" on a client, came to see us. At two that afternoon he had us out on a writ, free.

From that day on St. Louis Frank smiled no more. He became snarly, short spoken, and ugly. We got our money and parted. He went out on the road "bull simple," simple on the subject of shooting policemen. The stories told about him are almost unbelievable. Years later I saw him in the San Francisco county jail where he was waiting trial for the murder of a police officer in Valencia Street. The day he went to San Quentin where he was hanged, he sang out to me "So long, Blacky. If I could have got Corbett I wouldn't care."

All Corbett's beating did for me was to make me a little more careful. I got a boat to San Francisco, not knowing just what to do, but with a notion of killing time till old Foot-and-a-half George finished his time in Utah, and meeting him. I dug up the hotel keys Sanc and I had planted and experimented a little in hotel prowling. I hadn't the sure touch that came in later years with experience, and didn't do much good.

One night in the Baldwin Hotel Annex I got a roll of bills that rather surprised me, and I was still more surprised when I read in the next evening's paper that George Dixon, the little colored champion fighter, had lost his money to a burglar. At the Baldwin bar the next night somebody asked him what he would have done had he been awakened by the burglar.

Dixon, always a good loser, smiled. "I'd 'a' done just what you'd 'a' done. I'd 'a' gone right back to sleep till that man went on out."

FIFTEEN

DURING my stay in San Francisco I lived at the Reno House, a small workingman's lodgings in Sacramento Street. It was owned by a man named Rolkin, a carpenter, who invested his small savings in it knowing nothing about the hotel business. He had a "crazy notion" that he could put clean linen on every bed every day in this cheap place and survive. His competitors said he was insane. He persisted, however, and on that "crazy idea" he built a string of fine hotels that he counts to-day like a barefoot Franciscan counting his beads.

I brought a terrible cold out of the Seattle jail that hung on for months. I got worried about it and went to a doctor. After looking me over carefully he pronounced one of my lungs bad and said I was in a fair way to fall into consumption. He advised me to go to a different climate, not to worry and get into a panic about it, and to take cod-liver oil. "Not the emulsion," he said, "but the raw oil. It's nasty stuff to take, but it will save you. Take it for a year if you can stomach it that long."

I followed his advice. The cold was gone in a week, and in a month I gained ten pounds. I stuck to the nauseating raw oil for a year, and to-day I firmly believe that if I hadn't I would have long ago succumbed to the dreaded prison scourge, T. B.

One night as I was meandering over Kearny Street toward the Coast somebody fell into step beside me. I looked around and saw Soldier Johnnie. We were well met, and I asked about his visit home. "Hell, I only got as far as 'Chi.' I bumped into a tribe of hungry bums, winter-bound and starving there. They were living off the free-lunch counters and the weather was so fierce they couldn't stay out on the street long enough to beg a dime for a ten-cent 'flop' in the Knickerbocker Hotel. They were so miserable and forlorn that I went over to the West Side and rented a housekeeping joint and gave them an indoor 'convention.' In six weeks my thousand dollars was gone and I put in the rest of the winter hanging around Hinky Dink's and Bathhouse John's. When the weather got right I rambled west to Salt Lake. I was going to hold it down in 'The Lake' till George came out, but I met a beggar that had put in the winter here in the city and he implored me to come out here and take one look at the 'box' in the Wigwam Theater. I've looked it over and it's the softest thing I ever saw. It's older than I am and I can beat it with a fifty-cent hammer."

"Do you need any help?"

"No. An outside man would only attract the cops. I'll plant inside before the place closes and get out some way after I get the coin."

Johnnie didn't even waste fifty cents for a hammer. He found one in the stage carpenter's kit. He got something over a thousand dollars, all in gold, and I persuaded him to let me buy tickets to Sacramento, where I exchanged it for paper money. We got "under" a night passenger train and held it into Truckee, where we spent a few days fishing and drinking mickies of alcohol with some congenial bums we found by the river. The weather was fine, and we journeyed through Nevada on slow freight trains, sitting in the open side door of a clean box car, with our legs dangling outside, looking for the scenery.

If the brakeman came along and wanted fifty cents apiece from us, we refused and got off at the next stop, where we drank cool beers in the saloon and waited for another train. We waited a week at Ogden for Foot-and-a-half George who showed up on the day. His head looked a little more pointed, his eyes a little deader, and his limp a little more pronounced. He was in good spirits and condition after "stopping his jolt" in the stir and anxious to start "rooting."

Sanc failed to appear, and the three of us jumped into Pocatello to pay our respects to Salt Chunk Mary. In a few days her hospitality palled, and George voted that we move down to the jungle and celebrate his release from prison.

Bums, thieves, beggars, and yeggs appeared as if they had magic carpets. In no time the thing assumed the proportions of a convention. Everybody had money. The crowd soon split up into units. Each unit had its cook and cooking outfit. The "captain" of each unit collected from the individuals and sent the younger bums into the town to buy alcohol, beer, and the "makin's" of mulligans. There was drinking, fast and furious, eating, washing, shaving, while some of the older bums mended their clothes with expert needle. Cripples discarded their crutches and hopped about the camp fires grotesquely. "Crawlers" with cut-off legs swung themselves along on their hands drunkenly, like huge toads.

Because of George our unit easily had all the class of the convention. He sat in state on a coal-oil can by the fire, bottle in hand, royally receiving the congratulations of bums from the four points of the compass.

Somewhere near by at another fire a bum sang in a raucous, beery voice, "Oh, Where Is My Wandering Boy To-night?" "The Face on the Barroom Floor," "My Blue Velvet Band," and "Ostler Joe" were alcoholically recited by a fat, red-faced bum in a greasy coat, after which the convention stretched out on the warm ground and slumbered peacefully in the balmy summer air.

The cook of our party was a stranger to me. A tall, lank man of fifty with a straggly black beard and matted black hair hanging to his shoulder. He never spoke except when the bottle was passed to him. Then he would hold it aloft and in a dead, empty voice offer his unfailing toast, "The stool pigeon is the coming race."

"Kid," said George when I asked him about the cook. "He's crazy as a bed bug and the best 'mulligan' maker on the road. 'Montana Blacky' is welcome at any bum camp anywhere, and he spends his life going from jungle to jungle."

Each day the bums drank more and ate less. The cooks were drunk and would prepare no food. The fiery alcohol had done its work. The bums that could stand up were fighting or snapping and snarling at each other. Many lay on their backs helpless, glass-eyed and open-mouthed, while others crawled about on all fours like big spiders. No more laughter, songs or recitations. Gloom settled over the camp and Tragedy waited in the wings for his cue to stalk upon the stage.

Just when the convention was about to close for the want of able drinkers a fresh contingent of bums arrived from over the Oregon State Line. They were brass peddlers and had a big assortment of "solid gold" wedding rings. A big young fellow they called 'Gold Tooth' seemed to be "captain" of the outfit. Along toward dark they finished the last of our liquor, and Gold Tooth and his tribe prepared to go into the town to make a "plunge." He detailed a couple of them to take the main "drag," another to make the railroad men's boarding houses, another to the saloons.

"I'll make the cribs myself. I'm dynamite with them old brums in the cribs," he declared, with a satisfied, confident air.

The "brass" was portioned out and they started uptown to "tell the natives how it happened." There is no more industrious person than a half-drunk brass peddler out on the street "making a plunge" for enough coin to buy himself another micky of alcohol. The first peddler returned in an hour with his quota of "Dr. Hall" (alcohol), and the drinking began afresh. George, Johnnie, and I had enough; we drank sparingly. One by one they straggled in with their bottles till all had arrived but Gold Tooth.

There was much speculation as to what had happened to him, and his "tribe" finally decided he had been "yaffled by the town whittler." In the language of the bums "yaffled" is arrested, and the "town whittler" is the constable, so-called because he is usually found sitting in some comfortable place whittling a stick.

When Gold Tooth did show up it was evident that he would have been lucky had the town whittler got him first. Blood was running down his face from wounds on his head, his shirt was in strands, and he was raving.

"Look at me," he screamed, "this is the rankest deal I've got in my ten years on the road. And where do you think I got it ? In Salt Chunk Mary's. I go in her joint and drop a hoop to one of her frowsy little brums for nine dollars. I'm decent enough to buy her a bottle of beer when she pays me for my brass. When she goes out for the beer she shows the hoop to Mary. She comes in and deliberately orders me to blow back the jane's nine bucks. I tells her there's nothing doin' and starts for the door. Mary hits me in the back of the head with a bottle of beer, and when I go down she puts the boots to me."

George sat up and looked at the speaker curiously.

Still standing by the fire, he continued "That's what I get for bein' a good bum. I'm goin' back up there to-night and burn down her shack; the dirty, big, red-headed Amazonian battle-ax. I'll —"

"Hey, you," said George from across the fire, "you're a liar." His little dead blue eyes were blazing like a wounded wild boar's. "You was a good bum, but you're dog meat now." A gun flashed from beneath his coat, and he fired into Gold Tooth twice. Six feet away, I could feel the slugs hit him. His head fell forward and both hands went to his chest, where he was hit. He turned round, like a dog getting ready to lie down and fell on his face. His hat rolled into the fire. His hands were clawing the red-hot coals.

Soldier Johnnie ran around and pulled him away from the fire by the feet. George stood, with the gun smoking, glaring at the others of Gold Tooth's tribe. They slunk away into the dark, gibbering drunkenly. Some of the drunken sleepers by the fire were not even aroused by the shots. Johnnie kicked them awake; they got up and staggered away. Montana Blacky, our crazy cook, reeled unsteadily into the circle of firelight, wobbling like an old crow on a dead limb. Holding his bottle aloft, he croaked: "Oh, then the bums began to fight, and there was murder right and tight." Waving his arm over the scene as if conferring his benediction on the fire, the dead man, George, Johnnie, and myself, he disappeared, muttering: "The stool pigeon's the coming race."

George handed me his pistol. "Throw this in the river, Kid." I broke it open, took out the slugs and empty shells, threw them into the water at one place, and the gun at another. We hurried away toward the railroad yards. On the way up, we decided that Johnnie should stay in Pocatello and intimidate any of the weaker bums who might talk, and also try to shoo them all out of town.

In the railroad yards, I had my eyes opened to one of the safest getaways ever discovered – that of "springing" into a loaded box car. Johnnie got an iron bar out of a scrap pile. Equipped with this, we went through the long lines of loaded cars waiting to be routed out of Pocatello, and in a few minutes found a car of merchandise billed to Great Falls, Montana. The process of "springing in" was simple. With the iron bar Johnnie lifted the bottom of a side door till it was clear of the hasps that held it in place. Placing one foot against the car, he pulled the bottom of the door out, away from its position, making space enough for us to crawl up into the opening. When we were safely inside, he sprang the door back into its place with his bar. Usually one or both end doors were fastened on the inside, making it easy to get out.

In those days this was the bums' best getaway, and it never failed unless they went to sleep and snored so loud that the brakeman heard them when the train was on a sidetrack. Supplied with food and water, men have traveled across the continent in safety while sheriffs and posses beat up the jungles for them in vain.

Luckily enough, we got into a train that was already "made up" for departure, and it pulled out in an hour. Making ourselves comfortable on top of the cases of merchandise, we took turn about sleeping, and after a ride of almost twenty-four hours, got into Silver Bow Junction, where we opened an end door and crawled out, hungry and thirsty. Then a walk of six miles, and we were in Butte City, where we got food and a room.

George was well known to the police in Butte, but took no pains to hide himself, feeling sure that the masonry of the road and jungle would protect him against the common enemy – the law.

The next afternoon we were picked up on the street by plain-clothes men and taken before the chief of police.

"What's wrong now, chief?" queried George.

"Oh, nothing much, Foot-'n'-a-half, just a telegram from Pocatello – murder charge," smiled the chief.

"What about me ?" I asked.

He looked at a telegram on his desk. "Hold anybody found with him."

They searched us thoroughly and held everything found on us. We were locked up alone, in separate cells. "You've got plenty of money, boys," said the jailer, "you can buy anything you want in the way of food and tobacco."

I sat on the side of my iron cot, wondering who had kicked over the bean pot. A rat-eyed trusty came down the corridor and stopped in front of George's cell, directly across from mine. "What's the trouble, old-timer?"

George looked at him coldly. "Oh, nothing much. I just bit a baby's arm off."

The trusty went way. Something told him to ask no more questions.

Idaho officers came the next day and we went back with them to Pocatello, not caring to waste our money fighting extradition, and feeling confident there was nothing more than a suspicion of guilt against us. We were taken straight from the train at Pocatello to an undertaker's. Every town official was there. Inside, in the back room, they led George up to a table where his victim was laid out under a white cloth. He knew what was coming, and so did I. The cloth was jerked off the body and one of the officers pointed his finger at George.

"There's the poor devil you shot, you damned, murdering – , and we'll hang you for it."

George coolly and calmly placed his right hand on the dead man's brow for an instant. Then, taking it away, he held his arm out full length with the palm of his hand up and said to the officer:

"If I killed that man, there's the hand that held the gun, and there's the finger that pulled the trigger" jerking his index finger back and forth, and, pulling up his coat sleeve, "there's my pulse ! Do you want to feel it?"

They weakened. The old yegg had beaten them at their own game.

"Lock them up!" ordered somebody in authority. The marshal and a crowd of citizens took us to the calaboose, a small, one-room shack in the middle of a big lot. They waited around till a pair of villainous-looking Bannock Indians appeared with rifles. They were hired to watch us and took turn about, sitting on a box outside by the door, day and night, silent, motionless. At evening the marshal brought a basket of food from a near-by restaurant, and a bundle of clean, new blankets.

Pocatello boasted of two lawyers, brothers. One prosecuted cases in the magistrate's court, and the other defended anybody foolish enough to hire him. Salt Chunk Mary sent the defender over to see us the next day. He hadn't influence enough to have us brought to his office, so he talked to us through the calaboose-door wicket. We were not going to waste any money on him. We decided to wait and see if we needed a lawyer first. George thanked him for coming, told him we had done nothing, and didn't need an attorney.

Every day for a week we were taken out and questioned. At the end of that time, having exhausted their stock of questions and patience, the marshal and his deputy had us into the justice's court charged with vagrancy. In ten minutes we were tried, convicted, and sentenced to six months each in the county jail at Blackfoot.

No matter how small the town is, somebody can be found to fix things. Mary was on the job and got the town fixer to "see the judge." He consented to suspend the sentences if we would get out of the town and stay out, warning us that if we ever came back we would automatically start serving our time.

We went over to Mary's to get out of sight till train-time, and find out what had caused our arrest. Soldier Johnnie had not appeared at her place. He folded his tent and stole away with other members of the convention, and so precarious was the life we led that it was fifteen years till I saw him again. All Mary had gathered was that the marshal, noting the scarcity of bums about town, had gone down to the jungle, where he found a dead man sprawled beside a burnt-out fire. Searching the jungle further, he came upon poor old Montana Blacky raving mad. He was taken in and later sent to an asylum. He was the only bum in Pocatello the day after the convention's tragic close. We never knew what caused our arrest, but surmised that Blacky in his ravings might have named George as the killer.

When our train pulled out, the marshal was there to see that we got aboard and to ascertain where we were going. We foiled him by neglecting to buy tickets, and at the same time saved ourselves money by paying a hungry conductor half-fare cash to ride us into Butte.

There I began my apprenticeship at the dangerous and fascinating business of breaking open safes. As was proper, I did all the fetching and carrying. I stole the dan, bought the drills, got railroad timetables, and guidebooks. I was sent out to make the preliminary survey of the "spot" George had designs on. I reported to him whether the spot was "flopped" in. I looked up the getaway, the all-important thing. No place is fat enough to tempt unless some feasible getaway can be figured out.

I located the blacksmith shop, where heavy tools could be had if needed, and the livery stable, where saddle horses could be got if required. I learned what trains passed, and when. I checked the town whittler's comings and goings. I was careful to look over the place for dogs, the bane of the burglar's life. If my report satisfied George, he looked it over once to make sure. When we went against a spot he did the "blacksmithing" inside, while I covered the outside.

We traveled on foot, on horseback, or on trains as the occasion required. A hike of twenty, thirty, or even forty miles was not rare. We never got any such great amounts of money as burglars get today. A thousand dollars was considered a good "touch." I believe a thief could get more out of a thousand dollars thirty years ago than he could out of five thousand to-day. Living was cheaper, police fewer and less active, shyster lawyers not so greedy and well organized, and the fences and fixers not so rapacious. "Justice" was not so expensive.

Only the large cities attempted anything in the way of identification. The Bertillon system was in the experimental stage and finger printing unknown in police work. We jumped from one state to another, kept away from the cities, lived almost entirely on the road except in the dead of winter, and spent our money in the jungles with the bums or played it in against faro bank in the mining towns. When we got a decent piece of money we quit stealing till it was almost spent, but while we were spending it we always tried to locate new spots against the day when we would be broke. George although past fifty, never spoke of quitting. I doubt if the thought ever entered his mind. He was as much attached to his trade as any carpenter or bricklayer, and went about it as methodically as any mechanic.

His cold-blooded shooting of Gold Tooth caused many bums to avoid him. After he was dead, I learned by accident why he did it, but it was too late then to shake hands with him over it.

A year after we were banished from Pocatello a letter from Mary told us that the Sanctimonious Kid was arrested in Denver, charged with a tough burglary, and wanted help. She wanted to help him, but didn't know how to go about it. I sneaked into Pocatello for her generous contribution, and with what we could spare we went to Denver and got him the best lawyer there – Tom Patterson, afterward Senator Patterson from Colorado. We stayed in the state, turning every dollar we could steal into his lawyer's office, but in vain. Sanc got everything Patterson had in the way of service, and finished with fifteen years at Canon City.

A small post office in Utah yielded us a few dollars and a big bundle of "stickers." I had no fear of Pocatello after getting in and out of it once, and we thought it only right that Mary should have the stamps and get the profit on them. I got into her place with them, but she hadn't enough money and I had to wait till morning for her to get it from the bank. Instead of staying quietly in her house, as she advised, I went out for a look at the town and the whittler got me.

He threw me in the calaboose, promising to take me to Blackfoot the next day to start on my six months. He hired no Indians this time, but just locked the door and went back uptown, probably to look for George. I paced up and down the length of the calaboose, cursing my carelessness.

About midnight there came a rap on the door.

"Are you in there, Kid?" It was Salt Chunk Mary. She passed in a small bottle of whisky and some sandwiches. I implored her to go over by the depot and try to find some bum that would break the lock and let me out.

"No use, Kid," she said. "The town has been hostile ever since the convention. A bum can't light here any more. I'll try to get some gambler to do it."

She hurried away. In an hour she came back alone, armed with a crowbar. She put the pointed end of it into the neck of the lock and with a mighty wrench twisted it off and threw the door open. I stepped out. That pale, light-fingered ghost "The lady that's known as Lou," would have fainted in my arms. Not Mary. When I reached for her hand, she pushed me away.

"Don't waste time thanking me. Here's the coin for your stickers. I borrowed it from the girls. You've got to hurry; there's a train leaving in ten minutes."

While I was still pouring out my thanks to Mary she turned away, and I hastened to the railroad yards where I hid myself till the train pulled in. I didn't go near the depot to buy a ticket, but crawled under a coach and deposited myself on the rods. Before daylight I crawled out at Ogden and hiked straight out of the town. I waited at the first station out, and in a few hours got a train into Salt Lake, where George was waiting for me.

He had seen Judge Powers, who defended me when I ran away from the verdict of not guilty. The judge assured him that there was no claim on me and the worst I need fear was a charge of "vag" from some sore-head copper. I at once told him of my troubles at Pocatello and my delivery from the calaboose by Mary.

"You don't have to tell me what a grand character she is, Kid. I know all about that. She's righter than April rain. If you knew half what I know about her you'd have put a couple of slugs into Gold Tooth yourself. You probably thought I 'smoked him off' because I was full of 'Hall' (alcohol) and wanted to cut some crazy caper. I croaked him because he was slandering the best woman that ever stood in two shoes. I'm not lookin' for a chance to kill anybody. I got my belly full of that in the war, an' that ain't all. No matter what they say, dead men do tell tales. Robbery and burglary are soon forgotten and outlawed, but when you leave a dead man behind you they've got the balance of your life to catch you and hang you. A couple of those bums could go into the Salvation Army ten years from now and get religion and hang me.

"I've packed a gun for thirty years, and every time I fired it I was in the wrong except, maybe, when I let that Gold Tooth have it. That's because my business is wrong. But it don't include murder and I won't travel with anybody that deliberately shoots people.

'When the town 'bull' interferes with you at night, shoot at him, of course, and shoot at him first; but don't hit him. He thinks you're tryin' to kill him and that's enough. He'll go after reinforcements and you get away. If he shoots at you that's just a common incident; if he hits you it's a rare accident.

"You're only beginning at this racket, Kid," finished the veteran yegg. "Take my advice and be careful with your gun. It's a good servant, but don't let it become your master or it will hang you."

We hadn't been in Salt Lake ten days till one of the "dicks" that put me on trial in Smiler's case came into the "Gold Room," a gambling house we hung out in, and took me off to jail. They held me all day and that night, trying to dig up some charge to put against me. Judge Powers came the following day, and after a lot of palaver they charged me with vagrancy. He got me a bond and I was later dismissed.

Harry Hinds, who kept the Gold Room, saw the police and came back with the good news that we could stay in Salt Lake as long as we didn't "bother" anybody in the city and that they didn't care what we did outside the city limits.

We made our headquarters in the city for more than a year. We hung out in the Gold Room and our persistent attempts to beat the faro game kept us continually jumping into the near-by towns to replenish our bankroll. Dynamite was easy to get and we didn't trouble ourselves to go to Ogden for the parcel I had left in the safety vault. We became quite established in Salt Lake and came to know many people. We lived at a quiet, second-class hotel, and went about our business in a decent, orderly manner.

George lost interest in bums and their gatherings after the convention at Pocatello, and kept away from them. They still attracted me, and occasionally I went down to the jungle on the banks of the river Jordan that empties into the Great Salt Lake.

On one of those visits I fell in with a crippled beggar who had been down on the "poultice route" in southern Utah. He had formerly been a very capable thief, but the loss of a leg under a train at once disabled and reformed him, and he turned to begging, as many do when they can no longer steal. I had a bottle of "Dr. Hall" and as we passed it back and forth the beggar bewailed his misfortune in losing his leg and having to "dingdong" his way about the country for a few "lousy dimes." "There's a box," he wailed, "in the county treasurer's office in the courthouse at the town of —— that I could chop the back out of with an ax, if I was able-bodied. The town whittler goes to bed when the general store closes at nine o'clock at night. There ain't five hundred people in the town and they're all in bed before ten o'clock. I went in to beg the county treasurer and he gave me four bits. The 'box' was open and I saw a stack of 'soft stuff' (paper money) that would make Rockefeller's mouth water."

He drank himself speechless and went to sleep mumbling his misfortune.

I told George about it and we looked it up on the map and it was twenty miles off a railroad. "I don't like the way it's situated, Kid," said George, "but there's three or four thousand dollars there now while they're collecting taxes, and we'd better look at it."

We got a small roll of blankets each, and bought tickets to a town forty miles distant from the county seat. George went first, and I followed the next day. At this base he hired a saddle horse, and departed to look the spot over. He got back in a few days and reported that it was even "softer" than the cripple had pictured it.

"We'll hike the forty miles into the town, Kid, by easy stages, beat off the box, and get a couple of horses out of the livery stable. By daylight we ought to be thirty miles away, where we will ditch the horses and plant in the jungles till night. After that we will have to hike nights till we get back to 'The Lake.'"

The following Sunday night we got into the town, but found there was a social gathering in the church, next door to the courthouse. That delayed us till twelve o'clock. At one o'clock we went into the stables across the street, and saddled two gentle horses, leaving them in their stalls. The town was dark, dead, and we went into the courthouse and to a rear room where the safe stood.

The master coolly removed his coat, throwing it on top of the safe. On the coat he laid a big "cannon." I opened the small parcel containing the "dan" and "stems" (drills). From the blacksmith shop we had taken a carpenter's hand brace and a pinch bar. With this primitive outfit George attacked the box in a most workmanlike manner. I went outside, but there was nobody in sight, and the only sound was the pawing of a horse in the stable across the street. At two o'clock George came out to look around himself. He was ready to "shoot her." The make of the box required that the door be blown entirely out of place and the explosion seemed tremendous in the dead, quiet night with nerves on edge. But the town slumbered on.

George waited outside, but there was no alarm, and he went back, returning in five minutes with a small but heavy bag of gold pieces that clinked sweetly when he dropped it into his coat pocket.

"You carry this head of cabbage Kid," passing me a pack of greenbacks about the size of a brick.

Dawn was graying the east as we went into the stable and bridled the horses. George went out first, pulling his reluctant horse by the bridle rein pulled over his head. In the door his horse stopped, and George standing outside on the inclined platform, tugged with both hands while I slapped the horse on his rump. Suddenly George dropped the bridle rein and his hand went to the waistband of his trousers for a gun.

A voice shouted, "Here, you damned horse thief," and a shotgun belched murderously, then again. George got both barrels. He was almost blown off his feet. He toppled over sidewise and his body rolled slowly down the incline to the ground.

The man with the shotgun knew his bloody business. I plainly heard the sinister click of the breech-lock as he snapped it shut after reloading. Neither of the horses was gun-shy; they stood still. The gunshot echoes died away. A whiff of powder smoke drifted above and across George's body. The silence was awful. I could feel the shooter outside standing at "ready" with his murderous gun. I was trapped; my pistol was useless against such odds. Somewhere in the stable a horse, heaving heavily to his feet, shook the floor and roused me from my trance of fear and shock. I remembered having seen a door in the side of the barn opposite where the man with the gun was. I ran to it and out into a lot. Across the street was the courthouse and the general store. There was a cellar beneath the store. I had looked into it while George was working on the "box". Its old-fashioned inclined doors were open and it was piled full of farm implements, empty boxes, crates, kegs of nails, etc.

Half panicky, I dashed across the street and into the cellar, where I hid amongst the junk at the end farthest from the door. In a half hour the town was on fire with excitement. The store was opened and I heard loud voices and the tramp of many feet above me. There was a clattering of horses' hoofs in the street, and I knew the hue and cry was on. I burrowed deeper into boxes and bales, prepared for a long wait.

When daylight came I saw a pair of stairs leading up to a trapdoor in the store floor. There was much coming and going all day, and the steady hum of voices. I strained my ears, but couldn't make head or tail of the talk. I put in a long, hard day, and when night came and the store was closed I was famished for food and water. All day I had been debating in my mind whether I should sneak out at dark and try to hike away, or hold down the cellar for another twenty-four hours. I had just decided to go out and chance it when I heard the cellar doors banged down from the outside, then the click of a padlock. I was locked in.

About midnight I went up the steps and found the trapdoor unfastened. The store was dark, but I soon found the cheese and crackers and carefully "weeded" out a good portion of each. There was a bucket of water in the back of the store and I filled an empty bottle from it, after drinking all I could.

Letting myself out of a window at the back, I closed it carefully after me, and hiked out of the town. Before daylight I carefully planted my "head of cabbage" in a field and crawled into a clump of bushes a hundred yards away to sleep and rest up for the next night.

Between hunting in fields, gardens, and orchards at night for food, and walking as fast as I could, it took me four nights to get to the main line of the railroad sixty miles away. Counting the money, I found there was three thousand dollars of "green and greasy," worn paper money in small bills.

During my long hike I had plenty of time to decide what to do. I made up my mind not to go near Salt Lake, where I was known. This money had been the death of poor old George, and I felt that he would turn over in his grave if I lost it and my liberty, too. I took out a hundred dollars and buried the rest with the utmost care.

At Provo, Utah, I got some fresh clothes and settled down to wait till the business cooled off. From the papers I gathered that George was killed by the livery-stable owner, who had got up early to go duck shooting. Going to his stable to get a horse, he found the back door open and waited to see what was going on. He thought he had a horse thief, and only fired when George reached for his gun. Two thousand dollars in gold was found in George's coat pocket, and returned to the county. The hunt was still on for the burglar with the big end of the money. Nobody claimed the dead man's body and he was buried unnamed and unknown.

After a miserable month's wait, I dug up my money and bought a ticket to Chicago by the way of Denver and Omaha, going a roundabout way for fear of meeting my father and having to face his clear, cold eyes. If it had been honest money I would have gone to him and offered him any part of it, but I was afraid to face him with a lie.

I got into Chicago safely and immediately put my fortune in a safety box. Then I bought plenty of good clothes and got myself a nice room near the corner of Clark and Madison Streets. That seemed to be the center of the night life, and I instinctively anchored there. I put in the winter investigating the cheap dives, hurdy-gurdies, and dance halls. The tough Tenderloin district attracted me also. The beer bums and barrel-house five-cent whisky bums came under my notice. Not very different from the winos of San Francisco. I visited the five-cent barber shops of lower Clark Street and the ten-cent "flops" and dime ham-and-bean joints. Nothing escaped me. I nibbled at the faro games but was careful and never got hurt. Every night I looked into Hinky Dink's and Bathhouse John's bars and heard the same old alarm, "here comes the wagon." But those two kings of the First Ward were "Johnnie on the spot" and never allowed any of "their people" to languish in the "can" overnight.

I discovered the saloon of "Mush Mouth" Johnson, a negro politician of power and, fascinated, watched his patrons, each in turn trying to make the bone dice roll his way.

I stumbled upon the hop joint of "California Jack," an old Chinaman from Sacramento, who was waxing fat in his make-believe laundry in South State Street. Thieves, pickpockets, and pimps and their girls smoked unmolested day or night. Now and then a tired waiter or bartender threw himself wearily on a bunk.

I fell in with a wolfish-eyed girl of the streets, hungry and shivering in a doorway so shabby that men would not throw an appraising glance at her. Like Julia she was almost "ready for the river." I bought her food and clothes and a room. I gave her no advice and sought no profit from the transaction. With better clothes and food she plied her trade confidently and prospered. I saw her often on the streets. One night she paid me the money I had spent for her.

Then came a midnight when she knocked at my door, pale, panting with fear. "You must help me," she implored. "I have no friend but you. A man is dead in my room. If he is found there the police – you know – they'll say it's murder."

On the street we got a hack and in ten minutes were at her place. A shabby parlor fronted on the street; in back of it was a bedroom. On the bed, fully dressed, lying crosswise with feet on the floor, was the body of a man. Well dressed, about fifty, he might have been a clerk. I went out the back door and to the alley. There was no one in sight. When I came back she was shivering in a chair. I put the dead man's hat in my pocket and asked her to help me lift him to my shoulder. She refused to touch "the thing." With an effort I got it to my shoulder, the head and arms hanging down my back. Clasping my arms around its legs, I staggered out the back way toward the alley.

Stumbling up the dark alley over tins, wires, broken boxes, and other rubbish, I carried my dangerous burden almost to the cross street and threw it down, leaving the hat beside it. Annie Ireland, or "Irish Annie" as she was called by the street girls, was still huddled in the chair in a corner of the room farthest from the bed when I returned.

"Where did you leave it?" she whispered.

"Up the alley," I told her shortly. I had no stomach for this business, and wanted to be away and done with her. I felt sure she had dealt the man a jolt of chloral or some other stupefying drug.

"Look here, Annie," I warned her, "if you've got any of that guy's junk around here you'd better ditch it. They will find him in the morning, and every crib in the block might be searched."

"No, no," she protested. "I didn't touch him. I picked him up on the street. When we came in here he stretched out across the bed and went to sleep. I took my hat and coat off and tried to wake him, but couldn't. After a while his hands turned cold and I saw he was dead. Then I went for you."

I went out, and she followed me. "Where are you going now?" I asked.

"Oh, I don't know – outside, anywhere. I can't stay in there. I'll go down the line and get drunk, I guess."

I left her at the corner, resolved to see no more of her. But that wasn't to be, for there came a day, years after, when she held up her hand in a court and perjured me into prison. The next day I moved to another part of the city and kept away from the blocks she walked at night. I met her no more, and she soon fell into the background of my memory. I watched the papers, but saw nothing except a few lines reporting the finding of the body of an unidentified man in an alley. A dead man in an alley didn't mean much in Chicago then and his body probably went to the potter's field or a medical college.

SIXTEEN

SUMMER came and the memorable World's Fair. I saw it all, but it put an awful dent in my bankroll and winter was coming. I heard wonderful tales of New York City and its opportunities told by the hop smokers in California Jack's, and had almost made up my mind to go there for the winter when I met an intelligent young chap who knew all about it. He advised me to stay away from New York.

"It's the toughest town in the United States for an outsider to get by in," he said in answer to my questions. "I'll tell you what you're up against. You go in there single-handed. If you get by the wise coppers and the hungry fences, you've still got the gangs to beat. Almost all the thieves belong to gangs – the Irish, the Jews, and the dagoes. They fight each other, but they make common cause against an outsider, especially if he's from the West, and they'll know you in a minute with your soft hat and your Western talk.

"The gangs are made up of natives and 'home guards,' and some of them are not above snitching on you if you go in there and get too prosperous. If you show up in any of the hangouts with money they will beat you up and take it away from you like any sucker. Of course if you got into a gang they would protect you. The gang protects you, and the ward alderman protects the gang, see? But even then you'd never have anything, for the money's split too many ways.

"Those hop fiends are raving when they tell you New York is a simple spot to make a living in. Everything is simple and easy and rosy to them when they get a few pills under their belts; but you take my advice and stay away from it. I can get dollars in the West where I couldn't get dimes in New York, and I wouldn't go back there on a bet. I'm for Chicago and points west where you don't have to wear a derby hat to get by a policeman," he finished in disgust.

Turning this gloomy picture over in my mind for a few days, I decided to let New York alone and go back West. My spare clothes were left with the landlord, and after a soft, easy year I went back to the hardships of the road almost gladly. I made long jumps under fast trains into St. Paul and then on to the Dakota harvest fields.

Thousands of harvest hands were leaving with their season's earnings and a horde of yeggs, thieves, gamblers and their women beset them on every side. Some of the more wary and experienced laborers bought tickets and got out of the danger zone unscathed; others dallied with the games of chance and were shorn, or fell into the yeggs' clutches and got "catted up."

Harvest workers were called blanket stiffs or gay cats, and the process of pistoling them away from their money was known as catting them up. Train crews flourished by carrying the gay cats over their divisions in the box cars at a dollar each. Bands of yeggs worked with the brakemen, who let them into the cars, where they stuck up the cats, took their money, and forced them to jump out the side doors between stations. By the time they walked into a town and reported their losses, the train was far ahead, the money split with the train crew, and the yeggs were holding a convention in some safe jungle.

After several seasons the cats began buying tickets out of the harvest fields and the profitable industry of catting up went by the board.

I traveled along slowly now, uncertain where to go or what to do. Meeting many who had seen me and Foot-and-a-half George on the road, I told them freely the story of his finish and my getaway. My prestige grew and I came to be accepted everywhere as "Stetson," which, in the language of the road, means first class.

Being young I naturally got puffed up and superior. I looked wise and mysterious, said nothing, and "connected" only with the higher-ups among the knights of the road. Stepping out on the street one morning at Great Falls, Montana, an icy wind out of the north reminded me that winter had come. I was almost broke, and fearing a Montana winter without money, I made a dash for the coast. I traveled north through Lethbridge, at the Canadian line, and into Calgary, Alberta; then west over the Canadian Pacific toward Vancouver, where I hoped to spend the winter. The snow had piled up in the Selkirk range, delaying trains for days and making life on the road uncertain and very unpleasant. My money had dwindled till buying a ticket was out of the question. Riding the rods of passenger trains meant freezing and I was forced to take the slow and infrequent freights,with their open box cars. At one of the larger towns in British Columbia I stopped off to rest up, get a decent night's sleep, and thaw myself out.

In the office of the hotel I went to stand by a safe that attracted me. It was of a make that George always favored, and we had beaten a half dozen of them in the two years we were together.

No explosives were needed. It could be got "on the quiet." I put down my last dollar for a week's board and room, and began planning an assault on the ancient "box."

I was alone, almost broke, and here was opportunity. Opportunity not only to fortify myself with money, but to test myself and prove whether my years with George and the Sanctimonious Kid had fitted me to make my way alone at the profession I had drifted into. I went over the situation carefully. A westbound passenger train passed through the town at one o'clock A.M. The hotel closed at midnight. An hour was time enough for the mechanical work on the box. The time-tables showed that I could be on the "American side" in twelve hours if I got out on the night train. Here was a feasible getaway.

The next thing was to make sure that no one entered the hotel office between the hours of twelve and one. Several nights' watching satisfied me that I would not be interrupted in that way. The week was almost gone, so was my money, and I saw that more would be needed for my board and lodging before the arrival of my first big night alone. This forced me into a small room burglary that was almost fatal.

Prowling through the one other hotel in the town I found a room door unlocked and stepped inside. There were two beds in the room, both occupied. On a chair by the bed nearest the door was the sleeper's trousers, from which I got a purse. Pocketing it, I moved to a chair by the second bed, where I could distinguish something dark that appeared to be a bunch of clothes.

Right there I learned that a fair-sized, healthy dog sleeps sound as a human being. Instead of putting my hand on a pair of pants, it touched something furry that came to life with a start and a growl, and fastened a pair of strong jaws on my forearm. Both sleepers stirred. Before I got to the door, dragging the snarling, clawing brute that wouldn't let go his grip, the man whose purse I had sat up in bed. I was without a gun, but threatened to blow his head off just the same. Being a sensible man, he remained quiet.

I had put out the only light in the hall. Still burdened with the tenacious, growling dog, I was forced to feel my way with my feet toward the back stairway. I couldn't stop in the hall to choke him loose; my only hope was to drag him downstairs and deal with him outside the place.

At the top of the stairs his struggles and weight overbalanced me, and we rolled and bumped down the long, dark stairway to the landing below. On our way down he weakened, let go his grip on my arm, scrambled to his feet, and tore out into the alley, howling piteously. I gathered myself up and ran in the opposite direction. In my room, I took stock and found he hadn't injured me, and that I had enough money to carry me for another week.

I now moved into a small lodging house and paid for my room each night. As a transient roomer I could leave at any time without causing comment.

Curious to learn something about the dog I was tangled up with, I went into the office and barroom of the hotel, looking for him. One evening while I was getting a drink I heard a low, threatening growl across the room, and a look in the big mirror back of the bar showed me a good, big, husky shepherd dog standing under a card table. The hair on his neck and back bristled as he eyed me suspiciously. I thought he was going to attack me, and turned around to face him. When I did this, he backed still farther beneath the table, but never took his eyes off me. The room was crowded with loungers and card players, but none of them appeared to notice his actions. I went out of the place and stayed out.

At last the night came that I had decided was to be my last in the town. I had done everything possible in the way of precaution and protection. The stormy night favored me and the box gave up its contents after a few sturdy blows from a short-handled sledgehammer. The train arrived on time, and when it pulled out I got aboard without a ticket. That was part of my plan. I didn't want to be seen at the ticket office, where I knew inquiries would be made the next day.

The safe contained nothing of value to me but a roll of paper money. I had no chance to count or examine it while waiting for the train, but before the conductor got to me I fished out a worn twenty-dollar bill from which I paid my fare, about fifteen dollars, to Vancouver. I had no intention of going into that city now, but paid my fare there to mislead any one making inquiries from the trainmen. I planned to leave the train at a junction and take another across the border. Well satisfied with myself, I was reviewing the night's work when the train slowed down between stations, about twenty miles from where I got aboard.

After a long wait, the conductor appeared with the information that the train was blocked by an avalanche of snow and rock. "make yourselves comfortable," he said, "we won't get out of here before noon tomorrow."

My carefully laid plans crumbled. I wished myself back in the town. I thought of the bill I had given the conductor. I could see the constables with their heads together in the morning "deducing" and "inferring" with the result that they would deduce and infer that their burglar had left on the night train. I could see them arriving at our stalled train some time in the forenoon and buttonholing the conductor. I could see him pointing his finger at me.

It was suicide to leave the train. Not a hut or habitation within miles and a terrific storm raging, I went over every possibility and finished with a helpless, half-trapped feeling. I went into another coach, and, finding an empty seat, cut a slit in the cushion and planted the roll of money, keeping only the change from the twenty-dollar bill. There was nothing else I could do to protect myself. I tried to sleep in a seat, but couldn't, so I sat around, apprehensive and nervous, till morning. The storm abated at daylight and an hour later a work train pulled in behind us, prepared to dig us out. I got ready for a shock.

Sure enough, in a few minutes, two constables from the town I had left came slowly down the aisle behind the conductor. When he came to my seat, he stopped and nodded his head toward me. One officer stood by me, but said nothing. The other said something aside to the conductor, who took a roll of bills from his pocket, peeled off the top one and handed it to him. He turned the bill over, looked at it carefully, and then at a piece of paper he had in his hand. After more talk with the conductor that I couldn't hear, he turned and faced me with a gun in his hand.

"Put the irons on him, Mr. Stevens," he said to the officer beside me. "He is our man".

I protested against being handcuffed, pushed "Mr. Stevens" away, and demanded an explanation.

"You're arrested in the queen's name," said the officer in charge, "and anything you say will be used against you. You had better submit quietly. If you want force you can have it." He waved his big, serviceable-looking gun in my direction.

I submitted. They took me forward to a baggage car, removed my shoes and nearly all my clothes, and went through them slowly and thoroughly, but found nothing incriminating. When the train was dug clear it pulled out, carrying my roll of bills with it in the seat cushion, and I congratulated myself on getting rid of it. I was taken back to the town I left so suspiciously the night before, and thrown into the jail wondering what they had on me. They hadn't asked me any questions; that looked bad. They seemed too well satisfied with the thing.

All my speculations were put to rest the next morning when I was brought before the magistrate.

When I hear the word "technicality" I think of American jurisprudence. If there is any such term used in British courts I never heard it. The procedure in this magistrate's court was simple, alarmingly simple. The hotel man proved the burglary. The next witness, an old prospector who was wintering at the hotel, testified that he had changed a twenty-dollar bill at the hotel bar the evening before the burglary; that it was the only bill of that denomination he had that he had carried it with him for six months and had looked at it so many times he remembered the big serial numbers on the back of it. He swore further that he went to the hotel man the next morning and gave him the numbers. The arresting officers now told of following the train, getting the conductor's statement, and arresting me. They produced the fatal twenty-dollar bill the only one in the roll that could have hurt me, the prospector's bill. They testified that they got it from the conductor, who told them I had paid my fare out of it.

The prospector now identified his bill. On top of this it was shown that I had suddenly and suspiciously left the town, avoiding the ticket office and paying cash fare with the deadly twenty.

I hadn't a leg to stand on in the way of defense, but managed to get up and object to hearsay evidence and ask to have the conductor brought into court. The magistrate and Crown prosecutor laughed. "He'll appear when you go on trial at the next term of court," said the "cutor." "Any defense?" asked the magistrate.

I saw they had me right. "No, your worship, I'll save my defense till I get into a court where I will not be laughed at." He laughed again and made the order to hold me. This court proceeding didn't take an hour. I went back to the jail wishing the thing had happened in the good old U. S. A., where, with a smart lawyer, I would have got a continuance and sent somebody to the conductor who might listen to reason and not be so cocksure about getting the bill from me.

At the provincial jail I found a drunken Scotchman in charge. He was assisted by two half-breed Indian boys serving six months each. One of them cooked for the jailer and any prisoners that came in; the other scrubbed the jail. Both of them watched me faithfully and fed me regularly when the jailer was drunk. I was locked in a cell and never got out except for a bath once a week. The Indian boys slept on the floor in front of my cell by a big stove that was always hot and kept the jail warm.

There was not a fixture in the cell but a bucket. I had plenty of blankets and slept on the floor. My clothes were taken and I was dressed in a pair of white duck pants and a hickory shirt. They left me my shoes and hat. I was never so bare and helpless before or since. Not a smoke, nor a paper, book, nor magazine was allowed in the jail. When I asked the Scotchman for something to read, he got me a Bible which I read and reread with much interest but no profit. I was pestered daily for weeks by the Crown prosecutor to return the balance of the money taken from the hotel safe, eight hundred dollars. He offered me a short jail sentence if I would give it up, but I mistrusted him and decided to let some car cleaner find it rather than admit anything and get myself in deeper.

I gave my case a good thinking over and concluded there was no way out. Judge Powers, J. Hamilton Lewis, and Tom Patterson of Colorado, all rolled into one, couldn't have acquitted me. All day, every day, I read my Bible and prayed that the conductor might fall under his train before the day of my trial.

A priest visited the jail one day and gave me a pamphlet on which he had printed the Chinook language. In answer to my question he told me it contained about three hundred words – nouns, verbs, and adjectives. It was created by the Hudson Bay traders, years before, and taught to all the Northwest Indians to simplify trading with the different tribes.

I soon mastered Chinook, practicing on the two "breed" boys and any Indians that happened into the jail. I had given up hope of escape. I was barehanded. Even the tin spoon I ate my stew with was taken away when the meal was finished. The jailer disliked me from the first. He would come into the jail corridor roaring drunk at night, rout out the two "breeds," and have them unlock my cell and search "the damned Yank," while he stood away brandishing a big gun. They never found anything; there was nothing there.

One day he came in with a scared-looking China boy about twenty years old. "Yank, here's a cellmate for you." He locked the Chinese in, thinking he was punishing me. The China boy later proved the jailer's undoing and my deliverance. He knew some Chinook, but not one word of English. I learned from the Indian trusty that he was held for trial, charged with stealing a considerable sum of money from his employer, and that his case was about as hopeless as mine.

We got along great. I taught him the alphabet and many words of English while he instructed me in Chinese. I even humbled myself to ask the jailer for pencil and paper to teach the Chink writing. He went down to his office at once and brought me a lead pencil and pad of paper. I was surprised, and so grateful I thanked him half a dozen times.

Inside of a week he got drunk and ordered his Indians to take them away from me. I asked him no more for anything, and to this day I believe he gave them to me anticipating the warm, grateful, pleasant thrill he would get from depriving me of them.

The China boy's company got him a lawyer. When he came to the jail he called me out and offered to take my case. I could have got money by writing to Salt Chunk Mary, but it looked like waste to fight it. When I asked him straight out if he could do anything with the conductor, he was shocked, indignant. "Oh, ah, but, my man! Tamper with the Crown's witness, what?" He left as if I had the plague, and I don't doubt he reported me to the prosecutor.

I've had a lot of dealings with Chinamen and never got the worst of it from one. If a Chinese doesn't like you he will keep away from you; if he does like you he will go the route. By signs and a few words I conveyed to my cellmate that our only hope was to beat the jail. There was a barred window in our cell, the outside was not guarded. All we needed was a hack saw. He was for it. His "cousins" visited him regularly every week and if they could be made to understand what we needed they would get it.

There was but one hardware store in the town and to buy the saws there might cause talk. I had him tell his "cousins" to send to Vancouver to their company for them. After weeks of anxiety and uncertainty and much negotiating with their friends at Vancouver the precious saws were put into my cellmate's hands under the drunken jailer's nose. My plan was simple. Wait till spring when, if we got out and failed to get a train we could take a chance on foot in the country away from the railroad. Night after night we listened to the trains arriving and departing, checking the time. A freight train departed immediately after the one o'clock passenger. If I could "spring" into a box car, we could make Vancouver in safety. I secreted the saws and we settled down to wait for softer weather.

SEVENTEEN

WHEN spring came, my Chinese "tillicum," which is Chinook for friend, and I were the only felony prisoners in the "skookum house," or jail. The two half-breeds had finished their time and a couple of others had been brought in to take their places, four prisoners in all. The Indians watched us and we watched them. The tough end of our job was not to beat the jail or the drunken jailer, but the watchful trusties, our fellow prisoners.

I decided to cut the bars in the daytime and have my cellmate keep a lookout at the door against the appearance of our jailer or the Indians. The saws were dug up out of a crack and day after day, slowly, noiselessly, they bit into the thick bars. At night I put them away safely in their hiding place, and we slept as usual. Our jailer drank more and more, and we were searched oftener, but never once did he or his Indians look at the bars in our window. We were so closely watched and the jail was so tight the thought of our getting anything to "crush out" with never entered his foggy mind.

Strangely enough the China boy's "cousins" never appeared at the jail after the day they brought him the saws. Whether they were afraid or thought they had done enough for him I never knew. To all my queries about them he "no sabied." At the start I had figured on help in the way of money and food from them. Now I had to dismiss this. I determined not to go near the Chinese if we got out, but to get into a train and stay in it till hunger forced me out.

After weary weeks the work was done; the bars cut so nearly through I was afraid they would fall out every time the cell door was slammed shut. I hid the worn saws, and waited patiently till our jailer got drunk and gave us our searching. On those nights he never made a second appearance. Satisfied, he always went direct to bed and we could hear his alcoholic snores in another part of the building. The Indian trusties went to sleep and I rolled our blankets into dummies that looked passable. At twelve o'clock the freight train pulled in and went on a side track to get a fresh engine and allow the passenger train to go by at one o'clock. I broke the bars out and hid them under the blankets. The China boy's knees were shaking as he crawled out and dropped to the ground. I followed him, not any too calm and cool myself. He had no hat, otherwise he was dressed as I was – duck pants and a thin shirt.

There was no time to try to steal clothing, food, or money. As we hurried toward the freight yards where the train stood I had but one comforting thought – we wouldn't be missed till seven in the morning.

The Chinaman was helpless. At the side track I ran frantically about in search of something to spring a car door with. At last I found a pile of scrap iron and dug a fishplate out of it. The train was an all-through freight, billed to Vancouver, the terminus. I soon discovered a battered box car that suited, and sprang a side door away from its bearings. Then I showed the Chinaman the end door and tried to explain to him, mostly by signs, that he should get in the side door while I pulled it out, and then unfasten the end door from the inside to admit me after I put the side door back in place. He refused to budge. At last I made him pull the door out while I got into the car. When I got the end door open I had to get out, go down, and get him and put him in. Then I sprang the side door back in position, went to the end door, crawled in, and fastened it on the inside the way I found it.

We didn't have a pocketknife, not a dime, not a match; but we were safe, and I wouldn't have exchanged the security of that box car for a soft berth in the sleeper on the departing passenger train. We were barely settled inside when there was a bumping and jolting of cars and our train slowly got under way. We were in a car loaded with barrels of lime. They stood on end and it was painful to stretch out on them. The ride was a nightmare. Hungry, thirsty, cold, racked with fear and suspense, we got into Vancouver after twenty-four hours.

Clothes were the first problem, any kind of rags to cover our jail uniforms. I got out of the car with the half-dead China boy at once, and went directly back to the caboose on the train we rode. The conductor and brakeman were already gone. The caboose was deserted. The boy hid between box cars while I went to the top of the caboose, through the cupola, and down inside. In a locker were greasy coats and pants, and a cap for the Chink. The clothes were too big for him and the cap too small. He knew Vancouver and wanted to take me to his "cousins" in Chinatown, but I was afraid we couldn't get by a copper together, so he struck out alone after making me promise to hunt him up at his company's headquarters. I crawled into an empty car to wait for daylight, when it would be safer to go through the streets.

It was Sunday morning. I heard a church bell ring and knew it was somewhere around six o'clock. When I looked out of the car I saw that a heavy fog had settled over the city like a blessed benediction. I melted into it, making my way out of the freight yards and into the streets. The fog was so dense that I couldn't have found my way if I had known the town. After walking blocks along a street I saw that the stores were getting smaller and farther apart. Vacant lots became more numerous and everything indicated that I was going in the wrong direction. A few doors ahead of me an old, rheumatic, mongrel dog appeared out of a hallway. He was the only living thing in sight, and when I got abreast of him I stopped and looked at him idly. He came over to me, gave me a rather doubtful look, and sat back on his haunches. After balancing himself carefully, he lifted a stiff hind leg and made a futile effort to dislodge the hungry fleas from under his collar. Failing at this, he got up slowly, gave me another looking-over, and limped back to his doorway. As he went in he glanced at me out of the tail of his eye.

It sounds strange to say that I was suspicious of a mangy, old cur dog; but it's true. There was something so human in his glance that I followed him into the doorway to see what he was up to.

In the entrance behind the door, with his head on the lower step, a man was sprawled. A second look convinced me that he was a Saturday night drunk who had got that far and no farther. He was lying on his back, open-mouthed, and breathing heavily. The old dog stood beside him watching me.

I could see he was a workingman and ordinarily wouldn't have given him a look, but I was now broke, hungry, wolfish. The dog growled a feeble protest as I began exploring his master's clothes. He had money in every pocket. I left some silver in his vest for him to get a drink with when he woke up. The devoted old mongrel stood in the door as if to bar me from going out, and eyed me reproachfully when I gently pushed him aside.

Out in the street I cleansed my conscience by repeating the Sanctimonious Kid's favorite parody: "Oh, room rent, what crimes are committed in thy name!"

Turning the nearest corner, a glance over my shoulder showed me the loyal dog out on the sidewalk, still accusing me with his tired old eyes. The town was awake now and I soon found a sailor's boarding house where I got a couple of bracing drinks and sat at a long table where sailors and stevedores were breakfasting in free-for-all, family style. I didn't join in the conversation, didn't have to. The quantity of food I put away convinced them I belonged on the water front. Paying for a room in the place, I got into it and took stock. There was enough money to get an outfit of clothes and feed me for a couple of weeks. I made a bundle of the jail pants and threw it off a wharf at once. The next day I bought new clothes, shoes, and hat, got cleaned up, and, dismissing the burglary charge and broken jail from my mind, proceeded to look about me.

I had not been photographed or measured in the small town I escaped from; it didn't look reasonable that the authorities would travel five hundred miles on the chance of finding me in Vancouver, so I decided to stay there till I could get hold of something worth while. Moreover I was curious to know how my Chinese cellmate had fared, and being young and somewhat fond of myself, perhaps I wanted to meet his "cousins" and be admired by them.

After looking over the town, my experience told me the police were not to be feared and I went into Chinatown in search of my friend. Finding the company store he described, I went in and bought a small package of ginger candy. About a dozen Chinese were sitting around, talking or playing dominos, but the minute I appeared the dominos quit rattling and the Chinese stopped talking. I looked as mysterious as I could without making it too strong and surveyed them one by one. Not one uttered a syllable till I went out; then they all fell to talking and gesticulating at once. The following night I went back and bought more candy. A smart-looking, middle-aged Chinaman in European clothes was behind the counter.

"What you come here for?" he asked in very good English.

"I look for Chew Chee, China boy, my friend. We come Vancouver Sunday morning in box car. Before – we stop skookum house. Skookum house not very 'skookum' we come Vancouver – very cold, very hungry. Chew Chee tell me come this house. All right come. Now I go. Good-by!"

He remained silent, his face expressionless to me. I knew the Chinese mistrust of white men, and many of their good reasons for it, and was not offended or discouraged. He was protecting his countryman; I admired him for it. At the door I gave him a final dig. "My friend tell me come your house; I come. You think me 'luc zhe.' You very smart man. You think me policeman. All right. Good-by!"

This was too much for the stoical Chinaman. He followed me out and, catching up, said in a low voice:

"You no 'luc zhe'; you good man. You come 'fi fi' (quickly)."

I followed him into the next block, then down a narrow, dark lane between buildings and up shaky stairs where he knocked on a door. An old man admitted us and barred the door. The place was a big loft.The foggy air was hot, stifling, and laden with every Chinese smell – opium, tobacco, fish, and damp clothes drying. Chinamen were cooking, eating, smoking hop, gambling, or sleeping in curtained bunks that lined the walls. My conductor was evidently a considerable person. Silence fell on the room, and many Chinamen stood still in submissive attitudes.

He threw a mangy old cat out of a broken chair near the big stove in the middle of the room and told me to sit. After a few jerky gutturals to the old man that let us in, he disappeared in the haze of smoke. The gambling and chatter started again. Some of the younger Chinese passed and looked at me curiously.

I sat by the stove and watched the scene with interest. An old Chinaman – he must have been sixty – shuffled by me hastily with a hop layout and spread it in a near-by bunk. He was shaking with the "yen yen," the hop habit. His withered, clawlike hands trembled as he feverishly rolled the first "pill," a large one. His burning eyes devoured it. Half cooked, he stuck the pill in its place and turning his pipe to the lamp greedily sucked the smoke into his lungs. Now, with a long, grateful exhalation, the smoke is discharged, the cramped limbs relax and straighten out, the smoker heaves a sigh of satisfaction, and the hands, no longer shaking, turn with surer touch to another "pill." This is smaller, rolled and shaped with more care, better cooked, and inhaled with a slow "long draw." Each succeeding pill is smaller, more carefully browned over the lamp, and smoked with increased pleasure. At last the little horn container, the "hop toy," is empty. The last pill is finished with perfect stroke and flourish, the bamboo pipe is put aside with caressing touch, the lamp blown out with gentle breath, and the devotee, sighing softly, curls himself up for pleasant dreams.

I was so intent on watching the old man's magic transformation from a shattered wreck into a sleeping cherub that the boss Chinaman's return escaped me. He touched my shoulder and I followed him into a small room in a rear corner of the loft, where I found Chew Chee. He shook my hand awkwardly. His English was almost forgotten. All he could say was, "You good man, you good man."

The boss Chinaman was full of business. He drew out some American gold pieces. "I pay you. Chew Chee pay me some time."

I explained to him that I had not come for money; that I was there to see Chew Chee and make friends of his friends, and that if I ever needed money or help I would ask for it and expect it.

"Well, then," he said, returning the gold to his pocket, "I give you China letter to my company man. You come my store to-morrow night."

He went away and Chew Chee insisted that I go with him and meet his "cousins." We walked across the city to a laundry where I was royally received. Chew Chee was the only Chinese that had a word of English, but the party was a success anyway. They produced their finest liquor, their lichee nuts, their daintiest cakes, and choicest tea. The hop layout was spread, and Chew Chee rolled and toasted me a pill that I smoked just by way of being a sociable, good fellow. The pill made me drowsy. A bunk was prepared and I slept out the night peacefully and safely in the midst of my friends. I bade Chew Chee good-by in the morning, and never saw him again.

That night, having nothing else to do, I went down to the China store. The boss had my letter ready. I thanked him for it, and putting it in my pocket gave it no further thought. And yet that letter snatched me clear of the law's clutches on a night when I was caught in a burglary, overpowered, hog-tied, and waiting for "the wagon."

I marvel to this day I did not quit my stealing right then and there. I had all the best of it. I had escaped a sure conviction and sentence. I could have returned to the "American side" and the Canadian authorities would have given me good riddance. Yet the thought of turning to the right, squaring myself, and starting anew never entered my mind. Probably youthful egotism, which is nothing but confidence born of ignorance, whispered to me that I could beat a game I knew to be wrong and full of dangers. So without stopping to cast up accounts or take stock, I blithely looked about me for fresh endeavors. My money was fast dwindling, more must be had; and nightly I prowled the town with the single purpose of locating anything I could do by myself.

It's difficult to explain to a layman the pride of a professional thief. Nevertheless he must have pride or he would steal his clothes, beat his board bills, and borrow money with no thought of repaying it. He doesn't do those things day after day, but day after day he takes chances and is proud that he can keep his end up and pay for the things he needs. All wrong, of course, but there it is. If I had had brains enough to grease a griddle, I would have taken a hundred dollars from the boss Chinaman in the matter of Chew Chee and gone off somewhere, got a job, and tried to do the right thing by myself and others. But no, I was a journeyman; I had served a long and careful apprenticeship; professional pride – I don't know what else to call it – would not permit me to take the Chinaman's money for rescuing him from our common enemy, the law, and I went out to get money in my own way.

I was wrong. I knew I was wrong, and yet I persisted. If that is possible of any explanation it is this: From the day I left my father my lines had been cast, or I cast them myself, among crooked people. I had not spent one hour in the company of an honest person. I had lived in an atmosphere of larceny, theft, crime. I thought in terms of theft. Houses were built to be burglarized, citizens were to be robbed, police to be avoided and hated, stool pigeons to be chastised, and thieves to be cultivated and protected. That was my code; the code of my companions. That was the atmosphere I breathed. "If you live with wolves, you will learn to howl."

In my rambles about Vancouver, I met an acquaintance from Salt Lake. He and his wife were exiled from the Mormon city and could not return in safety till they got a "bunch of trouble fixed up." He fell on my neck, saying: "Just the party I'm looking for. I've got something soft for you; you can't go wrong." He invited me to his quarters, a cottage they had rented. They were both "smokers," and over the hop he explained the "soft" thing.

His wife, in buying a can of hop, had tendered the Chinese storekeeper a large bill. When he went into a rear room for the change, she saw that he had his money in a box concealed beneath the floor. He made a purchase later and verified her story.

"That's all there is to it," he said. "All you've got to do is go get it."

I investigated and found that his story wasn't altogether the rosy dream of a hop fiend. The storekeeper, an elderly Chinaman, did keep his money in a box under the floor, but he slept on top of it at night and in a room adjoining about a dozen Chinese laundry hands slept in bunks. It didn't look a bit soft to me. I convinced myself that the money was there, and that I could get into the place, but that was all I could be reasonably sure of.

My friend's wife was a resourceful woman. "Chloroform him, that's easy. I'll get you the chloroform," she cried.

I hesitated about that. I was practical, I knew nothing about chloroforming people. Sanc had never once mentioned chloroform and what he knew about burglary was plenty. In searching my mind for something to guide me I recalled having met a talkative chap in Chicago at California Jack's hop joint, who told me in great detail about his "ether outfit," how he injected the fluid through keyholes, putting his victims out before going into their rooms, how he chloroformed women sleepers by holding a saturated handkerchief to their noses, and how he stripped their fingers of rings while they were stupefied. I remembered his talk didn't ring just right and that he borrowed two dollars from me at the finish and never paid them. I had long since dismissed him from my mind as a magazine burglar, a reader and rehasher of crime stories, embellished and embroidered by daily devotion to the bamboo pipe.

Still his talk kept in my mind. There might be something in it. The old Chinaman had money there; I needed it. I was ambitious to learn. Chloroform seemed to be the only way and I decided to try it. I gave the place a final looking-over. It was a one-story shack between two larger buildings. A storeroom in front with its long counter, and shelves on both sides filled with merchandise, a small room directly back of it where the storekeeper slept on his pallet. I made sure of that by rousing him early one morning to make a purchase. The big rear room accommodated the Chinese laundry hands.

My friend's wife delivered the chloroform and a clean handkerchief. I rehearsed the whole business in my mind, and, feeling reasonably safe, put it to the touch. An open window let me into the bunk room, where I unfastened the back door, for a getaway.

On a long table in the center of the room a metal lamp in a dish burned dimly. The tired laundrymen snored or breathed heavily. Here a muscular brown arm hung limply over the side of a bunk below the curtain, and there a foot protruded. The door to the old man's room was open, and I stood there a long time till I could pick out his gentle, regular breathing from the chorus of wheezes, grunts, and snores in the bunk room. I had hoped to find him lying on his back. I don't know just why, but that was the way I had him in my rehearsals. Sure enough he was in that position, sleeping like a baby.

Holding the handkerchief at arm's length, I saturated it liberally with the chloroform and returned the bottle to my pocket. Then I knelt beside him and held the handkerchief above his nostrils. With the first breath of it he stirred uneasily, and slowly turned over, facing the wall. Here was something I hadn't anticipated. I was sure he hadn't enough; he breathed regularly again. I must give him more. Reaching over him, I held the stuff near his nose as before. One whiff, and he floundered away from it, turning over, facing me, but still asleep.

I grew alarmed. This tossing from side to side would soon wake him. I thought of giving it up and going away quietly. My heart was pounding with the suspense. It seemed to grow and expand till it filled my chest and almost stopped my breath. I must go through with it. Carefully this time, I held the handkerchief near his face with both hands. His body twitched nervously now. His breathing was labored. I was sure of him, and held it closer.

With a scream that woke every Chinaman in the bunk room, he sat bolt upright, and throwing his arms out fastened his clawlike fingers in my clothes.

Believing he was about to be murdered, the old man fought and screamed in a frenzy of fear. I saw red-handed capture in front of me, and tried desperately to throttle him. The noise of our struggle had roused the sleepers in the back room and I could hear their startled cries as they dropped out of their bunks. I had no thought of the money now; it was a question of getting away. Just when the old man was exhausted and I was in a fair way to get out of his clutches, some of the more daring Chinamen from the back room rushed in. I got a blow on the head that knocked me half out, and they fell on me like a pack of wolves, smothering me with kicks, cuffs, digs, and scratches. The whole thing was over quicker than I can write it. I was stretched out on my back on the floor with two Chinamen holding each of my arms down, two sitting on each leg, and another with both hands in my hair. They all chattered at once. Then one came with a lamp, and I was inspected curiously, like some strange, fearsome monster that had been trapped.

The old man, now recovered from the battle, gave a sharp order. A short, muscular, knotty-legged China boy went to the back room and returned with a rope. I was carefully raised to a sitting position and my arms held to my sides while the boy threw a couple of half hitches around my body, pinioning me safely. The rope was then run to my ankles, where he deftly tied some more strange and wonderful Chinese knots, and I was secured; scratched, bruised, bleeding, and asking myself if they were going to send for the police or execute me on the spot.

Another order from the boss and they lifted me bodily and sat me on a box in the corner of the little room. They stood by, eyeing me in silence now. The old man sat on his pallet. There was an odor of chloroform in the room, but he did not appear to be any the worse for what he had inhaled. Our struggle had probably worn it off. He picked the handkerchief from the floor where it had fallen and sniffed it.

Holding it out toward me, he asked in fair English:

"What for, him?"

Something told me I had a chance yet. I decided to tell the old man the truth. "Him medecine," I answered.

"What for medecine?"

"Make you sleep."

"What for sleep?"

"I think maybe take your money."

"How you know me money?"

"I come you store; I look see."

He got up, rolled his blankets away, and, raising up the small trapdoor in the floor, opened his box and made sure that it had not been disturbed. They all began talking again. I heard the fatal words "luc zhe," "luc zhe," which means policeman.

In desperation I cried, "No, no, no luc zhe. Him no good. I got plenty good China friends. Me good friend Chew Chee, China boy. Before –

Chew Chee stop 'skookum house' I bring him Vancouver. Me good man." I remembered my Chinese letter and cried out desperately: "You look my pocket; you see China letter; him good letter. You look my pocket."

The name of Chew Chee was like magic on them. They became silent and listened closely to my talk. I was tied up so that I couldn't reach the vest pocket the letter was in, but I managed to touch it with a finger. "You look my pocket," I cried frantically to the old man.

He came over to where I sat on the box and gingerly put his fingers into the pocket, bringing out the letter. By the lamplight he studied it long and carefully. Others then read it, and the powwowing started again, while I sat listening for the fatal "luc zhe," and picturing myself back in the jail I had so lately escaped from. The boss now got a box and sat opposite me with the letter in his hand and a thoughtful, puzzled look on his leathery, wrinkled old face. The other Chinamen stood behind him, silent again. I saw I was going to be tried or examined, and hoping for an out, I began to figure some kind of a defense.

His accusing words bit into me like an acid. They were laden with scorn. I turned hot with shame and confusion. Tapping the letter with a long, bony finger, he said: "Him letter talk you good man. What for, you good man?"

These were short, plain words and called for a plain answer. No use trying to deceive this old man after trying to rob him. No use putting up a crying talk for mercy. I could see he scorned me as a robber, a thief in the night, and made up my mind not to bring more contempt upon myself by pleading weakly and in fear. I answered him as I imagined he would have answered me if by any chance our positions had been reversed.

"Maybe me good man," I said. "Maybe bad man, I no know. Long time policeman make me plenty trouble. Long time I stop jail house. Then I come Vancouver. No more money, no more eat. I look see your money, I come your house steal your money. No can do; you catch me. You send me jail house, long time me no come home. More better you kill me now. Policeman talk me bad man; plenty Chinaman talk me good man. Maybe good man, maybe bad man; I no know."

I spoke firmly, looking him in the eyes frankly, and finished my argument for the defense with as much force and feeling as any barrister ever put into a plea for a client's life. His face was blank as a board. His little brownish-black eyes were fastened on mine but I saw no hope in them. I couldn't even tell whether he had understood what I said. After studying me for a long time he turned and said something to one of his boys. The boy went into the bunk room and came back with a heavy meat cleaver that the Chinese use to chop pork and fowl. Another order and I was lifted, box and all, out of the corner and placed in the middle of the room. The China boy with the cleaver stepped behind me.

Something in the pit of my stomach seemed to collapse. I tried to say something to the old boss, but the words wouldn't come; they just rattled around in my throat. The old man bored into me with his eyes like a blacksnake "charming" a bird. Suddenly he uttered a short, sharp exclamation that sounded like "Chut." I snatched my eyes away from his and closed them, prepared for the fatal blow that my guilty mind told me was about to fall on my head from behind. The blow did not fall, but I was almost dead anyway and swayed on my box till the China boys had to support me. I felt a fumbling at my ankles and opened my eyes to find the knotty-legged boy kneeling at my feet, untying his knots. When the rope was taken off me, I turned my head and saw the boy standing behind me, holding his cleaver at "ready," prepared to strike me down only if I started anything rough. One of them handed me my hat. I put it on, and stood up slowly and with an effort. The old man waved his arm toward the back room.

"You go ou'," he ordered sternly.

"My letter?" I asked meekly and respectfully.

"No more letter," he said, crumpling it in his hand.

The Chinese boys stood aside as I started into the bunk room to go out the back door. I was shamed, humiliated, covered with confusion. Turning back, I took off my hat, and facing the old man held up my right hand.

"If I ever rob another Chink I hope I rot in the gutter." I was so intent on expressing my gratitude that I forgot my Chinese lingo.

He understood no word of it, I'm sure, but pointed again to the back. "You go ou'."

I went out, humble and crestfallen. In the alley I threw the bottle of chloroform against a building, and its crash somewhat relieved my feelings. That was my first and last experience with chloroform as an aid to burglary. As an agent for stupefying a sleeping person without waking him, I maintain, in spite of the opinions of fiction writers and romancing thieves, "it can't be done." Making my way to the cottage of my Salt Lake friends who had promoted me, I reported my disastrous and humiliating failure. Had they been inclined to entertain any doubts about my story, my appearance would have set them at rest. I was scratched, clawed, bruised, and had a big lump on my head.

They were very sympathetic. I was invited to "stick around a few days" till they could look up something else for me. I excused myself as tactfully as possible, resolving to locate my own work from there on. I went to my room and to bed, and stayed there several days because of the terrible mauling the Chinamen had given me. Yet, with all this, I couldn't but respect them for letting me go free, heaping coals of fire on my guilty head. I remembered Smiler and our resolve never to pester another Mormon when we had been captured in the Temple yard and released. I vowed never to molest another Chinaman, and never since have I imposed upon one except on one occasion, and that was under great necessity.

Years after, I got out of a train at Cheyenne, racked with the opium habit, after an all-day ride to escape the Denver police. Making a hasty survey of the gambling houses and joints I failed to find anybody I knew who could direct me to a place to "smoke." It was almost midnight, cold and storming, and I set out to find a laundry. There was one near by, the laundrymen were resting after the day's toil, and through the glass door I saw one lying in his bunk, smoking his day's ration of hop. The door was locked, and they refused to open up for me.

No hop fiend's wits ever fail to work when the "yen yen" arrives. In desperation I hastened to one of the gambling houses, and going into a rear room took off my vest and wrapped it in a newspaper. Hurrying out, I got a messenger and gave him fifty cents to take the bundle to the Chinese laundry. I was at his heels. The Chinamen seeing what they thought was a parcel of laundry opened the door and I shouldered myself in behind the boy. Once inside, I took my vest away from him and going directly to the bunk where the smoker lay threw down some silver, explaining what I wanted. The smoker turned out to be the boss laundryman. The sight of my money mollified him somewhat, and after much protesting and objecting he let me lie down on his bunk and smoke my fill. In an hour we were friends. He explained that he refused to open the door because he thought I was a "ketchum money man" – a robber.

In the days of my sad experience at the Chinese store, Vancouver was a much smaller town than it is now. There were few opportunities worth while, and I decided to leave. Moreover every Chinese store, laundry, and business house reminded me of that disastrous night. I was afraid of bumping into Chew Chee or the boss Chinaman that had given me the letter. I was sure they had heard about it, and didn't want to face them. I was nearly broke again, and had to bestir myself.

The American side seemed the only place to go, and not having enough money to buy a ticket, I went down to the railroad yards to get a train. The blind baggage, or "stormy end" as the bums call it, was so crowded when the train pulled out that I saw they would all be thrown off at the first stop. I didn't want to get underneath on the rods and ruin my clothes for a short jump of fifty miles to the junction, so I got on top of a coach. Something must have been wrong with the engine, for there was one continual shower of red-hot cinders falling on me that burned holes in my clothes, ruining them and blistering my skin.

At the first stop I got down, intending to go in a coach and steal a hat check, or crawl under a seat out of sight. Looking about I saw that the last coach was in darkness, and thinking it was a dead, empty car, I waited till it came along and boarded the front end, hoping to find the door unlocked. The door opened to my touch, but when I went inside I found myself in a luxuriously furnished private car instead of a dead coach.

There are only three degrees of tough luck – bad, worse, and worst. When you reach the worst you have the satisfaction of knowing that if your luck changes it has to change for the better. I considered my Waterloo at the Chinese store the direst degree of bad luck. Not only had I lost a big bunch of money; I was hurt somewhere else.

At that time I thought it was my professional pride that suffered because of failure. Now I know I was hurt because the old Chinaman had shown himself so superior to me. If he had sent me to jail I would have done my time and forgotten him, but to this day thinking about him and writing about him make me feel uneasy. I wonder what I would have done had he made me promise to quit stealing?

But I was in this private car, feeling that my luck was due for a change, and with a chance to heal my wounded pride. The air inside the car was warm, live, vibrating. I sensed an occupant. Making my way along the aisle toward a stateroom at the far end, I looked about closely for an attendant but there was none in sight. The stateroom door was open, with a chair against it, probably for better ventilation. A heavily shaded lamp was burning, and by its soft light I saw the form of a big man rolled in the blankets on a broad berth. His back was toward the door, and nothing but a shock of coarse gray hair showed above the covers. A glance told me I was in the presence of power, wealth, affluence. I hadn't enough money to pay for that man's breakfast.

On a small table at the head of the sleeper's berth there was a large silver pitcher, a glass, two books, a fat leather pocketbook, a thick bill fold, a pocket purse, and a heavy gold watch, with a small, black ribbon guard. I took all the articles except the pitcher, glass, and books, and started for the door I entered, praying that the attendant wouldn't appear.

I saw nothing of him, and concluded he was somewhere forward, gossiping or shooting dice with the porters.

It was but a minute's work to get back upon the top of a coach, where I lay and let the cinders do their worst. The next stop was a junction, where I intended to get off and cross the line into Washington. The only train in sight was a westbound passenger waiting on a sidetrack. I was afraid to hang around, and when it pulled out I went underneath on the rods and got back into Vancouver after an absence of five hours. I planted the watch in the railroad yards, and never saw it again.

On my way uptown to get a room, I emptied the bill fold and purse, throwing them away. In the room I looked over the money, and found I had enough to keep me six months, if I kept away from the faro tables.

The fat pocketbook held no money, but was bulging with valuable personal papers. Looking through them I saw that their owner was one of the higher officials of the Canadian Pacific Railway. I realized there would be a terrific roar in the morning, and was on the point of burning the papers and destroying the pocketbook when the thought came to me that I could gain nothing by that, while I would be causing the owner an immense loss and no end of inconvenience. I secreted the pocketbook in the rear of the hotel, and went to bed trying to think up some safe way of returning it to the owner. No use in inflicting a profitless injury on him; and its return might take the sharp edge off his resentment.

EIGHTEEN

DISCARDING my cinder-burnt clothes for a new outfit the next day, I bought a ticket for Victoria, B.C. On my way to the boat that evening I dropped the fat pocketbook into a mail box, where I knew it would be found, then examined, and returned to the loser.

When I first began stealing I had but a dim realization of its wrong. I accepted it as the thing to do because it was done by the people I was with; besides, it was adventurous and thrilling. Later it became an everyday, cold-blooded business, and while I went about it methodically, accepting the dangers and privations it entailed, I was fully aware of the gravity of my offenses. Every time I stole a dollar I knew I was breaking a law and working a hardship on the loser. Yet for years I kept on doing it. I wonder how many of us quit wronging others for the best reason of all – because it is wrong, and we know it. Any thief that can't or doesn't put himself in his victim's place, in the place of the copper that pinches him, or in the place of the judge who sentences him, is not a complete thief. His narrow-mindedness will prevent him from doing his best work and also shut him off from opportunities to help and protect himself when he is laid by the heels.

Nobody wants to live and die a criminal. They all hope to quit some day, usually when it's almost too late. I will say right here to any thief who thinks of quitting that if he can put himself in the other fellow's place he has something substantial to start on; and if he can't do it, he'll never get anywhere.

I always figured that when I had a man's money or valuables he had suffered enough. What sense in destroying his personal papers, or keeping heirlooms of no value except to him, or subjecting him to any loss that would be profitless to me? In the case of this sleeper in his private car, I saw the money and watch meant little to him. The papers meant much. On top of that, his peace of mind was disturbed, and his sense of safety and security shattered. He would probably lock his doors and sleep in a stuffy room the balance of his life, another great hardship. I had his valuables and intended to keep them. I could not restore his peace of mind or his sense of safety and security. I could restore his papers, and, at some small risk, did. Had I been chased or suspected I would have thrown them away, or in the fire without a thought. I took his property coolly, impersonally, as a picker removes the feathers from a fat goose. I returned his papers as the last touch to a workmanlike job, as the cabinetmaker softly gives the last nail its last light tap.

To any thief who reads this and criticizes me as being over-thoughtful of the "sucker," I reply that he is probably one of those guys that beats his victim up after robbing him; who strikes down women and children if they get in his way; who destroys paintings, vases, tapestries, and clothing wantonly, and winds up by letting some housewife chase him under a bed, where she holds him with her broomstick till the coppers arrive. He is not a thief, but a "mental case," and belongs in a psychopathic ward.

At Victoria I put in a few very pleasant months. I joined the colony of Chinese and opium smugglers, who ran their freight across the line in fast, small boats at night into Port Townsend, Anacortes, or Seattle, Washington. The manufacture of smoking opium was then a legalized industry in Canada, and the smugglers were welcomed and harbored because they brought much American gold to the Canadian side. Being in the company of these characters I was accepted by the police as one of them, and went my way unmolested.

One fatal evening, as I stood watching a faro game making mental bets and winning every one, the devilish hunch came to me that I was lucky and ought to make a play. My resistance reached the vanishing point. I made a bet, lost it, got stuck, and feverishly played in my last dollar.

This gambling habit is the curse of a thief's life. He loses his last dime and is forced to go out in haste for more money. Like a mechanic broke and out of a job, he takes the first one in sight. He has no time to pick and choose, or calculate carefully what he is about; he must eat, and the minute he goes broke he gets hungry. Gambling keeps him broke, forces him to steal small money on short notice and take prohibitive and unnatural chances.

I could have borrowed money enough to expense myself to Vancouver where I had the valuable watch planted, but there had been such a cry in the papers about the car burglary, the loser was so powerful and influential, and the danger of trying to sell it so great, that I decided to leave it there till later, and take it to the American side.

During my stay in Victoria I had strolled through the residence district and noted several homes that looked prosperous and easy of approach. House burglary was almost unknown there then; there was almost no police protection, none was needed. Householders left windows open and doors unlocked.

One o'clock found me in one of the most pretentious places on my list, but instead of picking up trifles right and left as I expected, I found but one room occupied. Later I learned the family, with the exception of the man of the house, was away for the summer. He was a good sleeper. I took nothing but money, and not much of that – less than fifty dollars in silver and bills – leaving his watch and some small articles of jewelry as not worth the chances I must take in trying to dispose of them in a strange town.

I went straight downtown to the only all-night bar and lunch counter to eat before going to bed. Before I had my meal finished two officers and two civilians came in and spoke to the sleepy bartender. He nodded toward me and they all came over to where I sat eating. One of the civilians looked at me closely and said to the other: "Looks very much like the man; same clothes, same hat, same build, same height."

"What do you mean?" I asked.

"This," spoke up the other. "If I am wrong you have an apology in advance; if I am right you are in for it. I was robbed not an hour ago in my bedroom in my house. This man, my servant, had occasion to get out of bed and, while standing at a window in his room, saw the prowler leaving stealthily by the rear way. Suspicious, he alarmed me, and I discovered my loss. I brought these officers here on a bare chance that the burglar might be here. You are the only one who has entered here, except us, in the last hour. I do not accuse you. I ask you if you will permit the officers to search you. If you are an honest man, you cannot take offense."

He was the man I had robbed; he was an Attorney; he was a smart man. I was in a bad hole. If I objected to search it would look bad, and they would do it anyway. "Certainly. Go ahead and search me," I said, making the best of a bad position. When the officers had finished searching me, they counted the money.

"Lock him up," ordered the lawyer. "He has the exact amount of money I lost. The paper corresponds, and so does the silver."

They handcuffed me. "You're arrested in the name of the Crown, and anything you say will be used against you."

I was taken to the city prison where I gave the booking officer a very brief and misleading biographical sketch. The jail I had fled from with the China boy loomed before me and my only thought was to cover up. I put in the balance of the night going over my case. It looked hopeless. The next morning my cell was not unlocked when the other prisoners were let out to wash. Later a jailer opened it, and a Siwash Indian boy handed me a bucket of water and a towel.

When I reached for them the boy looked at me and I turned cold.

He was one of the watchful trusty prisoners at the jail I had escaped from. He knew me. This was the first of a long and bitter series of experiences with stool pigeons, and in all my life I never witnessed a more gratuitous, barefaced, conscienceless exhibition of snitching.

Without waiting to walk out of my sight he grabbed the jailer by the arm and began pattering away in Chinook, pointing at me. He didn't "spill the beans." He just kicked the pot over and put out the fire.

"To understand is to forgive," it is said. I have long since forgiven the numberless, noisy stool pigeons that beset my crooked path because I don't want any poison in my mind, but as yet I am unable to understand them.

Immediately the jailer came back with another officer and they put a very hefty pair of leg irons on me. At ten o'clock I was taken into the magistrate's court. The attachés and loungers crowded close and stared at me curiously. The magistrate briefly and coldly remanded my case for three days. A photographer waiting at the jail took a number of pictures of me and I was locked up again. The jailer, a sad-eyed, solemn-faced Scotchman, gazed at me a long time through the barred door and smacked his lips as if enjoying the flavor of some delicious morsel or rare wine.

In a voice that seemed to come out of a sepulcher he said: "You escaped from the provincial jail in the town of —— ."

I already knew I was lost, but his solemn face and melancholy voice conveyed to me, as he probably intended, the full force and effect of my predicament. He made me feel like one buried alive; his measured words sounded to me like cold clods dropping on my coffin. I wasn't taken out of my cell and "sweated" or third-degreed, or beaten up. That looked bad for me. The more a prisoner is questioned the less they know; the less he is questioned the more they know. If he is not questioned at all they know it all, or enough. My captors asked me no questions; they knew enough.

At the expiration of the three days I was remanded again. Then came another remand, and before it expired the Scotch jailer I escaped from appeared to take me back for trial where there was a cinch case against me and the charge of jail breaking to boot. The lawyer whose house I entered and who so neatly trapped me came to the jail before I was taken away. He was a fine fellow, an Englishman, and to use an English expression in describing him, I'll say he was "a bit of all right." He brought me a book from his library, Charles Reade's "It's Never Too Late to Mend." He waived claim to the money found on me when I was arrested; told the jailer to see that I got it and wished me luck with my case. He neither lectured me nor asked any embarrassing questions. Shaking my hand heartily when he was leaving he said: "Do read that book, old man. And, I say, I'm not intimating that you're an authority on burglary, but I thought you might tell me how I could prevent it in future." I told him to buy himself a dollar-and-a-half dog, and let him sleep in the house.

He shook my hand again and thanked me. He was so downright decent and charming that an outsider, observing our interview, would have thought he had come to ask a favor of me, and was departing under a heavy obligation. I was ashamed of going into his house and would have taken a pledge not to rob any more Englishmen but it didn't seem necessary. From what I could see, there was a judge waiting in the jurisdiction I escaped who would attend to that.

The Scotchman loaded me with irons, put me on a boat to Vancouver, then on a train, and finally landed me back safely in his jail. He took the Englishman's book from me on the train and never gave it back. I had no chance to read the story till I got out of his clutches. Later I got it, read it, and was fascinated and read every other book by the author that I could lay hands on.

During my absence a new and securer cell had been built in the jail because of our escape. It adjoined the jailer's office, and its barred door was directly in front of his desk, not six feet away. He moved a camp cot into his office and slept where he could watch me. Day after day and night after night he drank his whisky, smoked his pipe, and rustled his paper under my nose.

Chew Chee, the Chinese boy, had stolen two thousand dollars cash from his employer. He told me he gambled it away before he got arrested. At any rate, the money was never recovered. My jailer spread the report around that I took the Chinese boy with me so I could get the two thousand, after which I had murdered him and secreted his body. Whether he believed it or only pretended to, I never knew. He never questioned me about Chew Chee, and now when he got drunk instead of calling me just plain "damned Yank," he chucked in another adjective, "murderous." To get even with him I began sleeping in the daytime and walking up and down the cell all night, clanking the leg irons to keep him awake. He retaliated by prodding me with a long stick every time he caught me sleeping in the daytime, and I gave it up.

He took my Bible away and when the Salvation Army came on Sunday I reported it to them. Somebody regulated him, and he grudgingly returned it.

I had some thought of taking a jury trial. One never can tell what a small-town jury will do. Sometimes they carry their neighborhood feuds into the jury room and the defendant gets a disagreement. But after my jailer spread his story about my murdering the China boy, I dismissed the jury from my mind and decided to go before the court under the Speedy Trials Act. A defendant electing for a speedy trial dispenses with a jury and saves time and money for the community. A speedy trial is almost equivalent to a plea of guilty, but when the defendant is found guilty the court, in passing sentence, considers the fact that there has been no expensive jury trial and is more lenient.

The Crown counsel called at the jail to ask what I wanted in the way of a trial. I told him, and he had the witnesses subpoenaed for a certain day. I could have got a young lawyer of the town with the money I brought from Victoria, but it looked to me like a willful waste, and I held it.

In due time the judge arrived at the town. My irons were struck off, and I went into court. I got a brief, dignified, orderly trial. The train conductor appeared and identified me and the fatal twenty-dollar I gave him. All the other witnesses testified, word for word, as they did at my examination. I removed any doubts there might have been as to my guilt by declining to go on the witness stand. This trial consumed almost an hour.

Then I was tried for escaping from Her Majesty's jail. That consumed fifteen minutes.

Having no lawyer, the judge asked me if I wanted to go over the points in the case. I thanked him and said I could not presume to instruct His Lordship on law points. He gave his verdict then, "Guilty, both charges."

"Anything to say before sentence?" he asked.

Thinking he might be feeling better after lunch I asked till one o'clock to prepare a very short statement. He adjourned court. At one o'clock I stood up and said: "Your Lordship, my trial was fair; your verdict just."

He looked at me a long time. "Two years in the provincial penitentiary for burglary; six months for jail breaking. Sentences concurrent – and thirty lashes."

The prison sentence was no surprise to me. I expected a heavier one. I had long before admitted to myself its possibility, even its probability. But I had accepted that as a business man accepts a chance of bankruptcy, or as a laborer foresees an injury. The court's order that I be lashed was a surprise and caused me no small concern. I couldn't get it off my mind. I wondered if I could stand it; day and night I could feel the lash on my bare back. After turning it over in my mind I decided to make the best of it, and found some consolation in the thought that if the judge hadn't ordered the flogging he would have sentenced me to five or ten years.

I dismissed all thought of escaping again from the jail. Even if I had my saws that were planted in the cell I got out of, I couldn't have used them, for my jailer was determined to land me in the penitentiary and watched me closer than ever. I was wretched and almost lost hope. I envied poor dead Smiler and Foot-and-a-half George. I wished myself back with the larcenous-eyed Tex and his crew of cheap gamblers. My mind ran back to Madam Singleton and Julia and the overworked widow at my boarding house. I thought of the Sanctimonious Kid doing his fifteen years in a tough "stir" and wondered what had become of Soldier Johnnie, and how Salt Chunk Mary was faring in far-away Pocatello.

I was the most miserable of them all, and humanlike I tried to fix the blame for all my troubles on some one else. I started in with the judge who sentenced me, then back to the Indian that pointed me out, then to the lawyer who had me arrested, and on back and back and through it all till I got to my father. The Sanctimonious Kid, who was something of a philosopher, said to me once: "Kid, ours is a crooked business, but we must not allow ourselves to think crooked. We've got to think straight, clearly and logically, or we are lost. Of course we'll lose anyway, sooner or later, but let us not hasten the day by loose and careless thinking."

His advice had not been altogether wasted on me. I got into the habit of thinking things over carefully. The trouble was I didn't always follow out my conclusions. I knew I was taking a chance staying in Canada after my escape; yet I stayed. I had long realized that my every act was wrong and criminal; yet I never thought of changing my ways. After thinking it all over with all the clarity and logic and fairness I could command, I was convinced that nobody but myself was to blame, and that I had just drifted along from one thing to another until I was on the rocks. I hadn't been forced into this life, and this predicament, by any set of circumstances or any power beyond my control. I had traveled along this road largely of my own free will, and it followed that I could get on the right road any time I willed it.

Strangely enough, I didn't will to do it then and there. It seemed enough to know and feel I could do it if I wanted to. No use making resolutions until my sentence of two years was in. I would wait and see what that brought forth.

The same train that I was arrested on, in charge of the conductor I gave the bill to, carried me to the prison at New Westminster. My Scotch jailer loaded me with irons and handcuffed me to a seat to make sure of me and he delivered me safely. At the town of New Westminster I looked about me with interest; it was my birthplace. My parents were married in the United States, but spent the first year of their married life in British

Columbia, where my father had some small business interests. He was a British subject and never took the trouble to become an American. That left me a subject of Great Britain, which I still am.

Like ninety per cent of the men arrested for felonies I had given a fictitious name and birthplace. My jailer called me a "damned Yank" because I registered at his jail as an American. At the prison a more complete biographical sketch was demanded of me, with the result that just so much more fiction found its way into the prison statistics. I was bathed, shaved, uniformed, measured, weighed, photographed, questioned at great length, and at last put in a cell by myself. I was notified that I would get fifteen lashes next day and that the remainder would be "laid on" one week before my sentence expired. I was further told very distinctly that by good conduct I could greatly soften the severity of the last installment, but that the first would be administered as the law provided.

Prisoners passing my cell looked in. Some gave me glances of sympathy, others grinned. One, a big, tough-looking gorilla, out of the British Navy, stopped and taunted me gleefully. "Oh, aye, Yank, I reckon an' calculate as 'ow you'll get a fawncy tampin' in the mornin'." I abused both him and his native language.

The convict librarian came along with his catalogue. I selected a book and he got it for me immediately.

My cell was furnished with an iron bed, a small table, a bookshelf, a three-legged wooden stool, and a galvanized iron bucket. On the bed, folded, were a heavy, clean pair of blankets and two sheets. On top of the folded blankets was a straw pillow in a clean slip. Later on a trusty brought me a gallon bucket of water, a tin cup, a small wooden vessel to wash in, and a clean towel. Every movable article in the cell had my prison number on it, and I kept them till the day of my discharge. On the wall was a card of "Rules and Regulations for the Guidance of Prisoners." My first act was to read the rules. This was prompted by curiosity to learn just what I was up against, rather than a desire to learn and obey.

I sat on my stool and tried to read, but my mind was on the morning. Every hour of the long night I woke up with the sting of the lash on my back.

In the morning, after the prisoners had gone to their tasks, a guard came and took me to a room in another part of the building where we found the prison physician waiting. He examined me, pronounced me "fit," and told me to take off my shirt. The room was bare, except for a bench along one wall, and an arrangement in the center of the room that resembled a photographer's tripod, only it was higher and stronger. Its three legs were secured to the floor.

A short, thick man in uniform, with a bristly brown beard and cold blue eyes, came in with a strap very much like a barber's strop, except it was longer and heavier and had a different handhold. He sat on the bench, eyeing me speculatively. The deputy warden now appeared and gave an order. The physician sat down beside the man with the strap. Two guards led me to the triangle. My wrists were strapped to the top of the tripod where the three pieces joined and my ankles lashed to the tripod's legs, leaving me with my arms up in the air and my legs far apart, helpless as any sheep in the shambles.

"Now, Mr. Burr," said the deputy warden.

The man with the strap got up off the bench and stepped behind me a little to my left. Out of the tail of my eye I saw him "winding up" like a ball pitcher. Then came the "woosh" of his strap as it cut the air.

It would not be fair to the reader for me to attempt a detailed description of this flogging. In writing these chronicles I have tried to be fair, reasonable, and rational, and rather than chance misleading anybody by overstating the case I will touch only the high points and leave out the details. No hangman can describe an execution where he has officiated. The best he can do is to describe his end of it, and you have but a one-sided case. The man at a whipping post or tripod can't relate all the details of his beating fully and fairly. He can't see what's going on behind him, and that's where most of the goings-on are. Furthermore, he does not approach the subject with that impersonal, detached mental attitude so necessary to correct observing and reporting. Mentally he is out of focus, and his perspective is blurred.

If I could go away to some lonely, desolate spot and concentrate deeply enough I might manage to put myself in the flogging master's place and make a better job of reporting the matter. But that would entail a mental strain I hesitate to accept, and I doubt if the result would justify the effort.

All along I had my mind made up to take my "tampin'" in as manly a way as possible and to bite my tongue rather than cry out. Also I had tried to hypnotize myself up to a pitch where I could bow my back out toward the blows and hold it there till the thing was done. The first blow was like a bolt of lightning; it shocked and burned. Looking back at it now, it seems to me I jumped six feet in the air. But I couldn't have jumped an inch, I was too securely trussed up. I got through it without squawking, but fell down sadly on the business of bowing my back out. With each succeeding blow I shrank farther from the blistering lash and when it was all over my back was concaved, my chest was bowed out, and I was trembling like a helpless calf under the hot branding iron.

It made no difference how I wriggled and squirmed, I got the full force and effect of every blow, and each one fell on a different spot. "Mr. Burr," God bless him! served his apprenticeship as a flogging master in the British Navy, and he knew his little book.

I was untied and stood there a little bit weak in the knees. My back was blistered, but the skin was not broken. The doctor took a look at it and went away. One of the guards threw my shirt over my shoulders and, holding it on with one hand, and my trousers up with the other, I was marched out and up a flight of stairs to the prison dispensary. The man in charge was dentist, apothecary, hospital steward, nurse and guard. He was a big, brawny, muscular Irishman with arms like an iceman's. While he was applying a liquid to my back, probably to prevent infection, I asked him what it was he was using. "You will speak when you're spoken to," he growled severely with a brogue that was triple X positive. He fixed my back in silence and locked me in a cell in the hospital.

It was a year before I spoke to him again and I waited till he spoke to me first then. Going into his place one day I found him tugging at a Chinaman's tooth. After he got it out and sent the patient away he came over to see what I wanted. He was puffing and perspiring, and, feeling rather pleased with his job on the tooth, wanted to talk to somebody. "Man," he said, "that was an awful tooth in that Chinaman. Sure I thought the jaw was comm' off of him."

"Yes?" I inquired. "Was it a molar?"

"No, man, 'twas no molar; 'twas a back tooth."

He was our prison dentist. He wasn't a bad fellow at that. He brought me a worn volume of Shakespeare and let me take it to my cell. I kept it for months and read it all, and often wondered while reading it what would have happened to the British Empire if the spirited Will Shakespeare had been flogged when he stole Mr. Lucey's venison.

I've heard a lot about the humiliation and degradation of flogging. If anybody was humbled and degraded in my case it was not I. It may sound strange when I say I am glad now, and was glad then, that they lashed me. It did me good. Not in the way it was intended to, of course, but in a better way. I went away from the tripod with fresh confidence, with my head up, with a clear eye and mind, and sustained with a thought from the German, Nietzsche, "What does not kill me strengthens me."

After three days I was returned to my cell and assigned to work on the farm gang. Mr. Burr, the flogging master, who turned out to be a very chatty Scotchman, came to my cell door the first night to have a talk with me, "so there would be no misunderstanding or hard feelings." I don't think he was afraid I would try to do him violence; he just came in a straight, manly way to explain the thing and his part in it. I didn't gather from his talk whether he was in favor of lashing or against it. He appeared an intelligent, fair-minded man.

"You'll find me bark is worse than me bite," he said when he was leaving. I had already made up my mind I ought to hate somebody over the flogging and had about settled on Mr. Burr. But when he was gone I thought it all over again and saw there was no more sense in hating him than any machine I had carelessly got my fingers into.

I settled down to my work and had a chance to look about me. The prison, a stone building, was on the finest site in New Westminster, a gently sloping eminence overlooking a broad sweep of the Fraser River where it widens to its delta. The prison contained one hundred single cells and the silent system obtained. There was never any overcrowding or haphazard makeshifts. When the cells were all filled, a batch of prisoners was at once shipped away to the eastern prisons at Kingston, Ontario, or Stony Mountain, Manitoba, to make room for newcomers. We were closely watched and guarded by the officers, who were nearly all ex-army and navy men, iron disciplinarians and sticklers for the enforcement of rules. I looked about for some way out of the place, but it seemed hopeless and I gave it up, settling down to do my time.

The prison population came from the four corners of the earth. Sailors and ex-soldiers, deserters from the navy, a few "Yanks," fugitives from the "American side," Indians from the Arctic Circle brought down by the Mounted Police to do time for violating laws they never could understand, and a sprinkling of Chinamen and Japs. The sixty acres of prison land were farmed intensively, yielding an abundance of fine vegetables, hay, and grain. Clothing, shoes, and socks were made by prisoners. The food was coarse but wholesome. An American prison commissary would not believe a penitentiary could be run without beans. In my two years at this prison I did not see a bean.

An English prison warden would not believe a prison could exist without peas. I never saw a pea in an American prison. I never saw a cup of coffee in the place. We had pea "coffee" twice a day. It was made from peas grown on the farm, threshed out on the barn floors with flails, roasted and ground like coffee. It was very nutritious and not at all unpalatable. We had plenty of vegetables, mush and pea soup, lots of bread, not too fresh, and not much meat. The food ration, even to the salt and pepper that seasoned it, was regulated by law. Every prisoner got just what the law allowed him and no more. We always had good appetites, never quite had them satisfied, had no smoking tobacco, no coffee, very little meat, and plenty of sleep – the hospital was always empty and there was not a death in the prison in my two years' time there.

The place was clean and well ventilated. We had coarse, warm clothing, enough blankets, plenty of light, lots of good books, and nothing to distract us when reading. I never saw a bug, flea, or mosquito while there. The guards were not brutal or overbearing. I never saw one strike a prisoner; I never saw a prisoner strike a guard.

One morning I glimpsed a familiar face and figure; it was Soldier Johnnie. I forgot the rules, and sang out, "How long are you doing?" Before he could answer I was snatched out of the line and locked in my cell.

The warden was a hardened man, old, sick, and cynical. His motto was "Break them first and make them over." The guard submitted a written report of my misconduct, talking. My punishment was three days on bread and water. The prison had no dungeon. The prisoner under punishment was kept in his cell, which was stripped of its furniture and darkened by placing a blank, wooden, movable door against the outer side of the cell door proper.

In my dark cell I thought of Soldier Johnnie, and wondered if he remembered how they bored a hole and fed me through it in the Utah prison. All the yeggs and "Johnsons" in Christendom couldn't have put a crumb of bread into this dark cell in this backwoods prison – it was English. In all the time I was there I never had a chance to talk to Johnnie. He was discharged before me, and we had no chance to compare notes for years.

My cell was darkened many times and I lived many days on bread and water before I got my time in. I came to learn that a satisfying meal may be made of two ounces of stale bread if it is eaten slowly and chewed thoroughly. I was chewing my ration of bread two hours, taking small bits and chewing them to liquid in my dark cell years before I heard of Fletcher and his system of Fletcherizing food. My experience with short rations in many places has convinced me that we would all be healthier and better nourished if we ate half as much food and chewed it twice as long.

I soon got into a feud with the officers and guards. I talked and laughed and whistled and sang; all of which outraged the ironbound system of silence. The Fourth of July came along, and as I was registered as an American I refused to work on that glorious day. This was a very serious offense, and I was sentenced to twelve days bread and water. They opened my cell every fourth day, put in the furniture, and fed me the regular prison fare. No prisoner may be kept on bread and water for more than three consecutive days. That's English, also.

When the Queen's birthday, the big holiday, came around, I wrote a note to the warden asking permission to work; twelve days more, in four installments.

I read about hay fever in the encyclopædia, and when haying time came I refused to make hay on the grounds that I was a hay-fever addict. The doctor disagreed, and my cell was darkened again. When I was sentenced there was a law under which all prisoners got a plug of "black strap" chewing tobacco every week. While I was in prison the law was repealed. Newcomers got no tobacco, but those sentenced while the law was in force, even if they were life-timers, continued to draw their ration every week. A rule was posted forbidding a prisoner who drew tobacco to give a chew of it to one who didn't. That's English, too. I was caught throwing a chew to a chap that arrived too late, and got another dose of bread and water.

At last I tired of bread and water, got on my good behavior, and took to reading. The prison had a splendid library, not a worthless book in it. All the best English authors were there and I went through them hungrily. I became so immersed in reading that I was careful not to break the rules lest I lose three days or more from the books. I got schoolbooks and studied them. Remembering my poor arithmetic, I tried mathematics but couldn't get anywhere. Then the grammar, but the rules seemed to have been made for no other purpose than to confuse the beginner and "repress his noble rage," so I gave that up, got intensely interested in a small dictionary, and almost went into the dark cell for carrying it out with me to work and looking into it when the guard's back was turned. I read the best books in the library, except the Bible, and would have taken that only I already had six months with it in the Scotchman's jail.

I went through Chambers's Encyclopedia from A to Z. Read all about acids and paper, metals and metallurgy, dies and molds. I studied the history of locks and lockmaking, poring over the pictures of locks and their escutcheons – all kinds of locks and keys, door locks, padlocks, combination locks, nothing was neglected. I read a most interesting paper on picklocks and lock-picking by a famous lock-maker of London. I followed the history of explosives from gunpowder down to nitroglycerin. I found a passage that told clearly and concisely which explosives did the greatest damage and made the least noise. What a mine of information! I was fascinated. I studied guns and pistols, drills and saws and files, braces and bits and drilling machines of high and low pressure and fast or slow motion.

I investigated poisons, herbs, and drugs. I discovered that the finest quality of morphine may be obtained from lettuce and proved it in the prison garden by extracting it and eating it. I read up on sleeping and dreaming and learned just what kind of noise is most apt to wake a sleeping person; just when he sleeps the deepest and at what hour of the night his courage is at its lowest ebb. I can sit in a hotel lobby today and pick out the sound sleeper, the medium sleeper, and light sleeper. I got it out of the encyclopedia, and proved it in practice later.

The time flew by. I read away the long evenings, Sundays, holidays, and rainy days. We ate in our cells and I always had a book propped up behind my pan of pea soup. My feud with guards was forgotten. I had no trouble with fellow prisoners; the silent system and single cells prohibited that. There was no whispering, plotting, scheming, and snitching as there is where the congregate system prevails. The stool pigeon, so fostered and encouraged in American prisons, did not flourish there. The silence obliterated him, made him unnecessary.

There was a little cloud on my mind that began to grow. My time was getting short, some of my credits had been forfeited, and not being able to find out how much, I was uncertain about the day of my discharge and expected to be called out any time for the last installment of my lashing. This made me very nervous, restless, and irritable. The books no longer held me.

NINETEEN

AT LAST I was sent for by the prison tailor to be fitted into a discharge suit, and knew that I hadn't more than a week or ten days to do. A day or two later the same guards took me to the same room, where I found the doctor, the deputy warden, the flogging master, and the triangle all ready for me. I saw I was in for it. The atmosphere was a little more "official" than on the former occasion. Mr. Burr's beard bristled more, and his eye was a little harder. The doctor looked me over with more interest. The guards turned their eyes away from mine as they trussed me up to the tripod, and the deputy warden's "Now, Mr. Burr," was ominously soft, smooth, oily.

The lashing is regulated by law as is every other detail of British penology The strap is just so long, so wide, so thick, and so heavy. The flogging master can swing it just so far and no farther. Mr. Burr did the best he could with those limitations and reservations, and it was plenty.

To make an unpleasant story short, I will say he beat me like a balky horse, and I took it like one – with my ears laid back and my teeth bared. All the philosophy and logic and clear reasoning I had got out of books and meditation in my two years were beaten out of me in thirty seconds, and I went out of that room foolishly hating everything a foot high. I had a chance to cool off during the remaining week of my time, and the day of my release found me halfway rational again.

On my way out of the prison grounds I passed the deputy warden directing a gang of prisoners. I had nothing against them; I was going out and feeling good. I waved them a farewell. He turned on me savagely, snarling, "Be on your way." I stopped, gave him my best dirty look, and turned my back on him and his prison forever.

I was in perfect physical condition; the regular sleep, regular work, and short ration of food had done that for me. I still had the money the lawyer at Victoria did not claim on me, the discharge money, and fare to the town I was sent from; in all enough to last me a month by careful management. My mind had been so unsettled during the last weeks of my time in prison that I hadn't decided where to go or just what I would do. There was no hurry about anything; it was a fine day; I had my liberty. I bought some tobacco and papers at a near-by store and lay down on the warm ground in the green grass under the Indian summer sun to think it over, take stock, and look to the future.

This would be a good place for me to say that I would have quit stealing then if the terrible lashing hadn't embittered me and sent me out looking for revenge, but that would not be the truth. I don't know to this day whether the law contemplates flogging as punishment, as a deterrent measure, or partly both. As a punishment it's a success; as a deterrent it's a failure; if it's half and half one offsets the other and there's nothing gained. The truth is I wouldn't have quit, no matter how I was treated. The flogging just hardened me more, that's all. I found myself somewhat more determined, more confident, and with a feeling that I would play this game of violence to the finish. I had taken everything they had in the way of violence and could take it again. Instead of going away in fear, I found my fears removed. The whipping post is a strange place to gather fresh confidence and courage, yet that's what it gave me, and in that dark cell I left behind many fears and misgivings.

I got up and went my way with the thought that I had got more out of that prison and its keepers than they got out of me. I think the same to-day of every prison I went into. There were times when I thought I got a bit more punishment than was coming to me, but I don't regret a minute of it now. Each of us must be tempered in some fire. Nobody had more to do with choosing the fire that tempered me than myself, and instead of finding fault with the fire I give thanks that I had the metal to take the temper and hold it.

I have hopes that these lines will be read by many convicts and ex-convicts, and they are nothing if not critical readers. I am not trying to lay down any "rules and regulations" for their guidance on the outside, but I want to say this – any prisoner who comes out of prison saying to himself, "I can't quit; it's too late; I'm wrecked and ruined; every man's hand's against me; if I get a job some copper will snitch on me to my boss, or if that don't happen the other 'cons' will blackmail me; there's no use trying, I can't quit"- any "ex-con" who says that is sentencing himself to a jolt that the most heartless and hard-boiled criminal-court judge couldn't conceive of.

The other "con" who comes out time after time saying to himself cold-bloodedly and calculatingly, "I won't quit," might change his mind some time and say, "I will quit." When he wills it, he does it, and no copper snitches him out of his job. If there is any such animal as the blackmailing "ex-con" he gives the "will" chap a wide berth.

I now went to Vancouver and took it easy for a week, resting up, reading papers, and trying to get my bearings. I saw nothing of Chew

Chee, the China boy. He didn't show up in the prison while I was there, and I have no doubt he quit stealing while he was all to the good and went on the square.

Falling in with an outfit of bums and beggars at Vancouver I heard glowing reports of the prosperous mining towns in the interior of British Columbia and decided to visit them. A week's journey over the Canadian Pacific Railway and down the Columbia River found me in the Kootenai mining district. Everything I touched turned to money. The sudden change from no liberty at all in prison to all the liberty in the world almost wrecked me. I didn't think of saving the money so dangerously earned, but squandered it drinking, gambling, and making many trips across the line into the states where there were more opportunities for spending and dissipating.

At last a very valuable parcel of stones found its way into my hands. It was suicide to try to dispose of them on the Canadian side, and I bought a ticket to Pocatello and Salt Chunk Mary. I had been away from there almost four years, and had no fear that the town whittler would remember me, even if he was still on the job, and besides I was hungry for a look at Mary and for a feed of her beans and salt pork.

Arriving at Pocatello I hastened to her place. There was no change in its appearance except that it looked more forlorn and weather-beaten by reason of its contrast with the new buildings that had sprung up around it. In answer to my confident knock on the door a very genteel and refined colored woman opened it and asked me to step in. She looked at me strangely when I asked for Mary. "Why, Miss Mary Howard went away more than three years ago. She sold me the place for almost nothing, settled her affairs, and disappeared. Nobody in Pocatello knows why she left or where she went."

I inquired at the bank, but they knew no more about her than the colored lady. I asked no more questions, but got the first train out for Butte, Montana, where I disposed of my stones and made the bums' hangouts determined to find out the whys and wherefores of Mary's disappearance. I remembered the night she crushed the calaboose for me, and if trouble had come to her I wanted to shoulder my end of it.

The bums all knew of Mary's disappearance, but none of them would even make a guess as to what became of her. Almost ready to give up, I met one of the oldest and best informed bums on the road. His "monoger" (a corruption of monogram), "Hannibal," was carved on every water tank between the two Portlands. I made his acquaintance in the Utah penitentiary, and had met him later on the road. He knew my connection with Foot-and-a-half George, but did not know I was with him when he was killed. I had not seen Hannibal since George's death, and naturally the talk turned to it.

The burglary was long since outlawed, there was no need for me to conceal my part in it, so I told him all about the caper. He listened very attentively, and when I was done said: "You must have been there, for that tallies exactly with what I heard. Over three years ago I met a bum by the name of 'Rochester Red' at 'Stew Junction' (Puyallup, Washington). Red was five miles outside of that county seat the night you and George got that box. This is what he tells me.

"He's just finished a long stretch in the stir at Canon City. His health ain't none too good, so he jumps over into Utah and down on the 'poultice route,' where he won't be pestered by bulls while he's recuperatin' on good fresh air an' green vegetables an' plenty of bread and milk. He flops in a haystack five miles out of the town where you people cut the caper. At daylight the next morning the hoosiers drag him out and he thinks they're goin' to lynch him. They take him into the town an' give him a look at the stiff laid out on the courthouse floor. He raps to George, an' just as you say, he is almost cut in half by the two shotgun loads. Red don't see any use in givin' himself a bawl-out by identifyin' any dead burglars, so he dummies up on the natives an in a couple of days they let him go, an' he keeps on goin', for they are proper hostile. When Roch' Red tells me this, I dash into Portland and out over the Short Line into Pocatello, an' tells Mary."

"What was all your hurry about?" I asked.

"Hah," Hannibal replied. "That's somethin' Red didn't know, an' somethin' you don't know. But you're all right, an' I don't mind tellin' you.

"George and Mary was raised in my home town, Hannibal, Missouri, an' George was her brother. They was a mysterious pair, an there's no use tryin to figure what become of Mary."

When my breath came back, I said: "Well, that explains to me why George 'sprayed' Gold Tooth with all that lead at Pocatello."

"Oh, yes. Tell me about that, Blacky. I never got the straight of it."

In return for Hannibal's tale, I ordered a fresh bottle, and over it told him the story of Gold Tooth's death at the hands of Foot-and-a-half George.

Unable to gather any more information about Mary, I turned to work again, making the towns of Spokane, Portland, Seattle, and Tacoma, confining myself strictly to house burglary, which is "one man" work. This kind of thievery is fast becoming a thing of the past. Better lighting, policing, and locking systems; the apartment house; the building of "tighter" residences; the better treatment of dogs which makes them more intelligent; and more efficient and careful servants have combined to put the old-time house burglar almost out of business. And that is well, for of all manner of theft it is the most nerve-racking on both the burglar and the householder.

I never crawled into a window that I didn't think of Smiler. I never stepped in or out of a door without thinking of old George. Yet I kept it up for years, and quit it only because I got tired of playing the peon for crooked pawnbrokers and getting "fifty fifty" from the professional "fences." The fences' notion of "fifty fifty" is to put a lead dollar in the Salvation Army tambourine and ask the lassie for fifty cents change.

In the midst of plenty I found myself starving, and in self-defense turned to the more direct business of highway robbery. My experience with house burglary in the small hours of the night left me a nervous wreck and an opium smoker. Almost every house prowler turns to booze or drugs. Reader, I'll ask you if you wouldn't take a jolt of booze or hop after an experience such as this?

You are a burglar; you have put in a week "tabbing up" a residence. You decide to "make" it; it looks all right; no children, you haven't seen a dog. The night arrives. You jump into the yard. It's two o'clock. You look the house over. Every door and window fastened, not even an open coal-hole, no porch to go up. You go back to a kitchen window and perform a very delicate operation – taking a pane of glass out piece by piece. Then you put your hand in, release the catch, and raise the window slowly, noiselessly. You find inside on the windowsill bottles, boxes, corkscrews, can openers, and a toothbrush. These you pick up, one at a time, and place outside, below the window.

Now you are in the window, and you find that below, inside, is the kitchen sink. You get in without disturbing dishes or pans and open the kitchen door, so you will have a getaway in case anything causes you to hurry out. You have been almost an hour getting in the house and you haven't started on the job yet.

It is very dark in the house, but you light no matches, nor do you use a flashlight; you are an expert, you know your business. Your years at this work have developed a "cat" sense in you. You can sense an object in front of you without seeing or feeling it. You feel your way slowly, silently into the dining room. Your eyes are getting accustomed to the dark and you distinguish a few objects – table, chairs, sideboard. You sit in a chair and remove your shoes, shoving them down in your back pockets, heels up.

You are going upstairs where the sleepers and valuables are. You button your coat and pull your hat down over your eyes to hide your face from the sleeper should he wake up on you and switch on a light. It takes you fifteen minutes to get up the stairs; they creak frightfully and you must find solid places to put your weight. You know your business, so you keep as close to the banister as possible, where the step boards are nailed down tight and can't shift and creak. You know the creaking won't wake sleeping people, but you don't know yet whether they are asleep. If they should be lying in bed awake, they would know what the creaking meant and you might get shot.

Now you are at a bedroom door, it's latched but not locked. You take hold of the doorknob in a certain way and turn it slowly till it won't turn any farther. The hall you are in is dark and dead silent. You push the door open an inch and you can hear the gentle, regular up-and-down breathing of the healthy sleeper. You wait a long time, maybe five minutes, with your hand on the doorknob, listening intently. Yes, there are two sleepers in the room.

Then out of this awful silence comes a coughing from a room at the back of the hall. You stiffen and your hand goes to your coat pocket. You hear a glass clink against a pitcher, and you know that man is awake. You hear him turn over in bed, and straighten out for another sleep. You remain rigid for another five minutes and then feel your way down the dark hall to make sure he has gone back to sleep.

His door is ajar, and now he is snoring. You wish he wouldn't snore; he might wake somebody else, he might wake himself. Snorers do wake themselves. The expert burglar doesn't fancy the heavy snorer; he likes the sleeper that wheezes gently, softly, regularly. You feel your way back to the front room. You want that first. That's where you have decided the best stuff is to be found. Your hand is on the doorknob again, and you open the door another inch, slowly, noiselessly.

Now something soft, yielding, obstructs it.

This thing that softly blocks the door is probably a rug or an article of clothing. That's easy. You release the doorknob, stoop slowly, and put your hand around inside. Yes, it's a rug, a fur rug. You nip a few strands of hair in your fingers and tug at it gently. The thing comes to life with a scared howl that turns your blood to ice water. You jump up, pull the door shut with a bang, and hasten to the top of the stairs with sure and certain step. It took you fifteen minutes to ascend that stairway. You know every inch of it. You straddle the banister and slide down – it's quicker and safer. In the dining room you slam the door shut, and none too soon. The man upstairs has released the big mastiff and he's roaring at the dining-room door. You made no mistake when you left the kitchen door open. You dash through it, pulling it shut behind you just as the man inside opens the dining-room door for his dog.

You take the back fence, tearing your clothes. The big dog is in the back yard now; you hear his ferocious growls plainer than ever. You run into a vacant lot, toward the next street. You hear the master urging his dog to follow you, but he is too well trained and refuses to leave his own yard.

The householder is a regular man; not to be balked of his burglar he opens up with a six-shooter and empties it at you. After the first shot you instinctively begin making side jumps like a bucking bronco. You don't make as much distance, but you reduce your chance of getting hit. Every time the gun goes off you can feel the slug boring a hole in your back. You don't realize it has already passed you when you hear the pistol crack. His gun empty, his shooting stops.

You feel like throwing a few slugs in his direction; but, well, you are in the wrong. You are safe now, it would only make matters worse if you hit him, and besides, he and his pistol and his dog have made enough noise already to rouse the neighborhood and you're lucky if you can get out of the block without bumping into Mr. "John Law."

You make a big detour and get downtown safely, so exhausted from the intense physical and mental concentration that you are barely able to drag one foot after the other. Yes, reader, I'll admit you might go to your room and to bed and drift off into sweet, refreshing slumbers; but I never could do it. I always had to hunt up a hop joint and roll myself a few pills, "just for the good of my nerves."

You are still a burglar, reader. You get up the next evening, put on a different suit and hat, and go out for your "breakfast." You dismiss from your mind the incident of last night as lightly as a gambler would forget the loss of a few dollars. You remember the dog that recognized you in the hotel barroom years before, and with the thought that it would be well to keep out of this mastiff's neighborhood you turn your mind to the business of the night. You take a long time to eat, looking through all the papers. You read about a burglar "shivering somewhere in his lair after escaping in a panic of fear from Mr.— and his mastiff and pistol."

This makes you mad. You say to yourself: "What do those reporters expect of a man? Do they want him to shoot everybody in sight, cut the dog's throat, carry out everything valuable, and burn the house down? Can't they understand that the burglar's first thought is the loot and his second thought is to get out of the house as quietly and quickly as possible without harming people when they wake up on him? And what madness for the householder to try to corner a burglar in the dark, prepared to resist capture but not to kill for loot. When he senses a burglar in his house, why can't he say in a loud voice, 'Is that you, Percy?' and give him a chance to fade away quietly? He'll do it. He knows there are plenty of other houses."

You give it up, put these idle speculations out of your mind, and go out into the street. You have been busy locating "prospects." Your thoughts turn to the most likely one. There's the gambler that runs the poker games in back of the cigar store. He turns the game over to an assistant at twelve o'clock, takes the bankroll, and goes home. You decide to "take him home" to-night. You hang around till he comes out and get in behind him. You "tail" him to a genteel-looking place with a "private board" sign in a downstairs window. He lets himself in with a key. You are across the street; you wait a while and observe that a dark room on the second floor has been lighted. Your man is at the window pulling down its shade. You have his room located, and you go away to kill the next two hours.

Two o'clock; you are in the dining room downstairs. You were lucky enough to find an open window. You don't open any doors here, you decide to retreat by the window, if necessary. This is a boarding house with a number of people in it, and you don't have to creep around so carefully. A noise on the stairs or in the hall of a boarding house doesn't mean much.

You go upstairs quickly and find a light in the hall. You put it out; not by pushing the button, but by unscrewing the globe a little. You are an expert; you don't want any light; you don't want any one to get a look at you in a lighted hallway. You prefer darkened rooms, because in the dark you have the best of the situation.

You find his door; more luck, it's not locked You must be careful with this chap; he is a bad sleeper, thin, nervous, "touchy," an incessant smoker and a heavy coffee drinker. You step into the room and close the door but don't latch it. He is asleep, breathing, as you expected, very softly. His clothes are on a big rocker – nothing in them but some silver and a watch. You take the silver, "heft" the watch and leave it; it's not solid. You're disappointed, the roll of bills should have been in his trousers' pocket. You feel on the table by the head of his bed; it's not there. On the dresser; not there. Oh, well, you'll have to go under his pillow after it, that's all. This operation calls for your best professional touch; your perfect technique is needed here; he's a light sleeper.

You are on one knee beside his pillow. You lay a gun on the floor within easy reach. If he wakes up on you that's his bad luck; you'll stick him up, take his money, and lock him in his room. He is lying on his side facing you and not eighteen inches away. You can feel his breath against your face. You pull up your right coat and shirt sleeves to the elbow, your left hand lifts the outer end of the pillow ever so little while your right, palm down, slowly, carefully, worms its way beneath his head. Your ear notes his breathing. So long as it is regular, he is asleep; if it breaks off he is waking up. While he sleeps he has no more control over his breathing than over his heartbeats, and you can plainly hear it, and when you cannot hear it you know he is awake. With your ear alert for the danger signal and your hand under his pillow your mind is racing all over the universe.

"No wonder," you think, "they hang men in some parts of the world for this kind of burglary – going into a man's sleeping room with a gun and taking his property from under his head while he sleeps. No wonder your hair is graying above your ears, and wrinkles showing up in your forehead."

You make up your mind to quit this racket – it's too tough – but your hand goes further under the pillow. Careful as you are, the slight movement beneath his head seems to disturb this catlike sleeper. His breathing catches, halts, and no longer reaches your ear. You become petrified, your mind on the gun beside you. With a jerky movement he turns over, and you wait till he goes sound asleep again.

His back is to you now, and his head on the farther end of his pillow. This makes it easier. You explore and explore, but feel nothing. Slowly you withdraw your arm. You must look farther; in his shoes, his hat, the dresser drawers, the clothes closet, and, that failing, you will put the gun on him, wake him, and make him dig it up. You have been there almost two hours. It will soon be dawn; you must hurry. You search everywhere, but no bankroll. You go around the bed and your arm is quickly thrust under the other pillow in the last hope of finding it. It's not there; no use looking farther. You decide to wake him and demand it.

Having made up your mind to stick him up, you must now transform yourself from the silent, stealthy prowler into the rough, confident, dominating stick-up man. You walk around to the back of the bed and stop to plan your new move. Now you have it all straight in your mind. You will go to the side of his bed where you first started in on him. That puts you between him and the door and leaves him no chance to get out into the hall. You will touch him gently on the shoulder. He will wake up in alarm.

"Eh, what? What is it? Who is it? Turn on the light."

Then you will say to him in a firm, kindly tone "Listen to me and don't get excited." You will put the cold muzzle of the gun against his neck and now your voice will be cold, hard, threatening. "Do you feel that? That's a gun. If you move I'll let it go. You just keep cool and don't get yourself killed over a few lousy dollars. I want that bankroll of yours; I know it's here. Tell me where it is and make it easy on yourself – and be quick about it."

Yes, that's the way you will handle him. You start on around to the side of his bed. You remember you have been in the room almost two hours and a half. It will soon be daylight. You look at the window. Yes, there it is; a faint line of gray down the edge of the curtain, the dawn. You must hurry. You are by his side now. You take a better grip on the gun, reach out to touch him, and – pandemonium breaks out in the adjoining room.

It's only an alarm clock going off, but it petrifies you standing up and tears every nerve in your body up by the roots. You don't bolt out of the room in a panic; you remain perfectly still. Your mind jumps into the other room. Your sleeping gambler kicks out his legs, turns over with a jerky movement, mutters a string of curses, pulls the covers over his head, and settles himself for more sleep.

You don't pay much attention to him now. The next room concerns you more. The noise of the alarm clock changes to a dull, empty, hollow protest. You know somebody has his hand on the bell, smothering it till he can turn it off. Now it stops. You hear somebody lumbering about, every step shakes the floor. He must be a big, heavy man who puts his heels down first when he walks. You hear him push a button and a vertical crack of light appears at the head of the bed you are standing by. You know what that is. This is an old house, and that's a folding door.

The man now unlocks his door and steps out into the hall. You step softly to your door and listen. He goes heavily down the hall, muttering to himself. You hear him push the light button a couple of times but he gets no light – you unscrewed the globe; he thinks it's burnt out. You hear him open and shut a door; he is in the bathroom. You turn back to your man. Then a window is thrown up with a bang in the room on your other side. Daylight is racing on you. You can see clearly now. You hear other noises. The place is becoming a hornet's nest. You must give it up and get out. You're not broke. You don't have to risk everything here. You step out of the room, close the door softly, go downstairs, and out the front way.

Yes, reader, you went down the street and into a restaurant where you ate heartily. Then to bed for a good, healthy, sound sleep.

Not me! I went back to the hop joint.

You get up the next evening, go to the same restaurant, get something to eat, and look over the papers. You find nothing about your doings; you didn't expect to. You know the gambler missed his silver. You know he will suspect somebody around the boarding house and lock his room door in future. You take stock and decide to lay off for a few nights and give your luck a chance to switch.

You are slowly making up your mind to get out of this burglary racket; it's too tough. Suppose you had stuck up the gambler. Maybe his money was downstairs in a safe and you wouldn't have got it. You would have had to dash out into the street whether you got it or not. How could you tell who would be in the street when you went out? The cop on the beat might be sitting on the front steps. You might bump into the milk man, the bread man, or the ice man. You decide that the whole thing is very uncertain, after all.

For the first time you see clearly this dangerous angle of this business of yours. You can plan and plot and scheme; you can figure out just what you'll do from the minute you step into a place till you step out of it, but the great weakness of it is – you can't tell who or what is going to be outside when you go out, and all your ingenuity can't overcome it. You toss the whole thing out of your mind and go to a theater. After that you go to your room. It's a warm night, you're in no hurry about going to bed, so you sit in the dark by the window getting the cool air.

You wonder who will occupy the transient room directly across the light well from you. Last night a woman and two children were in it. They talked all during the forenoon and kept you awake. You hope they have gone away. Just as you are ready to go to bed a light is switched on in the room across the way. Idly you look over. The window is open and the curtain is up. A fat man with a pink complexion and gray hair is standing in the middle of the room. His door is still open, you can see through his room and out into the hall. He stands facing you, his legs apart, hands in his pockets, and his hat on the back of his head.

You decide he is about half drunk. He takes his hat off and throws it out of your line of vision, probably at the dresser. Now he turns around, goes to the door, and kicks it shut with a bang. Back in the middle of his room he puts a fat hand in his capacious pants pocket and comes up with a small roll of paper money. He unrolls the bills, looking at them with a mysterious smile on his fat face. You don't understand his smile and wonder if he is thinking how he cheated somebody in a poker game; he looks like a gambler.

The roll interests you, the outside one is what you call a "salmon belly." It is a yellowback – a big bill. The fat man now gets a chair and places it directly in front of his window, but instead of sitting down he stands up on it unsteadily. You get alarmed and watch him intently. Surely he's not going to jump out? No, he takes the string and pulls the curtain halfway down. All you can see of him now is his bulky midsection. The upper part of him is silhouetted against the curtain. He raises one hand above his head, the hand that holds the bills. You can see its blurred shadow as he runs it along the roller at the top of the curtain. He takes hold of one edge of the curtain now, pulls it down a little till the ratchet is released, and lets it go up with a rattle and bang. He puts both hands on the windowsill to steady himself as he gets off the chair.

He is still smiling, but there's no mystery about it now. You sit in your room not fifteen feet away, open-mouthed in amazed admiration. What a fox he is, to roll his money up in the curtain! What a plant! What chance would a prowler have of finding his money?

He sits down with his back to you and you hear him drop one shoe on the floor; in about a minute you hear the other one drop. Then he goes over to the door, turns the key and snaps the light out. In fifteen minutes you can hear him breathing like a blacksmith's bellows.

He is healthy, he is a good eater and drinker, he is a sound sleeper. But the thing looks suspiciously soft to you and you wonder if the fat man might not be a smart dick framing for you. You decide he isn't because he locked his door.

"Well," you say to yourself, "bad luck or good luck, I'm going after that dough."

You don't mind his door being locked. You know your business you have three ways of opening it. You go out and down the hall to a small room where the Chinese bed maker keeps his brooms, buckets, loops, and other things and get a small parcel of delicate instruments you keep planted there. You go back to your room and wait till, say, four o'clock, when everything is dead and all the guests are in and abed. Then you go around into the fat man's hall, put out the light, and go to work on his door.

You go about the opening of his door confidently, and with a sure touch. You know he is sleeping, you can hear his gusty breathing from where you stand outside. Now you have it unlocked, you open it, step in and close it. The chair is still in place by the window. Your ear follows his regular breathing. You don't creep around this room as you did in the gambler's. You walk over to the chair, step upon it lightly, put one hand up against the roller, and pull the curtain down with the other. It makes a little noise. Your back is to the sleeper, but your ear tells you he is safe. When the curtain is about halfway down, your fingers touch the roll of bills, another little pull and you have it.

You step down off the chair and find his vest and trousers. His watch "hefts" heavy. You take it, and you take the silver out of his trousers – just to penalize him for trying to be foxy.

You go out, closing the door carefully behind you. Back in your room you examine the bills and silver carefullv – you remember the twenty-dollar bill that cost you two years and two lashings. You find you have more money than you would have got out of both the places you failed in; enough to last you six months if you are careful and don't gamble.

You plant your instruments in the little room down the hall. Then you go out the back way to dodge the night clerk, and down to an all-night saloon where you put the bills away in your compartment in the big safe. The night bartender is "square"; he knows you and your business. You want to get rid of the watch as quick as possible. It's worth a hundred dollars. You sell it to him for a twenty-dollar note, glad to be done with it.

Yes reader, I know what you say to yourself now. You are saying: "Well, he doesn't have to go to the hop joint this time."

You are right. I didn't have to go, but I went just the same. The opium smoker can always find a good excuse for an extra smoke. I went to the joint to celebrate my changed fortune and to propitiate whatever deformed deity it is that is supposed to look after the luck of a burglar. I must have propitiated to some purpose, for within a week another stroke of dumb luck more than doubled my bankroll, and I decided to take a lay-off.

Always in the back of my mind was the thought that some day I would go back and see my father. It was ten years since I ran away from him. Many things had happened to me. Something may have happened to him. He might need money or help. I was free to go; I had no associates to cling to; I was under no obligations to anybody. My time and money were my own. The hop habit was getting fastened on me, and this trip would give me a chance to break away from it. The notion of being respectable and feeling safe and secure for a few months took my fancy, so I started in to do the thing right.

My gun and burglar tools went to my bartender friend as presents. I was glad to get rid of the gun for a while. I could get another any time for ten dollars, and for another ten I could order by mail more instruments from an ex-burglar at Warsaw, Illinois, who manufactured them and advertised them in the Police Gazette as "novelties."

I had always followed the Sanctimonious Kid's advice in the matter of wearing careful clothes, but now I satisfied my hankering for a gray suit and hat. I thought of the leather trunk too, but it had no appeal any more. I remembered old Cy Near, and smiled to think how I had worshiped the twenty-dollar gold piece that dangled from the watch chain across his ample paunch.

I soon discovered that being respectable imposed many hardships and obligations I hadn't thought of. One of them is paying railroad fare. I played the game square while I was at it, and gave up my money for a ticket and a berth in the sleeper. Here I encountered another hardship. My professional eye told me there were many fat pocketbooks beneath the pillows of my fellow travelers that my professional hand could have taken when the porter was out of sight, but I forebore.

At Kansas City I prowled about the neighborhood I had lived and worked in, but asked no questions. The crabbed, cranky widow's boarding house was closed. Tex of the larcenous eye was gone, and so were the card and dice sharks. Cocky McAllister, the hack driver that helped me rescue Julia, was not around his old stand. The milkman I worked for, collecting bills from "them women," was not at his place. The theater where Julia worked was still going, but she was not there. I passed Madam Singleton's old place, but there was another name on the red-lighted pane of glass above the door. Still I asked no questions; they were all nothing to me. I could easily have found somebody to tell me what became of them all except, perhaps, Julia, but I was a stranger in my own town and preferred to remain one. My father was the only one I asked about. At the railroad offices, in the department where he had worked, I learned that he was dead.

A talkative old pensioner on the company who tended a door told me he had been dead three years; that he died after a long siege of sickness and had barely enough money left to bury him decently in the village graveyard beside my mother. I was not shocked to learn of his death; we had been too far apart for that. I wondered if my long silence and absence mightn't have aggravated his illness and hastened his end. I was sorry not to have been with him when he was sick and needed me. I was glad he died without knowing what I had done to my life.

That was many years ago, but I wasn't thoughtless even then, and I recall now, distinctly, how I realized with shame and regret that I had never done one thing to repay him for caring for me till I was able to shift, no matter how lamely, for myself. Looking back now, as I did then, I am forced to admit that the only consideration I ever showed for him was this: I never put his name, which is my name, on a police blotter or a prison register while he was alive, or after his death.

I had been dallying with the opium pipe almost daily for a year, yet I had no trouble when I gave it up. Just a few restless days and nights and

I forgot it. I gave this no thought then, but later when I saw an opium smoker doubled up with cramps and pleading for hop, and learned he had been "on the pipe" only three months, I got interested and began thinking it over and observing.

My observations and experience have convinced me that the drug habit like most of our other habits, is largely mental. In another chapter I shall submit a few facts in support of this opinion.

Kansas City had nothing of interest for me now, and I left it, never to return. A cheap excursion ticket took me back west to the town of Los Angeles, where I finished the winter, fraternizing with the bums and yeggs from the road, polishing up old acquaintances, and gathering gossip from the four quarters of the underworld.

TWENTY

SPRING came. For me that meant moving, and while I was trying to decide where to go I made by chance the acquaintance of a coal miner who had worked in a small mine in one of the middle-west provinces of Canada. In the course of our talks I learned by asking a few casual questions that the mine worked between thirty and forty men; that it was on a short branch road of the Canadian Pacific; that the pay-off was in cash, on or about the first of every month, and that the money was shipped by express from the city of Winnipeg, Manitoba. The fact that the payroll had to be held one night at the point where it was transferred to the branch road into the mine interested me. I knew the place, and that there was little or no police protection. There were four or five thousand dollars that had to lie somewhere in a small town overnight, practically unprotected. The two thousand miles I would have to travel meant nothing. If the thing couldn't be handled, I would still be in the midst of fertile fields where I could make a living without taking tough chances against wised-up city police and the busy stool pigeon.

Bidding farewell to the bums and yeggs at "Mother Moustaches" wine dump in "Sonora Town," where they all hung out and did their drinking, I discarded my gray suit for a pair of overalls, a rough coat, a blue shirt, and a cap, and took to the road for a three-week jump. Through California, across Oregon, and into Spokane, Washington, where I found my bartender friend and recovered my "instruments," which had been lying unused in the safe. The gun I left with him, as it was cumbersome and useless to me on the road. I could get one when I got nearer my destination.

On through Butte, Great Falls, and to the Canadian line I traveled; on north to Calgary again, but this time I turned eastward and soon arrived at the town where the mine payroll had to be transferred.

I had managed my money carefully during the winter and still had enough to carry me for a few months by economizing. The first thing I did was to take a look at the "box" in the depot, which was the express office as well. I had confidently expected to find a safe of cheap or obsolete make, such as was generally in use then in the smaller towns.

One look at this "box" made me regret that I had ever met the talkative coal miner. It was of the latest make and belonged in a bank instead of an express office in a town of two thousand people. It was as near burglar-proof as any safe could be, and in addition to this it was "chested," which, in terms of burglary, means it had a steel chest inside – a safe within a safe. I was dismayed. I saw at a glance that it was too much for me. It was the kind of safe that discourages the "heavy man" (safe breaker). He looks it over and says to his mob: "Yes, I can beat her all right," and explains to them in detail just how it can be done. "But," he finishes, "it would take three or four shots to get into the guts of her and, you know, the first shot wakes the natives up. If they don't hear another they don't know what woke them, and go back to sleep; but when they do hear the second shot they get up to find out what it's about. Then comes the last one, and they're on top of you with shotguns and pitchforks. You've got to stand them off and dash out. Where? Why, nowhere. There's no getaway here, and I don't want the coin bad enough to go against it."

I knew if they put the payroll in that "box" it would be as safe from me as if it was in the bank at Winnipeg. I couldn't have opened it if I had it in the town blacksmith shop for twenty-four hours. Discouraging as the business looked, I decided to stay in the place and have a look at the money when it arrived.

I got a room at the hotel, hung my coat up on a rack, and went about in my shirt sleeves trying to appear like a miner or ranch hand and attract no attention. Every night at nine o'clock, when the train came in from the east, I was on the depot platform with the town loungers and did as much staring around as any of them. At last the end of the month came, and with it the payroll. This night the station agent, who was telegraph operator, express agent, and everything else about the depot, was a bit more alert, walking around with an air of importance, responsibility. When the train pulled in, he was at the door of the express car, and, sure enough, out came the payroll in a small leather container, about the size of a woman's hand bag.

When the train departed, the agent, with a firm grip on the leather pouch, returned to his office escorted by the depot loungers. The payroll was locked securely in the inner compartment of the big safe, and then the heavy outer door closed upon it, shutting out any hopes I had of getting my hands on it that night. I went off to bed sad and thoughtful.

The next morning at ten o'clock I followed the payroll aboard the jerkwater train that carried it to the waiting miners. At twelve o'clock I sat on the sidewalk across from the mine office and gloomily watched the paymaster portioning it out to the joyful miners. In the afternoon I rode back to the main line with my mind made up to let the thing go and look elsewhere for something not so tough.

There was a Chinese laundry in the town and I had often thought of going into it for a smoke to kill off the dull hours, and now, both dull and despondent, I made my way to it and into the confidence of the boss Chinaman, who made me welcome. He was hospitable and kindly as all Chinese are who have not become sour and suspicious under the impositions of their white brothers.

A moderate quantity of opium will not inflame or distort the imagination. I do not say it is an aid to clear thinking, but it is a fact that I left the laundry with what I thought, and still think, was nothing less than an inspiration.

The next day I went over the town thoroughly and looked at every "box" in it. There was not one that I couldn't beat. My "inspiration" told me that if I could put the depot safe out of business a few days before the payroll arrived again, the agent would be forced to lock it in one of the other safes in the town and I might get a chance at it. After traveling the great distance and spending so much time and money, I hated to quit without making a try for this money.

I jumped fifty miles farther east, where I got dynamite and drills, stealing them at a mine, and returned to wait another month before I could do anything more. A week before the payroll was due, I went into the depot one night with a sledge hammer, knocked the combination knob off the "box," battered the spindle in, and smashed the handle on the door. Adding another touch to the "burglary," I left a couple of crowbars behind, broke open the till, smashed things generally, and threw cigarette and cigar snipes and pipe scrapings on the floor. When the station man opened up the next morning, his office looked as if it had been raided by a tribe of yeggs that had tried to wreck it when they failed to open the "box." There was a tremendous hue and cry, and a fruitless man hunt. An inspector of police came, looked at the safe, and declared the job was done by a band of thieves that had been ravaging depots and post offices farther east. The battered safe was shipped to Toronto to be opened and repaired by its makers.

I waited with much anxiety and not a little curiosity to see what would be done with the leather pouch when it arrived at the end of the month.

Two days after the safe and express office were wrecked, a "redcoat," as the Mounted Police are called, was killed by a drunken Indian. Every idle able-bodied man in town joined the man hunt that lasted ten days, and my "burglary" was forgotten in the new excitement. I kept a careful watch on the depot agent, and saw he was taking the day's small receipts home with him every night. I looked over his house and prepared to enter it in case he did the same with the payroll instead of leaving it in one of the safes. My most careful check on his residence showed he had no children, no dog, no old people in it. He and his wife were all I would have to contend with.

On the evening the money was due I went over the whole thing carefully and satisfied myself that nothing had been left undone in the way of precaution and protection. Not a glance of suspicion had turned in my direction so far, and I was sure that if I got my hands on the money I could plant it, stand pat, and weather the storm.

At last the train pulled in. A mail sack was thrown out to a small boy, who ran off to the post office with it. The leather pouch was put into the agent's hands and a few of the "regulars" at the depot followed him to his office. As usual he at once put out the lights, locked the place up, and walked across the street to the post office, surrounded by the depot loungers. The small mail was distributed in five minutes, and he turned toward home with the payroll under his arm, a neighbor on each side of him, and I half a block behind.

His neighbors left him at his front gate, and his wife met him at the front door. I was relieved when the business resolved itself into a house burglary, for forcing safes with explosives is an uphill job for one man and is seldom attempted. The house was new, well built, and small – three rooms downstairs and two above. It was in a large lot with a few small trees and some plants around it. I took up my watch at once, and from the vacant lot adjoining I saw them sit down to dinner. After a half hour at the table, they got up and I could hear them shutting doors, putting windows down, and fastening them. For a minute the house was dark, then a light appeared upstairs, which meant they were going to bed. Another half hour and the upstairs light was doused. I walked away. I had "put them to bed" and could do nothing more till after midnight.

In the city the burglar finds most people asleep at dawn; in the country most people wake with the dawn. I knew I must start early and set one o'clock as the hour to begin. Allowing myself two hours to get in, get action, and get out, I could have it over by three o'clock, which would give me time to plant the money and be in my room before daylight. My parcel of instruments and a gun were planted a few blocks away. I went after them, returned to the house, and found a place in the yard where I could watch and wait without being seen by any chance passer-by. With two hours to kill, I went over the thing again and could think of nothing more in the way of precaution. I had even picked a place in a lot near by to plant the money.

At one o'clock I took off my shoes and put them in my back pockets. There in that house was a big piece of money. I had put in almost two months planning to get it, and now that I was ready to "step" I summoned everything in the way of professional skill that I had acquired in the years since the Smiler gave me my first lesson. I found the kitchen door locked. The key inside was soon displaced and the door unlocked with one of my own. Once inside I shut the door; this was in the country and I could not chance stray, hungry dogs or cats coming in for food and knocking pans around while I was upstairs. The door to the dining room was shut, but not locked. There was a rocking-chair in line between the front and back dining-room doors. I carefully pushed it to one side, making the way clear in case of a hasty leaving.

At the foot of the stairs in the hall I could hear the man breathing. The bedroom door upstairs was open. The stairs were solid, well put together, and did not creak, but I took a long time in doing them, wondering all the while where I would find the leather bag. No such luck as getting it off the dresser. No, he would surely have it under his pillow. After a long wait at the door of their room my ears picked up the woman's gentler breathing. They both slept the sleep of young, healthy, tired workers, and I could wish for nothing more. There was light enough from the window to enable me to look over the dresser. The pouch was not there and I prayed it wouldn't be in one of the drawers, for all the abominable obstacles that balk the burglar of a sleeping room the bureau drawer is the first and worst.

After wasting the better part of an hour going through the room, I concluded the thing was under his head. Kneeling beside his pillow, I put the gun beside me on the floor, ready to my hand, where I could get it and stick him up if he woke up on me. The sleeper was lying on his back. His head was on the middle of his pillow, and directly beneath it was the leather bag.

A watch or purse may be taken from under a pillow with ease, but an object the size of this bag I wanted will shift the pillow when it is withdrawn. It pulls the pillow with it, the pillow pulls the sleeper's head with it, and he wakes up. When the burglar gets up against this, he has to put one hand against he end of the pillow, holding it in place, while he tugs gently at the spoils below.

Whether it was my pulling on the pouch I don't know, but the sleeping man stirred uneasily and his regular breathing stopped. I shrank down lower beside the bed, one hand under his head and the other at the pillow, breathless from the intense concentration and suspense. He stirred again and then floundered heavily over on his side, his back to me and his head off the leather. I could not hear him breathe. I was sure he was awake, but not alarmed. After a heart-breaking fifteen minutes his sleep became natural again, and I slowly, softly pulled the pouch free from under his pillow. It was mine now, and it was my business to hold on to it.

I took as long going downstairs as I did going up, and at last made my way out of the house, closing the kitchen door softly behind me. Putting my shoes on, I hastened away to plant the money. In the neighborhood was a big vacant lot, its boundaries marked by a row of broken and leaning fence posts from which the boards had been taken for firewood or other uses. Pulling one of the loose posts from its place, I threw the pouch in the hole and jammed the post down on top of it. The gun and instruments I threw into a small stream near by. I wanted to be entirely clean of anything incriminating in case I was suspected, arrested, and searched.

In the security of my room I went over the night's work. After an hour's thought I could think of but one more thing I ought to do. My socks might have picked up dirt or dust around the house. A particle of dust, a piece of thread or lint or raveling of cloth might convict me if suspicion fell on me. Taking the socks off my feet, I went out and threw them in a lot.

Fully satisfied that I had done everything possible to insure safety, I returned to the hotel. Daylight was coming on. Going upstairs I met the porter coming down to open up. He gave me a sleepy "goodmorning," and I went on to my room and to bed, but not to sleep. I was in the dining room as usual about seven o'clock. The room was noisy, every one was talking at once. A tall man got up from the table, saying in a loud Western drawl : "Waal, I'm fer lynchin em if we git 'em." A quiet-spoken Englishman next me at the long table told me all about the burglary. Out in the street I saw with some concern that the town was on fire with excitement.

I got through the forenoon all right, standing around the street discussing the burglary with acquaintances I had made in the town, doing more listening than talking. At noon, when I went into the hotel for dinner, the constable, the hotel men, and the porter I met on the stairs in the early morning were standing at the bar with their heads together talking earnestly. When they saw me they quit talking and went out on the sidewalk. One glance from the constable told me I was suspected. I saw that the porter had done his deadly work; I was due for a lot of questioning. Along in the afternoon the superintendent of the mine where the payroll belonged got into town and took charge of things. There was a powwow in the magistrate's office. I saw the hotel porter go in, and braced myself to take the blow.

In a few minutes the constable came out and over to me where I stood with a crowd of natives. "Please step inside, young man," he said. Inside a group of men were seated and I was given a chair. I was determined to answer no questions. No use in going into long, detailed explanations of my movements and have them exploded and discredited on investigation, and thus strengthen the case against myself.

The magistrate began on me. "Young man, we want you to explain your business here. Who you are, where you're from, and what you do for a living? You are suspected as the burglar who last night entered the express agent's house and made off with four thousand and eight hundred dollars cash. You were seen entering your hotel at daylight this morning. Explain that to us.

My mind jumped back to the floggings, the dark cells with their bread and water, to my escape from jail, and to every other hardship I had accepted without weakening, and I laughed at him. Here was a little, pompous fat man blustering under his black skullcap behind a cheap table with a few legal papers on it, trying to make me talk.

I said to him "Did you ever sleep in my hotel?"

"Yes," he answered, forgetting his dignity.

"Well, then, you know that the wash room and toilet are in a covered space between the two wings of the building, outside and at the rear, and to get to them you go down the back stairs and out a back door."

"Very well," he replied "now tell us why you were at the depot the last two times the payroll was left off. Why you followed it up to the mine, and why you followed the agent home last night."

I brazened it out with all the indignation I could muster, reminding him that I was a British subject and it was my right to stand mute and answer no questions. The mine superintendent said to the others so I could hear him: "My men want to lynch somebody; I don't know whether I can control them." I knew all about miners and knew they never lynched anybody anywhere. I knew I was in Canada where lynching never flourished.

I turned to a group of miners at the back of the room. "This man says you want to lynch me. Before you do it, I want to know why."

One of them, a giant, red-headed Irishman with shaggy, white eyebrows and pebbly blue eyes, said:

"Don't worry, me boy, there'll be no lynchin' here." Turning to the magistrate, I said: "You telegraph, at my expense, the Minister of Justice at Ottawa that this man," pointing to the superintendent, "is trying to incite these miners to lynch me. And I want a copy of the telegram and my request made a matter of record in your office."

The magistrate looked confused. The superintendent said, "I'll make the complaint. I want this man held." The constable arrested me "In the queen's name," searched me and locked me in the town jail, a one-room affair in a lot back of his house. He brought me blankets and supper, and left me to meditate in silence and privacy. I went over everything again. The shoe was on the other foot this time; they hadn't a thing on me. No court in Christendom would convict me on those shreds of suspicion. I rolled up in the blankets and went to sleep with the comfortable thought that the forty-eight hundred dollars might help me to forget the awful lashing I took at New Westminster when I got to San Francisco or Chicago with them.

Next morning in court it was shown by witnesses that I was at the depot twice when the money arrived; that I went to the mine once on the same train with it; and a woman testified that she saw me walking behind the station agent and his neighbors as they went home the night of the burglary. The porter who spilled the beans finished the trial by testifying that he met me on the stairs in the early morning; that I was nervous, acted suspiciously, and tried to avoid him.

I made no defense, but set up a loud and long protest that did no good. I was held for trial and whisked away to the provincial jail. I was convinced that the mine superintendent had engineered the thing on the theory that I was guilty and in hopes that something would transpire in his favor while I was waiting to be tried.

The provincial jail was like the one I escaped from. The jailer was sober and decent, giving me plenty of books and fair treatment. I had a cell to myself, kept away from the other prisoners, tried my case mentally every day, and got acquitted every time; and at night I spent large chunks of the payroll that was so securely planted in the post hole.

After three months of leisure, reading and pleasant anticipations, I went to court. A judge had arrived for the fall assizes and mine was the only felony case. The witnesses were all there. I pleaded not guilty and my case was set for trial at two o'clock in the afternoon. The judge asked if I had counsel. I told him I had no lawyer and didn't want one; that I had but little money and would need it when I was acquitted.

"Better get counsel," he snapped. "A defendant that tries his own case has a fool for a lawyer."

I replied by asking him to read the testimony from the lower court before wasting his time trying me.

While I was eating dinner the mine superintendent came to my cell and said if I would give up the money I could go free. I threatened to sue him for false imprisonment when I got out. He went away mad. I decided they wanted me to get a local lawyer in hopes I would unbosom myself to him so he could do the same with them.

At two o'clock I was back in court. The judge was a brusque, businesslike little old man with the brisk, aggressive air of a terrier. His hair was clipped short and his cropped beard grew in every direction. He wore a coarse suit of tweeds, hobnailed shoes, and a cheap flannel shirt, with a linen collar and no tie. He had two sheets of paper in his hand, looking at them.

"Have you anything more than this?" he asked the Crown counsel.

"Nothing, Your Lordship."

"And do you expect me to try a man on this ragged rot?" Throwing the papers on his desk, he turned toward me. "Defendant discharged."

I walked out and over to the jail, where I got my belongings – forty dollars a pocketknife, and a lead pencil. The constable who made the arrest followed me all over town – to the barber's, the restaurant, and at last to the depot. A train came in going in the opposite direction from the scene of the burglary, and I boarded it without buying a ticket. He watched the train leave, but did not get on. At a junction I got off and traveled south to a stage-line connection, where I took the stage back in the direction of my money. After ten days of maneuvering and detouring, I reached a settlement off the railroad about thirty miles away from where I was arrested.

Hiring a saddle horse there, I jogged away in high spirits, timing myself to get into the town about midnight, when I could lift the plant and be far away before daylight. Everything favored me as I rode into the town. There wasn't a stray dog or cat on the back streets, and every soul was in bed asleep. Turning a corner, I came in sight of the big, vacant lot. Yes. there it was. My eye took in the row of leaning, rotten posts down one side and across the front, then to the inner line of the lot where I put the leather pouch in its post hole. There seemed to be a change there. Was I at the right lot? Yes, there, a block away, was the house I entered, plain in the moonlight. My eye followed the route I took from the house to the lot. I pulled up the tired horse, certain I was at the right spot; and I was.

But on top of the spot, directly on top of it, stood a long, wide, well-built, substantial, two-story frame building.

That hour when I saw the money was lost to me was probably the saddest of my life. I never got a greater shock. I am telling this story because it is an interesting incident, not to cause anybody misery or mirth. Yet I know that any thief reading it will groan in sympathy with me. The honest reader will laugh and say: "It served him right."

In the last ten years I have learned money-honesty. I have come to like it, it has become a habit. I practice it daily. Some day I may learn to laugh at the loss of that forty-eight hundred, but I'll never learn to like laughing over it. It will never become a habit to be practiced daily.

Slumping off the horse, I threw the bridle rein over his head, left him standing patiently in the street, and walked stiffly over to the building. As near as I could judge one corner of it was directly over the spot where I made my plant. The front and one side of it covered the line where the decayed fence had formerly marked the boundary of the lot. Small barred windows in the cement foundation showed there was a basement and crushed my hopes that the money might be under the building. A careful survey of the place convinced me that the payroll was gone and there was no use in hanging around and inviting another pinch. Right here I should have muttered a string of oaths, thrown myself into the saddle, sunk my spurs, rowel deep, into the flanks of my horse, and dashed madly out of town. Sore from the long ride, I was barely able to throw a stiff leg over the saddle and settle down in it. Turning the horse's head in the direction of his home, I threw the reins on his neck and let him jog along as he liked. I was crushed. It was an hour before I could think rationally. Then the question came into my mind that is in your mind now, reader. Who got the money?

I wish I could tell you, but I can't. I don't know. I wish I could tell what became of Julia, the girl from Madam Singleton's. I wish I could tell you what was done at the Diamond Palace when the tray of stones was missed, and whether Chew Chee, the Chinese boy, was recaptured and had to go to prison.

I can't answer any of those questions. The nature of my business was such that I preferred to leave them unanswered rather than bring disaster by inquiring too closely. I know the mine payroll never got back into the owner's hands. I assume it was found by a laborer, who kept it. The reconstruction of the finding of my money and the picturing of its finder furnished me with many hours of mental relaxation. Lying in the dungeon or in the hop joint or on the grass in the public parks, I pieced it together painfully. But never could I see the lucky finder as an honest man; nor by any effort of imagination could I ever picture him as putting the money to any good use.

In the end, he always turned out to be a drunken, dissolute day laborer, sweating in the sun as he dug out the ditch for the foundation of that building. I saw him turn up the leather pouch with his shovel, seize it, open it stealthily, and thrust it inside his shirt. Then he threw down his shovel, walked over to the boss, and demanded his "time."

I heard the foreman say : "All right, you're no good anyway. I was going to fire you to-night."

I followed the finder to the little depot where he bought a ticket to the wide-open joyful town of Montreal. There I watched him dissipate my money riotously in the slums. At last, and with great satisfaction, I saw him dead in the gutter without a dime, and followed his body to the morgue, where the coroner pronounced it a case of "acute alcoholism."

After a long tiresome ride I delivered the fagged horse to his owner and went off to a quiet spot to sum up and see how I stood with the world. My loss was not put down to poetic justice or attributed to the law of compensation. I just classified it as a mess of tough luck and tried to forget it. An inventory of my possessions showed one pocketknife, one pencil, a bandanna handkerchief, tobacco and papers, and nine dollars. I was a hundred miles away from any place where I could put my hands on a dollar without getting arrested at sunrise. I had no gun, no keys, no instruments. I was a shorn lamb. No one but myself was to blame for the shearing, and it was up to me to get busy and temper the wind as quickly as possible.

In the way of clothes I had those I left Los Angeles in – overalls, blue shirt, a stout coat, and a cheap cap.

After bumming a stage ride, beating my way over a jerkwater branch road, and stowing away on a Columbia River boat loaded with dynamite and explosive oil for the mines, I got into one of the prosperous camps with a lone dollar in my pocket. The town was booming; crowded with miners, prospectors, and speculators. Beds were two dollars a night and meals a dollar. This caused me no uneasiness, for I knew it would be easier to get three dollars there than fifteen cents in the big cities where, in those days, a "chicken dinner" could be had for a dime and a "flop" on a bare floor for a "jit," as the Southern negro affectionately calls his nickel.

In a restaurant I met an old friend in the person of the waiter, who had formerly been a very active member of the "Johnson" family. He was still in good standing, although he had retired from the road after several unfortunate experiments with burglary and robbery. It was late at night; I took an hour to eat, and he listened with genuine sympathy to all the harrowing details of my latest experience. At the cash register, where he also officiated, my dollar was no good. He offered to share his room with me, and when I declined, explaining that I would be too busy to sleep, he magnanimously suggested that I "prowl the joint" he lived in. This looked all right, and I took his room key with the understanding that if anything went wrong in the place I could say I was looking for his room and he would alibi for me.

It was late when I started to look through his hotel. I lost half an hour locating a sleeper with his door unlocked, and another half hour pulling his moneyless trousers from under his head, where he had placed them from force of habit. I fared better in another room, and, calling it a night, hastened to my friend's place to return his key and look over my takings.

The restaurant was deserted. I joined him at a back table, where he sat cleaning a row of water glasses. Blowing his breath into one, like a housewife with a lamp chimney, he polished it carefully with a soiled napkin. "Did you score?" he inquired.

"Yes," I said.

I spread my money on the table to look it over. My sad experience with the twenty-dollar bill had made me careful. The paper money looked safe enough, and so did the silver except one fifty-cent piece that was worn smooth and had a monogram engraved on one side of it – a pocket piece or keepsake.

"Take this out in the back and throw it away," I said to him ; "it's deadly poison."

Instead, he rang it up on the register, saying, "That will pay your check; no use wasting it. It will go to the bank in the morning."

I went to his room and to bed. At seven o'clock he came in with this amazing story, and I suggest a careful study of it by any young man who thinks stealing is an exact science, and all he has to do is outwit the coppers.

"Thirty minutes after you left the restaurant," said he, "a guy came in and ate his breakfast in silence. He laid down a five-dollar bill to pay his check and the four-bit piece you threw me was in the change I gave him. He jumped stiff-legged and began frothing at the mouth when he saw it.

"I was robbed last night in my room. I had to wake the clerk up this morning and borrow five dollars. This fifty-cent piece is mine. I had it last night. It has my initials on it. I've carried it five years. How did it get into your till?"

"I told him I took it in an hour before from a short, stout, red-headed man with a broken nose and about forty years old. He is going to have a policeman at the place until the redhead shows up again. I promised to point him out if I see him anywhere.You're safe; but you had better eat somewhere else for a while."

TWENTY-ONE

THIS strange coincidence of the marked piece of silver more than ever convinced me of the necessity for keeping something ahead so I wouldn't be forced to go out and take long chances for short money. With enough in my pocket now to last me a month, I gave the town a thorough canvassing for something worth while. I found many places that appeared to be advertising for a bursar, and the most promising was the big general store. It was packed to the roof with merchandise, and the owners, to save floor space, had placed the safe behind stairs, where it could not be seen from the street. I "pegged" the spot for a week and satisfied myself that after the store was closed at night no one entered it till opening-up time in the morning.

The expression, "I have him pegged," which has crept into common usage, is thieves' slang pure and simple, and has nothing to do with the game of cribbage as many suppose. The thief, to save himself the trouble of staying up all night watching a spot to make sure no one enters after closing hours, puts a small wooden peg in the door jamb after the place is locked up. At five or six o'clock in the morning he takes a look. If the peg is in place the door has not been opened. If it is found lying in the doorway, that means somebody has opened the door in the night. If he finds the place is visited in the night he must then stay out and learn why and at what time and how often. He now has the place "pegged" and plans accordingly or passes it up as too tough.

Dynamite and drills were to be had for the taking at any mine. I invited my friend, the waiter, to "come in on the caper," but he declined for the very good reason that he had "done enough time." Compared with the work I had put in getting the mine payroll this was simple and I went against it alone, confident of success and glad I wouldn't have to split the money with anybody. The "box" was of a make that has long been extinct. It was an experiment on the part of the manufacturers, and a costly one, for the "box men" soon found a fatal weakness in its make-up and hungrily sought them out till the last one went into the junk pile.

The one I had designs on looked more like an old-fashioned clothes closet than a receptacle for money. Its four wheels rested on a heavy wooden platform that served to reinforce the thin floor of the storeroom. The work of putting a hole in it, placing the "shot," and laying a five-minute fuse took an hour. The man that does this kind of work alone must now take a look at the street to be sure there are no late stragglers around. When he satisfies himself on this point he returns and lights his fuse. While it is burning he goes back to the street some distance away and plants himself in a hall or doorway till he hears the explosion. Then when he is satisfied there is no alarm, he goes after his money.

I was in the door of an all-night saloon when my explosion arrived. Nobody appeared on the street and after a few minutes I went back to the store to finish the business. Inside, I saw that my "shot" had resulted in something entirely unforeseen. The outer plate of the door was torn from its place and lying to one side, bent and twisted. The force of the explosion had shifted the ponderous box from its platform. It had fallen forward on its face and ten sturdy burglars couldn't have turned it over. Had it remained upright the money would have been mine in five minutes. Lying on its face, its contents were as safe from me as if they had been in the town bank. The next day a gang of men turned it partly over and one of the clerks finished opening it with a crowbar I left in the store.

The storekeepers said "there was nothing in the safe anyway." My friend, the waiter, who stood by when it was opened, said they hurried to the bank with a fat package and "what was in it was plenty."

This failure took the heart out of me for a few days, and I don't know what depths of despondency I might have wallowed in but for my friend. He suggested, with the best intentions I am sure, that I take a job washing dishes in the place where he worked. This was a jolt to my pride. Of course I had nothing against dishwashers or dishwashing. I saw that any able-bodied dishwasher would have more to show for his ten years' hard work than I had for mine, and if I had been in the notion of going to work I would have taken that kind of job as quick as any. But the thought of working was as foreign to me as the thought of burglary or robbery would be to a settled printer or plumber after ten years at his trade. I wasn't lazy or indolent; I knew there were lots of easier and safer ways of making a living but they were the ways of other people, people I didn't know or understand, and didn't want to. I didn't call them suckers or saps because they were different and worked for a living. They represented society. Society represented law, order, discipline, punishment. Society was a machine geared to grind me to pieces. Society was an enemy. There was a high wall between me and society; a wall reared by myself, maybe – I wasn't sure. Anyway I wasn't going to crawl over the wall and join the enemy just because I had taken a few jolts of hard luck.

I did go over the wall in the end and take my hat off to society and admit I was wrong, but I didn't do it because of discouragement, because

I was afraid of the future, because of the police. I didn't do it because I realized I was wrong; I knew I was wrong years before. I did it because – but that's a separate story, to be told later, in its place.

So, instead of following the waiter's advice, I busied myself with a few careful hotel burglaries, got a small bankroll together again, bought some presentable clothes, and kept looking around for a decent piece of money. The booming mining town had its share of gamblers, women of the night, thieves, and hop fiends – nearly all of them renegades or fugitives from the "American side." Their leisure time was given to drinking or smoking hop. I had weaned myself from gambling. I was naturally a light drinker. So it fell out that, in this town of no amusements, the hop joint claimed me.

One afternoon as I lay smoking my day's portion of hop, a voice, a woman's voice, strangely familiar, came to me through a thin partition from the adjoining room. When she finished talking to the Chinese boy that attended the hop layouts, I fell to wondering who the speaker could be. My contact with women had been very limited and it didn't take much elimination to fix the voice as that of the street girl of Chicago, the girl from whose crib I had carried the dead man; the girl I avoided because I believed she had carelessly killed him with an overdose of some drug. Just to satisfy myself that I was right, more than anything I got up and stepped into her room. No mistake; it was she. She knew me instantly and I needed no introduction, no sponsor.

Irish Annie had changed. She was now a well-poised, confident woman. The world had treated her better than it does most of her kind, and yet she was not spoiled. She instantly referred to "that awful night" and sincerely acknowledged the service I had done her. We compared notes roughly. She had left Chicago to avoid going to jail for a theft, and after many hardships and adventures found herself in this British Columbia mining camp. A lucky prospector in the mines finding himself rich overnight, had bought an establishment for her and she was prospering.

To show her gratitude to me, she gave a blowout at her place, introduced me to her "girls" as "an old friend from the States," set a room apart for me, and insisted upon me making her home my home. The Chinese boy brought meals to my room, a hop layout was procured so I could smoke in peace and security. My room was more comfortable than any I could have had in a hotel, the meals were better than at the restaurants, I was treated with deference by everybody in the place, so I remained there. I paid the rent on rent day, ordered the liquors and provisions, and "slipped" the town marshal his "once a week." The

Tenderloin, the marshal, and his deputies accepted me as Annie's protector and the man about the place – something I was not and did not aspire to be. I didn't take the trouble to enlighten them. I preferred to have them believe anything rather than the truth. This would make my stealing easier.

This soft life that loomed before me in Irish Annie's had about as much lure for me as the dishwashing job. Without taking her into my confidence, I went on with my burgling. That was my trade and I would not leave it for a job in a restaurant, a "job" in Annie's, or a position in a bank.

Winter came with a rush and a roar. I had thought of getting away from the North, but it came before I was prepared and there was nothing to do but stick it out with the others.

Of all the gamblers that found their way into this camp "Swede Pete" was probably the cleverest. I knew him from towns on the "American side," where he played in all the big poker games with more or less success. He submitted a scheme to me that looked very good. His plan was to buy a box of playing cards, mark each deck, and have me, as a capable burglar, go into one of the big poker rooms, open the card locker, and substitute his box of marked cards for a box of legitimate cards belonging to the house.

I looked at the place and saw my end of the business would be simple. He went to work on his cards, and after many days and nights of patient toil put his "work" on them so he could read them from the back as easily as from the front. When he had replaced the seals on each deck and on the box that contained them, he put them in my hands and it was but an hour's work for me to put them in the locker and return to him the full box that his had replaced.

The following night he sat in the game as usual. Whenever he lost a pot he threw the unlucky deck on the floor and ordered a fresh one. After a night or two of this, the gamekeeper had to open a fresh box. This was our box and Pete's luck changed at once. In a couple of nights' play he got the long end of the money in the game. From what I heard and saw I estimated his winnings, or stealings, at three thousand dollars. It was understood that the money should be split evenly between us. When he gave me my end of it he declared he had won but fifteen hundred and that he had to have a man in the game with him and the money had to go three ways. I took the five hundred dollars knowing I was getting the worst of it and wondering how I could get even.

Pete was a big, six-foot, blond giant, good-natured, generous, and with a laugh you could hear a block. Everybody liked him; he was a good spender and a good loser. He carried a bankroll of several thousand dollars, as I knew, but the thought of robbing him never entered my mind till he burnt me in the marked-card transaction. He was interested in a saloon and had a game of his own in a rear room. I watched him carefully and learned that when the game and the bar were closed for the night he put his bankroll in the cash register, locked it, and went to bed in a comfortable little room that adjoined the big barroom. Apparently his money was safe. He left his room door open; the register could not be opened without waking him.

After thinking the matter over pro and con, I decided to beat off the barroom, carry the register out and into the alley and smash it open with an ax. Every night for a week I watched him from across the street and saw him make up his cash for the day, then put his own money in the register, lock it carefully, and go into his bedroom. Satisfied on this point, I now kept away from his place so as not to be too fresh in his mind on the morning after I got his money.

At last a stormy night came that drove everybody off the street. I kept out of the neighborhood of Pete's place till four o'clock in the morning. I had no trouble getting into the barroom through a door opening into the hall that separated the saloon from the hotel office. Carefully removing a lot of glasses from around the register, I lifted it and placed it on the bar. Then I had to go around the bar, pick it up again, and carry it out into the hall where I put it on a table while I went back to close the door. All the while Swede Pete was snoring like a horse.

Lifting the heavy weight again, I made my way slowly to the sidewalk. Groping along in the blinding storm of snow and sleet I missed my footing and fell flat on my back with the heavy register fair on my chest. Its sharp edge dug into my ribs and although I never went to a doctor, I believe to this day a couple of them were cracked or splintered. Unable to lift it again, I tied my handkerchief in the grill work at the top of the thing and painfully dragged it to an opening between two buildings and down into the alley where I had planted an ax.

I was morally certain Pete's money was in it. I saw him put it there the night before, but on this last night I had kept away, not caring to be seen about his place. There was one chance in a million that he hadn't locked the register, so before attacking it with the ax I touched one of the keys. The bell did not ring, but the cash drawer opened. But to my dismay it did not slide out with the slow, labored, obese movement of a cash drawer loaded with heavy gold and silver; instead it shot out with a thin, empty hollow jerk that told me there was nothing in it.

With numb and freezing fingers I explored the little cups only to find them bare of coin. The compartments in the back gave up no fat bankroll. The thing was as empty and as inviting as a new-dug grave. This last blow was too much for my philosophy. Cursing the snow and sleet and every organic thing, I started back determined to go into Pete's bedroom and search for his money. I was too late. At the door I looked into the hall and saw the porter limbering up for another day's work.

Sad and sore I turned away and trudged through the storm to my room at Irish Annie's where I found food and drink and light and heat and the consoling hop layout.

I was out early the next afternoon to find out what had happened at Swede Pete's that caused him to shift his money. He was around town drunk as a ragman, going from one bar to another, buying drinks for all hands, and telling with great relish how he had saved his bankroll from the "burglars." I heard his boisterous laugh as I was passing one of the saloons and went in to get an earful. He threw an American twentydollar piece on the bar, and as it bounced up and down, roared: "Yump, you beggar, yump! Many times I ha' to yump for you." Then everybody was invited to drink and listen to his tale.

I gathered from it that his cash register "bane on the bum." Something got wrong with its locking arrangement the night before, and Pete took his money to bed with him. "Ay take the old bankroll and throw her under the mattress and lay my two hundred pounds Swede beef on her," he finished with a roar. Then, bouncing another gold piece on the bar, he ordered it to "yump" and the house to drink. If he suspected me he didn't show it, and I went out not relishing his talk or his liquor. I thought of sticking him up, but he knew my voice and that wouldn't do. I thought of chloroform, but my awful experience with the Chinamen warned me against it. I had no desire to get tangled up with Pete's "two hundred pounds Swede beef" that wasn't beef at all, but bone and muscle he put on in his youth as a laborer in the Northwest lumber camps. After much thought, I let him go and gave him up as a total loss.

I don't know what the statistics show, but I should say that for every five hundred burglaries one burglar gets arrested. On the other hand, my experiences showed that if the burglar gets what he is after one time in five he is lucky.

After my bad luck with the big Swede I sat down and gave my system of stealing a good overhauling. As near as I could calculate ten thousand dollars had slipped out of my hands since I left Los Angeles. I wasn't satisfied to put this down to tough luck entirely. I saw that carelessness had something to do with it. I should have planted the mine payroll in a safer place. A more careful and experienced "blacksmith" would have taken measures to prevent that big safe from falling on its face and burying the money beyond reach, and in the matter of Swede Pete I was careless and overconfident, in not checking on him the night I went after his money. Figuring that my luck was about due to change for the better, I resolved to pull myself together, tighten up my system, and look around me for something else.

If business houses took as much precaution in protecting themselves from thieves as thieves do in protecting themselves from the police, the business of burglary and robbery would reach the vanishing point in no time. Thieves are occasionally careless; business men are habitually so; both pay for their carelessness sooner or later.

In looking about for some worth-while endeavor, I came upon an instance of carelessness on the part of a business man that I never saw equaled in all my years of stealing. It cost him a small fortune in diamonds and sent him into the bankruptcy court. The Christmas holidays were coming on, and the jewelry store in this mining camp spread out a display of stones that would have done credit to any large city. I was naturally attracted, and began investigating the jeweler's system. I found that he slept on the premises in a room back of his storeroom. He testified in court later that he carried no burglary insurance, that he could not get fire insurance because the town had no fire department, and that he slept in his store to protect himself in case of fire or attempted theft. I watched him closely through every business hour of the day – from seven to eight o'clock one day, from eight to nine the next, from nine to ten the next – and so on through the entire day from his opening hour till he closed at night. I found that he left his store in darkness to save on the light bill, and to my amazement I also found that, instead of locking his safe carefully and completely at night, he gave the combination knob only a quarter turn, leaving it "on the quarter," or only partly locked and at the mercy of any one with a working knowledge of combination locks.

This putting out of the lights and careless locking of his safe was entirely due to a feeling of security because he slept in his place of business.

After gathering every scrap of information available, I was sure I could "take" the spot if I got a fair break on the luck. The rear room of the place was used as a workshop. This made it possible to enter the back door without waking the owner, who slept in a small room between the shop and the big front storeroom. When I decided to go against this thing, I sat down and looked far ahead.

The stones would have to go to the "American side" to be disposed of in some big city. I decided on San Francisco and planned my route there. Irish Annie was no small problem. I had no intention of confiding in her or giving her any part of the junk, if I got it. I was under no obligation to her. Our relations were just those of two social outcasts, thrown together by chance, and our parting could mean nothing to either of us. To disarm any suspicions she might have later on, I told her I planned to go to Carson City, Nevada, for the big fight between Fitzsimmons and Corbett. This would give me a reasonable excuse for leaving after the burglary.

With the five hundred dollars I got from Swede Pete and more I had picked up around the hotels, I was amply supplied with expense money and had no worry on that point. Two weeks ahead I bought an old Indian cayuse and a cheap secondhand saddle and bridle, planning to ride across the boundary line fifteen miles distant, plant the junk, and return before the burglary was discovered.

The old horse was staked out in a corral where I could get him at any time. I even rode to the "American side," crossing the Columbia River, which marked the boundary, on the ice, and picked out a place to plant my stuff. A week ahead I rented a front room in a lodging house across the street and from my window watched every move in the store every evening. I saw the boss go out to dinner, leaving the place in charge of his clerk and an apprentice boy. I saw his man in the repair shop go out and away. I saw the boy go home after the boss returned, and later saw the clerk depart. An hour after, the owner began gathering the most valuable articles from show window and show cases, placing them in specially made trays and boxes that fitted snugly in the safe. Then the big door swung shut, and a quarter turn of the knob locked it so that it could be opened quickly in the morning by the lazy, careless owner, or just as quickly at night by an industrious, careful burglar.

My mistake in not checking Swede Pete the night before was not repeated here. When the final night came I stood in the snowstorm outside the window, cap pulled down and overcoat buttoned up, looking carelessly at the cheap articles he left there overnight. When he locked his safe as usual, I went back to my room across the street and saw him secure his front door, put out the lights, and go back into his bedroom.

At one o'clock I was at the back door of the store and after a few minutes of the most careful work I stood in the warm workshop where a big stove still glowed in the dark. The doors inside were open to allow the warm air passage into the sleeper's room and the front room beyond. I had all the luck at last.

There was no serious obstacle. The sleeper slept on. The safe door opened as easy for me as for him. The inside of the safe was like a beehive – fifty watches, wound up, ticked noisily. Some years ago jewelers thought watches should be kept running all or part of the time to insure perfection. I believe this is no longer done. For fear their ticking should wake the sleeper when I passed through his room on my way out, I wrapped them in their box in my overcoat. Taking nothing else except some gold rings, all the stones, and what money was in the cash drawer, I closed the safe, went back out the rear door and, closing it carefully departed unseen.

All my junk went into a grain bag at the corral, where I kept the old cayuse. He was gentle as a dog, but the ticking of the watches almost drove him frantic. He reared and pawed and snorted in fear. I couldn't get into the saddle, and had to snub him up to a tree where, for ten or fifteen minutes, I let him listen to the ticks and get over his fright. At last he cooled off and allowed me to mount him and turn his head south toward the "line." Riding away I looked back over the night's work and thought with satisfaction that no human being could possibly suspect me of it.

In the small town across the line I planted the stones and cash carefully in the plant I had prepared, but put the watches in another place where they could tick themselves out in security. At seven o'clock in the morning the faithful old horse was back in the corral, well fed and rubbed down, and I was in my room at Irish Annie's. In the afternoon she came in with the small town "Extra" paper. I saw that this burglary, one of the simplest and easiest of my life, was by far the most profitable. Diamonds valued at twenty thousand dollars, wholesale price, fifty watches, five hundred dollars cash, and a parcel of gold wedding rings roughly outlined the loss. I immediately "pooh-poohed" the business to her, telling her I knew enough about burglary to see that it was an inside job and that it was done by the storekeeper to beat his creditors. She believed me and no suspicion whatever found lodgment in her mind.

The next day's paper questioned the burglary. It was hard to believe that any sane man could be guilty of such carelessness as the jeweler frankly admitted. He also admitted that the stock was taken on consignment, that the stones were not paid for, and that if they were not recovered he would be broke and bankrupted. The town was divided as to whether he had robbed himself, and the marshal and his deputies remained dormant.

I paid another week's board for the old horse, and another week's rent for the room opposite the jeweler's. I had no use for them any more, but thought it safest not to give either of them up too soon and chance arousing suspicion.

After a restless month I said good-by to Annie and to the "Canadian side." Leaving the watches and rings where they were, I dug up the plant of stones and cash, and went into Spokane, where I threw away my good clothes, put on overalls, a mackinaw coat, a lumberjack's cap, and bought a cheap ticket to Seattle. There I changed again, buying an expensive outfit of clothes and other things necessary for the traveler. Three days later I was in San Francisco, safe, secure, and unsuspected.

My first act was to put the stones in a safety box, tear up the receipt, and plant the key in a safe, convenient place. Then began the toughest part of the business, getting the stones off my hands and into cash. Day after day I sorted out the larger ones and in my room "unharnessed" them from their settings. Other articles, clusters and sunbursts, were left intact in their settings – to remove them would depreciate the value. I had many of the best stones reset and sold them for fair prices openly to bookmakers, prize fighters, jockeys, gamblers, and women about town. My money went into the bank, and for the first time in my life I carried a check book.

I was careful, kept clean and sober and away from the hop joints and thieves' hangouts. For once in my life I managed to get a fair price from pawnshops for some of my junk. Taking one of the reset rings that was perfectly safe and impossible of identification, I would step into the pawnbroker's at lunch time and always when there were other patrons in his place. The average thief is duck soup for the hockshop man. He will walk by the hockshop and look in. The hockshop man sees him and knows he has something "hot," or crooked. If there is anybody in the place but the employees, the thief waits till they go out before going in. This convinces the pawnbroker he has a thief to deal with and he offers him half what he would offer an honest man with a legitimate article.

Instead of sneaking into a hockshop, taking a ring out of my pocket, and saying, "How much can I get on this?" I walked in confidently, held out my finger with the ring on, and said: "I want to pledge this ring for one hundred dollars till pay day. My name is so-and-so. I work for such and such a firm. I lost some of my employer's money at the race track and must have it to-night."

I always asked for a sum far in excess of what I expected, but that served to convince the pawnbroker I knew nothing about pawning things, that I was honest, that the ring was mine and that I would probably redeem it. After inspecting it he would offer me much more than if he thought it was crooked. If it was redeemed he would get his big interest, and if not he would still be safely below the wholesale price, which is the dead line for him.

In one way and another I unloaded most of my stones to advantage. I could go about with them one at a time in safety; they were impossible of identification when out of their original settings. While I was trying to find some safe way of selling the pieces I had left in their settings, I met by chance a young chap I had known on the road. He had settled down, got married, and was making a semi-legitimate and uncertain living gambling. He was square enough, and I arranged with him to sell them for me. He was in San Francisco when the burglary was committed and was in no danger of being charged with it if he did get arrested.

He got rid of them quickly to his friends in the Tenderloin and to small pawnshops, getting a price that satisfied me and left him a good profit. I cleaned everything up and quit with eight thousand dollars in the bank and several very nice stones that I wanted to keep. Of late I had thought of buying a saloon some time and leaving the burglary business. Now, as I looked over the small dives and joints with their hangers-around, their discordant pianos and beery-voiced singers, and drunken, bedraggled women, I found they had no attraction. Now that I could have one of those places I didn't want it.

The notion of going into any decent business never occurred to me. Without any definite notion of what to do, I settled down to have a few months of ease and relaxation. The race tracks and gambling houses were running wide open, but I kept away from them and didn't get hurt. The wine dumps, the "Coast," Chinatown, and the dingy dives that fascinated me when I first saw them, no longer held anything of interest.

I'm not finding fault with these brave days of jungle music, synthetic liquor, and dimple-kneed maids, and anybody that thinks the world is going to the bowwows because of them ought to think back to San Francisco or any other big city of twenty years ago – when train conductors steered suckers against the bunko men; when coppers located "work" for burglars and stalled for them while they worked; when pickpockets paid the police so much a day for "exclusive privileges" and had to put a substitute "mob" in their district if they wanted to go out of town to a country fair for a week. Those were the days when there were saloons by the thousand; when the saloonkeeper ordered the police to pinch the Salvation Army for disturbing his peace by singing hymns in the street; when there were race tracks, gambling unrestricted, crooked prize fights; when there were cribs by the mile and hop joints by the score. These things may exist now, but if they do, I don't know where. I knew where they were then, and with plenty of money and leisure I did them all.

TWENTY-TWO

THE YOUNG fellow that helped me dispose of the stones was the wayward son of a fine family and it would not be right to them to use his name. I will call him "Spokane," the monoger he was known by among his associates. He had been in San Francisco for years and was familiar with an underworld that I had seen very little of. Most of my life had been spent on the road or roughing it in out-of-the-way places, broken by a few months now and then in city slums. He introduced me into the elegant hop joints where we smoked daily, into the hangouts of polished bunko men and clever pickpockets, into the gilded cafes and other exclusive and refined places of entertainment.

I grew tired of this life after a few months and suggested to Spokane that he go up to the Canadian line and lift the plant of watches and rings. The burglary cry had died out and I had arranged to sell them all where they would never rise up to accuse me. This trip suited him, as it would give him a chance to visit his people in Spokane, Washington, and it pleased me to have him go because I didn't want to take chances with the watches which were all numbered and easy of identification. I had left them behind me rather than carry the bulky package around and chance losing the more valuable stones because of it. I gave him a diagram of the spot where the plant was, supplied him with tickets and traveling expenses, and sent him on his way with instructions to express the parcel to the San Francisco express office, value it at twenty-five dollars, and tell the express agent it contained samples of ore.

To make everything safe and sure, I further instructed him to stand at the depot when the train was in and make sure the parcel went into the express car, then to take a train the next day and come back to San Francisco by an indirect route which would protect him in case anything happened to the package en route.

I put in a couple of anxious weeks, but he showed up in due time with the good news that he had located the junk without trouble and sent it along exactly as he had promised. He called for it at the express office the next day, but it hadn't arrived. Not caring to make too much fuss over a package valued at twenty-five dollars, we waited a few days before he went back for it. The express office was in Montgomery Street then, and I stood in the Palace Hotel entrance where I could look across the street and see him showing the receipt and arguing with the clerks. His willingness to go to the office every day convinced me he was on the square. He had a receipt for the package; I assumed it had gone astray.

We talked the thing over and decided there was nothing to be afraid of. If the parcel had been seized by the police he would have been pinched at the express office. I began to get suspicious after a week and was for abandoning the whole thing, but Spokane insisted on making another call. From my spot across the street I saw two men fall on him when he spoke to the clerk and knew he was arrested.

I went straight to my room, got everything and moved to another, where I sat down and tried to figure out what had happened and what to do. His arrest was a mystery, but it was plain to me that I must either jump out on him or stay and help. I was clean, there wasn't a scrap of evidence against me. If I deserted him that might cause him to squawk, and with his testimony they could convict me if they got me. I knew the police would accuse him of the burglary and that he could and would convince them in an hour that he was in San Francisco when it occurred. That would start them on a hunt for another man, and that would bring them to me, for I had been seen with him daily for months. I saw I would be picked up; I saw they could prove I was in the town where the burglary was committed, and at the time. But they could get no further. The evidence to convict me was not in existence. I could not be convicted without Spokane's testimony.

I was reasonably certain he would protect me if I protected him. I sent and found that the police had not been to the room I deserted; that meant he was standing up. I decided to stay and take a pinch and have the business settled while I had money to fight. After making this decision I cleaned up a few odds and ends of jewelry, put them away in my safety box, and left the key in a secure place. I took a thousand dollars in hundred-dollar bills and secreted it in different parts of my clothes. The pawn tickets had all been destroyed the minute we got them. I felt perfectly secure, and went openly around the hangouts waiting for the blow to fall.

It came in a hurry, and to my surprise I was put in the cell occupied by Spokane. I learned later that the cell had some kind of listening arrangement, but we did not discuss our troubles. We were both "on the small book," which meant incommunicado, but I promised a trusty prisoner a dollar if he would get word out to an attorney I had in mind. He was one of the leading criminal lawyers at that time, and had us both out to talk to him the next morning. The evening papers carried the story of my arrest and of the burglary. The attorney had read it and seeing it was a case of considerable magnitude he came at once. He did not believe in any fat fees being held incommunicado.

I gave him a substantial retainer and asked him to find out what we were charged with and what we were being held on. Spokane had got barely an hour's sleep at one time in the three days he had been in. Policemen and detectives took turn about questioning him, trying to wear him down to the weakening point. They now started on me, threatening, blustering, cajoling, wheedling, and promising. I made no statement except that I was innocent. There was no local interest in the case, and we were not mistreated. Captain Lindheimer, long dead now, was in charge of the city prison. He frowned on the beating-up of prisoners, and there was very little of it done when he was in charge. He was a very humane man, and of all the prisoners that passed through his hands I don't recall ever hearing one with a harsh word for him.

Our attorney had influence enough to get our meals sent from the outside; we bought clean, new blankets from the head trusty and plenty of opium, which we ate. Spokane's wife was permitted to visit us, the police probably figuring they could follow her to something that would convict us. She had not been told anything, knew nothing, and could do us no harm.

Out of my thousand dollars I got in with, I saw to it that she was taken care of. This was only fair to Spokane, and helped him to help me by keeping his mouth shut.

The attorney could learn nothing except that we were being held on telegrams. "This is soft," he said. "They can't hold you on that. I'll take you out on a writ of habeas corpus."

The next morning we went into court on the writ. The court gave the police twenty-four hours to get something more substantial than telegrams, threatening to liberate us if they failed. When we appeared the next day they had nothing except more telegrams, and we were discharged from custody.

I grabbed the attorney's hand. "Don't get excited," he said, "they're not done with you yet."

Although the judge released us we were promptly rearrested at the courtroom door and put in our cell. The attorney applied for another writ. This was granted and we went to court again the next day, but were put over twenty-four hours on the plea of the police that witnesses were on their way from Canada. No witnesses appeared, and we were discharged only to be arrested again. The court warned the police that they would be in contempt if we were held longer without evidence.

On our next day in court we were confronted by the chief of provincial detectives from Victoria with a warrant of extradition and a day was set for him to make his showing. One night a strange attorney came to me in the prison, told me he had had a talk with the judge, and that for a sum of money he would point out a flaw in the case that would upset the extradition plea. I sent for my attorney and asked his advice. He investigated, and told me to put up the money.

When we went into court the Canadian officer produced his warrant. It was the biggest document I ever saw – a piece of parchment about three feet long, embossed, engraved, and signed and sealed with the seal of Queen Victoria – a formal demand from the British Government on the Secretary of State to deliver us over to the Canadian authorities. He had it in a bag carefully rolled and wrapped in paper. Taking it out carefully, reverently, he placed it in the judge's hands.

"Where did you get this document?" the court asked.

"From Ottawa, the capital of Canada," the officer answered.

"Did you go to Ottawa yourself for it?"

"No, it came to Victoria by mail."

Looking at it closely the judge pointed to a name signed at the bottom. "What's this?" he asked.

"That is the signature of Lord Aberdeen, governor general of Canada."

"Did you see him sign it?"

"No."

"Hm," said the judge, laying it down.

Our lawyer picked it up and appeared to read it carefully. Turning to the officer, he asked: "How do you know that is Lord Aberdeen's signature? Were you there when he signed it? Did you ever see him sign his name to any paper? Did you ever see Lord Aberdeen? What's this thing?" he tapped the seal, the big red seal half as large as your hand.

"That is the seal of Her Majesty, Queen Victoria of England," the man answered, getting indignant and red in the face.

"Oh, it is, is it? How do you know it is? Did you see her put it there? Is she here to identify it? There's no Victoria here in this court, is there? This might be the seal of Jane Doe, a waitress. Anybody can have a seal. Do you think the court is going to recognize this thing? You'll have to come in here with something better than that," he said, throwing it on the floor and kicking it under a table.

The officer got down from the witness stand, picked it up, brushed it off, and carefully put it away.

The judge then said: "This court cannot recognize that as a valid document. You come here with a paper demanding custody of these defendants, but we have here no proof that it is genuine. It might be a forgery. We know there is such a person as Lord Aberdeen, of Canada, but we have no proof that his signature is on that warrant. I cannot hold defendants on such evidence."

We were discharged again. I don't know where the money went that I gave the lawyer who sold us the point that beat the extradition; I know the judge didn't give us any the worst of it.

We were arrested again at the door. That night we were indicted by the grand jury; I for bringing stolen property into the state of California, and Spokane for receiving it from me. The police saw we were framing and using money, so they, rather than be beaten, began framing us. Our cases were transferred into another court where they could do some fixing, and we couldn't. The indictments meant that we would have to wait for trial. I began to get uneasy about the stones I had in the safety box. The police were tearing the town open for them, not knowing that nearly all of them had been sold. I told our lawyer where to get the key to the box, gave him a password and told him to take the junk out and put it in some safe place. The police "tailed" every visitor we had and even the lawyer in hopes of locating the stones, and he had to be careful.

Making another application for a writ of habeas corpus, which he knew would not avail us, he had the hearing set for ten o'clock in the morning. This alarmed the coppers and every one of them was at the courtroom when the case was called. Everybody was there but our attorney. The hearing was held up for fifteen minutes. During this fifteen minutes he was at the safety vault lifting the plant while every detective on the case was waiting in court. He came in, nodded to us, apologized to the court, and went on with the case with the parcel of loot in his pocket. The writ was denied, of course. I told him to put the stuff away, and he did.

When I asked him about it later, he looked me straight in the eye and said: "Did you think I was damn fool enough to keep that stuff around me? Say, when court adjourned that day I went straight down to the foot of Powell Street and threw it in the bay."

This didn't look just right to me, but what could I do? I was only a poor, honest burglar in the hands of a highway lawyer. He got us a copy of the testimony given the grand jury, and from it I learned what had caused our arrest – Spokane's passion for gambling.

After lifting the watches and rings in the little Northern town, he tried his luck at the faro table and lost his expense money. This forced him to open the parcel and sell a couple of the watches to a gambler for enough money to buy his return ticket. The next day the gambler took them to the town where I stole them, fifteen miles away, across the line, and tried to pawn them. He was arrested and told where he got them. In an hour the police learned about the express package of "sample ore" Spokane shipped. It was seized en route to San Francisco. There was a big reward for the burglar, and the Northern police, wanting it, decided to capture him. Instead of wiring to have him arrested the first time he went to the express office, they hurried here and got him themselves.

Spokane was repentant, but it was too late. I did not reproach him.

His wife was faithful, and devoted to him, and visited us daily at the prison, bringing papers and small delicacies. One evening, while we were chatting on a bench in the visiting room, an officer came and took him out to another room. Several policemen were standing around, and there seemed to be something stagy going on that I couldn't understand. Suddenly, as I sat talking to Mrs. Spokane, a screen at the other side of the room was knocked aside and Irish Annie dashed from behind it, heaping abuse on me and trying to get her hands on my friend's wife.

Annie's furious appearance was like a thunderbolt out of a clear sky. I saw instantly that she had been poisoned against me. I tried to talk to her but she wouldn't listen, and the coppers stood between us pushing me away to make her think I was trying to get my hands on her and strangle her. Mrs. Spokane had collapsed on the bench, almost fainting from fear and wondering what it was about. Annie was led away screaming threats. Spokane's wife went home, and we back to our cell where we tried to piece together this unexpected angle.

I saw the police were playing my game better than I could. They knew I was trying to frame myself out; they began framing me in, and with Irish Annie they had a dangerous lead on me. It was plain to me that they had told her she was discarded for another woman; that they had called Spokane away to leave me alone with his wife while Annie watched from behind the screen. I could almost hear them saying to her: "There you are. There's the woman he left you for. There's the woman he hung his diamonds on, and spends his money on. How he got her is a mystery to us; she's a decent woman. She's crazy about him and believes he is innocent."

Then Annie, too ready to believe herself "a woman scorned," turned copper on me, knocked the screen away, and poured out the vials of her wrath. Still I wasn't much alarmed about the case and I couldn't help admiring the coppers for the way they tooled Annie and chiseled her out of her right senses. They assumed I was guilty; that gave them the right to assume that she, being my companion, knew something about the burglary. They were justified in getting it out of her by fair or unfair means. I knew she was ignorant of the least detail of it, and felt like laughing at them for wasting time on their elaborate scheme.

Our attorney made many efforts to see her, but the police had her in a hotel under the eye of a matron, and he and his runners failed.

At last he subpoenaed her as our witness and had her brought to his office. All his eloquence got nothing out of her. She was mute and stayed mute till the day of my trial. She had not been before the grand jury. We had no police-court examination and there was no way of finding out what she was going to say till she went into court. The attorney was apprehensive. I wasn't. I told him of the night I first met her shivering in a Chicago doorway, of the warm clothing I got for her, and of the night I staggered out of her crib with the dead man over my shoulder. I told him in detail of our meeting in the North by chance, and of our relations there. He was old and wise. He shook his head thoughtfully and quoted the poet's line about scorned women and their hellish fury.

The prosecution clamored for a speedy trial of the case. Almost ten thousand dollars had been spent by the Canadian authorities in retaining a firm of high-priced lawyers to prosecute; in transporting witnesses and paying hotel and other bills, and for private detectives hired to spy on the local police. Still no diamonds showed up. Spokane was offered a job with the Pinkerton Detective Agency if he would turn on me. I was promised my liberty if I would turn up the stones. We kept up our cry of innocence and made no statements at any time. A week before the day set for my trial, our attorney was stricken in his study and died in his chair, of heart failure.

We had to get another lawyer and pay another stiff fee. I went over the case with him, but somehow was unable to convince him that I had not talked too much to Irish Annie.

At my trial she swore, and she wasn't mealy-mouthed about it, either, that I told her of the burglary when I was planning it; that I offered her part of the stones when I got them; that she was afraid to take them because they were stolen. She added that she would have notified the police then, but was afraid I would kill her or have her killed. On cross-examination she said she was not testifying in hope of a reward or in revenge; that she was glad to be rid of me, and hoped I would be sentenced to life so I couldn't get out and murder her.

The next witness was a pawnbroker the police dug up. Spokane had sold him a piece of jewelry. It was identified by the loser and put in evidence. The witness identified me as the one who sold it to him and produced his book showing a fictitious name Spokane had signed. I got alarmed and protested loudly. Spokane, who was in court, jumped up and cried out to the judge that he pawned the article. The court ordered him to sit down, and my lawyer told him if he testified to that, he would be convicted on his own statement of receiving it from me, when his trial came on. Our attorney tried to get a sample of my handwriting before the jury. The prosecutors objected, and the judge ruled that no exemplars could be admitted in evidence unless they were written before the burglary was committed. I could not dig up any that old, and the case went to the jury with no defense except my sworn denial of guilt.

When the jury disappeared in their room and court was adjourned, I lit a cigarette. Before I had half finished, the jury was back with their verdict, "Guilty, as charged."

Spokane's trial was set, but I made affidavit that he was an innocent tool in the matter, and he was dismissed. He worried himself sick because of his carelessness in getting me arrested and in a few months fell a victim of tuberculosis. His devoted wife contracted it in nursing him and long before I was at liberty they were both dead and buried.

In due time I was sentenced to eight years at Folsom. The case went on appeal to the supreme court and I settled down for a long wait in the old Broadway county jail. My case gave me food for much interesting thought. I was guilty. Justice had overtaken me. But let us see how justice fared. It seemed to me that the blind goddess got a tough deal herself. Everybody connected with the case outraged her. The first judge took money. The coppers framed me in. The witnesses perjured themselves. The second judge was so feloniously righteous that he stood in with the framing. My lawyer was a receiver of stolen goods – even stole some from me. And the police told me that the Jewelers' Association beat them out of the reward.

That's one side of the case; here's another. The jeweler was bankrupt. The Canadian authorities spent ten thousand dollars. The state of California had to feed and clothe me while I was in prison.

Here's another side of it. Spokane and his wife died of T. B. that he contracted while in jail and "justice" overtook Irish Annie for what she had done to me.

Not very pleasant reflections; especially when I had to admit to myself that I was the cause of everything from the burglary to the punishment of Annie, and all that happened in between them. Yet this burglary is by no means unique. It frequently happens that the initial loss in dollars and cents is as nothing compared to the wrong and injury that radiate from such crimes like ripples on a pond.

TWENTY-THREE

MY FIRST few months in the county jail were put in hard enough. About all I did was hate Irish Annie, and plan ways and means to revenge myself on her. I kept close track of her through friends and learned that her punishment began the day she got back to Canada. Her girls left her establishment when they saw her turn copper; her friends in the Tenderloin shunned her as if she had the leprosy. Finding herself cast out by these outcasts, she gathered up what she could and joined the gold rush to Alaska.

Then, just when my bankroll had melted away under the heavy expense of two attorneys' fees and incidentals, and I was beginning to wonder if I would finish by having to eat the jail fare, a number of mysterious money orders came to me from Nome and Skagway. I couldn't but think this was conscience money from Annie. This took the edge off my hatred and I began making excuses for her. After I had several hundred dollars, the money orders stopped coming. No letter or explanation came, and I remained mystified. At last a prisoner who was brought into the jail en route to San Quentin from Alaska put an end to my guessing.

Irish Annie was dead. My informant was very discreet and mentioned no names. "Certain people," he said, "and good people, too, found out that she had a bunch of dough. They went into her crib, tied her up, and took it. When they went out, one of them said to the others: 'Black is in the county jail in San Francisco. He ought to have one end of this money. That woman put him there.'

"They didn't know she had snitched on you and objected to splitting you in with the coin. The first party, your friend, went back into the crib, and croaked her. When he came out he said: 'I've done that for Black. Now, does he get his end?'

"You got it, didn't you?"

I acknowledged the money and asked no questions.

My attorney learned later, and told me, that when she was found dead and her body identified, the police began a search for me, and the only thing that saved me was my jail alibi, the only alibi that ever convinced anybody.

With Annie off my mind I then began hating the pawnbroker. But before I went to Folsom he was charged with perjury in another case and went broke saving himself from a prison sentence, and I put him out of my mind.

I didn't worry about the coppers framing me in. I started it. It was their business to put me away if they could, and if they hadn't played my game I would have beaten the case on them. It has always been a question with me where this framing and jobbing started; whether the defense originally began it and forced the prosecutor and police to do it in self-defense, or whether it was the other way around. I never could find the answer; long ago I gave it up and filed it away with that other old question about the hen and the egg.

My attorney knew his business. He held me in the county jail till my last dollar was gone, and I refused to "write for more money" as he suggested. When I was leaving for Folsom he showed up at the jail and asked me for my watch, the only thing of value I had left.

"You won't have any use for it up there." he said. "Give it to me and I'll get you a job in the warden's where you'll get something to eat."

I told him to go plumb to hell.

I went to prison without any plans for the future. With good conduct I would have to do five years and four months and there was no use trying to look that far ahead. Two other prisoners arrived the morning I did, and the three of us were taken out to the office to have our prison biographies written – name, age, birthplace, occupation, etc. We were then photographed, measured, and weighed, and turned over to the captain to be assigned to work.

Richard Murphy ("Dirty Dick" the "cons" called him) was captain at that time. He had worked his way up from the guard line by cunning and brutality. He believed in "throwing the fear of God" into a prisoner the minute he arrived, by browbeating and bullying him, and every man went out of his office hating him. It's more than twenty years since I left Folsom, but I can still see Dirty Dick's short, squat figure on the flagstones in front of his filthy office. I can still see his pop-eyes and pasty face, his frog belly, his knock knees, and his flat feet.

I was the first to be questioned. "Where are you from?" he asked.

"San Francisco," I replied.

"How long did you do in San Quentin?"

"Never was in San Quentin."

"What other penitentiary were you in?"

"Never was in any penitentiary," I lied, and I knew he knew I was lying but wouldn't give him the satisfaction of thinking he had bullied me into telling the truth.

"Hah, you're a liar, and you know it. You can't get anything like that by me. I'll dig you up, and find out all about you. Use hop?"

"No." I did use hop, had eaten it all the time in the county jail, and had a small portion secreted about me then. He again called me a liar and said to a convict runner: "Here, Shorty, take this fellow to the stoneyard. Search him, and if you find anything you want, keep it."

I had already been searched and had nothing but a handkerchief and a pipe. "No prisoner will keep anything belonging to me," I said, looking at Shorty. He didn't search me.

The captain called up the second man. "Where are you from?"

"Sacramento," he answered.

"How long do you bring?"

"Ten years:"

"What for?"

"Grand larceny."

"What kind of grand larceny?"

The little runner, Shorty, stepped up and said: "Pickpocket, captain."

"Where do you belong?" Murphy continued.

"Chicago."

"What's your name?"

"James Brown."

"You're from Chicago, eh? And your name is Brown? What do they call you? What's your monoger?"

The little runner stepped up again and said: " 'Chi Jimmy,' captain."

"Chi Jimmy, eh? Pickpocket, eh? The rock crusher for you," said the captain. "Maybe you'll be 'Chi' a few fingers before you get out."

Which he probably would be. This was Murphy's idea of a joke.

The third chap got about the same deal, and was waved away. "To the crusher with him, too."

At that time prisoners were allowed, for economy, to keep the coats, vests and hats they brought in with them, but were made to wear striped pants and shirts. As the last man turned away. Murphy saw he had a good hat. Calling him back he took it and threw it to his runner. "Here's a hat for you, Shorty. If you can't wear it give it to somebody else; it's too good for the rock crusher."

He knew all about us before we were brought to his office and had us out there only to "throw the fear" into us and get a line on us by the way we answered his questions. He made three enemies right there. He received all prisoners that way and if they got insolent under his badgering he had them thrown into the dungeon for thirty days "to cool off."

The dungeon was an empty cell with a solid door to darken it and contained nothing but a thin blanket, and a bucket strong with chloride of lime. In cases of this kind the captain signed the punishment order which included bread and water. Every third day the prisoner got a pan of beans. Most of them were so hungry they bolted the beans without stopping to chew them and a few dungeon sentences brought on stomach troubles that added to their misery.

My eight-year sentence was considered a short one at Folsom. I found nine hundred prisoners there whose sentences averaged twelve years. They were all hopeless. The parole law was a dead letter, inoperative. Only at Christmas or on the Fourth of July did any one get a parole. The place was a seething volcano of hatred and suspicion. Dirty Dick had in the twenty years he was there developed a perfect stool-pigeon system. A visiting warden, surprised because there was no wall around Folsom, asked Murphy how he managed to keep the "cons" there. "That's simple," he said. "I've got one half of them watching the other half." His system caused many murders and assaults and at last it climaxed in the bloodiest prison break in the history of California.

Opium was the medium of exchange in the prison. About three hundred men used it habitually and a hundred more, occasionally. Incoming prisoners smuggled money in and we bribed the poorly paid guards to buy hop at Sacramento. No prisoner was allowed to buy anything through the office. The trusties stole every movable article they could from the guards' and warden's quarters and peddled them to us in the prison for their rations of hop. The "cons" were divided roughly into three groups. One group played the officers' game, working in the offices or holding down other soft jobs where they could loaf about the place and spy and snitch on the others. Murphy rewarded them all. He gave the best snitches the biggest beefsteaks. Another and larger group openly antagonized the officers, engineering hop deals, planning the murder of stool pigeons, and promoting escapes.

Between these two groups was a small bunch of convicts who did not handle hop or curry favor with the officers. They were the best conducted prisoners there, yet they were ground to pieces by the two stronger factions. They got fag ends of food in the convict mess and wore the patched-up clothes of the others.

I had some thought of getting off the hop when I got to Folsom and of keeping my nose clean and trying to shorten my time by making a parole. But I saw quickly all that was impossible for me and that I would be lucky if I earned my credits. I joined the schemers and soon had my share of the opium which meant power and influence. We sold the hop to those who had money and with the money we bought more. Also we paid guards to smuggle in sugar, butter, and other food.

Conditions at San Quentin were the same. Martin Aguirre became warden there under Governor Gage. Aguirre introduced the strait-jacket punishment and I have been told he did it on the suggestion of a convict. This brutal and inhuman form of torture had been condemned in English prisons years before as dangerous to life and limb. Yet this man was permitted to revive it in California and its use was continued until Hiram Johnson became governor.

Let it be said to this humane and enlightened gentleman's everlasting credit that one of his first official acts was to banish the jacket and other brutalities from California prisons forever. Captain Murphy welcomed the jacket as something superior to anything he had at Folsom in the way of punishment. Up to that time the prisoners were "regulated" by long terms in the dungeons on bread and water, loss of credits, or by hanging them up by the wrists till they were on tiptoe. When Dirty Dick saw what could be done with the jacket he came into the stoneyard and declared himself openly, "I've got something now that will make you tough birds snitch on yourselves."

The killing and maiming of convicts in the straitjackets are matters of record and too well known to call for any notice in this story. At Folsom I saw the jacket making beasts of the convicts and brutes of their keepers. I saw Jakey Oppenheimer transformed from a well-intentioned prisoner into a murder maniac whose wanton killings and assaults in prison brought him "under the rope" in the end. I saw the convicts throw their hats in the air and shout for joy when Warden Charles Aull died.

Thomas Wilkinson followed him as warden.

The tasks were increased, the food rations cut, and even the convict stripes were made thinner and cheaper. These abuses, coupled with brutal strait-jacketings for the slightest infraction of rules, crystallized all the hatred, despair, and hopelessness in the prison. All the convicts needed was an organizer, a leader. He appeared in the person of Dick Gordon. With a sentence of forty-five years and a prior prison experience, Gordon saw no chance of getting out on the square and began planning to escape. He was young – about twenty-three – modest, kindly, intelligent. He came to Folsom with a reputation for doing things on the outside and for being on the square. With great care and diplomacy he sorted out a dozen men and his plan was laid down for the getaway. It was simple and direct. Every Monday morning there was at least a dozen officers and guards at the prison office.

The warden was always there to get everything under way; the captain to try all prisoners for offenses committed between Saturday evening and Monday morning; the overseer to plan the week's work; the commissary to give out clothing, and the turnkey to listen to requests for changing of cells. This meant there were always thirty or forty prisoners at the office.

The plan was for Gordon and his men to mingle with others at the captain's office. When the signal was given they were to rush the officers, who were unarmed, put a knife at the throat of every one, and march them all out through the guard line, using them as shields against the gatling-gun fire from guard towers that encircled the prison. For once Captain Murphy's carefully built-up system of spying failed him; it toppled on him, crushed him, and brought about his dismissal from the prison.

His spies, when things were dull, often fabricated plots and stories to hold their jobs. Sunday, before the break, they reported to Murphy that something was brewing in the prison. He ordered fifty suspected men searched but nothing was found. The knives Gordon and his men were to use were being carried about by a "harmless" short-time convict, who kept by himself and was not suspected.

Murphy, finding nothing wrong after the search, put the reports down to over-zealousness by his stool pigeons and forgot them.

The next morning the knives were distributed and the dozen men dropped out of the line at the captain's office as the men went out to work. Every officer in the prison except the doctor was captured.

The only guard that resisted was killed instantly, cut to pieces. The only officer that resisted was Cochrane, the turnkey, the man who personally laced up the strait-jacket victims. He was hated bitterly and every man that got near enough put a knife into him. He was cut a dozen times and left for dead. He recovered, and later took his grudge out by brutalities to prisoners who had never harmed him.

Gordon and his men marched their captives to the prison armory. Under threat of death the warden ordered the guard in charge to open it. Taking all the arms and ammunition they could carry they destroyed the balance and still using the officers as shields marched them off the prison grounds and into the woods. Here some of the escapes demanded Dirty Dick's life for the things he had done to them, but Gordon had this way. "No murder" was his order and he enforced it. At sundown the captives were released. The escapes scattered. Gordon went his way alone and, though hunted for years, was never taken.

Five others of the twelve are still at liberty. The other six were captured here and there. Three of them were hanged, and the remaining three sentenced to life imprisonment, paroled after many years, and are living within the law.

When things cooled down the people of California wanted to know how men could be driven to such desperation that they captured and cut down officers and guards, rushed and took a gatling-gun tower with nothing but crude knives made in the prison blacksmith shop. This bloody affair called attention to the terrible conditions and proved the beginning of the end of prison cruelty in California.

After the break Folsom was a hell. The warden and Captain Murphy began taking revenge on friends of the escapes. We were brought into the office and questioned. I answered all questions respectfully, disclaimed any knowledge of the break, and avoided punishment at that time. Warden Wilkinson was removed and Archibald Yell of Sacramento, took his place. He had no experience and was forced to feel his way slowly. He had to depend on Murphy. This put him in virtual control of the convicts and his lust for revenge went unchecked. I was on his list and he soon got me. I had but three months to serve when I was slated for the strait-jacket. I knew the captain wanted to get my credits, which amounted to two years and eight months. Murphy had me brought into his office, where he said he had information that I was holding opium. If I had admitted this they could have taken away my entire good time. I denied it.

"Take him to the doctor," the captain ordered. That meant I was to be examined as to my physical condition before they put me in the jacket. This worried me; I was not sure whether I would snitch on myself and give up the hop. Some staunch men had weakened in the jacket. I thought I could stick it out and made up my mind to. I had been flogged and starved and third-degreed before going to Folsom and had taken them all with a grin, but I was not sure of myself in the jacket. Many prisoners claimed they gave up information on themselves and friends while delirious or semiconscious in the jacket, and that was what alarmed me. I preferred death to the loss of my credits.

While waiting for the doctor I got word to a friend who was holding my hop to throw it in the canal at once. In this way I figured I was protecting my credits even from myself. The doctor OK-ed me and I was taken into the dungeon, where Cochrane, now recovered from his terrible wounds, was waiting with the jacket. I saw it was a piece of heavy canvas about four feet long and wide enough to go around a man's body. There were long pockets sewed to the inner side of it into which my arms were thrust. I was then thrown on the floor face down and the jacket was laced up the back. The edges of the jacket were fitted with eyeholes and the thing was tightened up with a soft, stout rope just as a lady's shoe is laced. It can be drawn tight enough to stop the circulation of blood, or the breath.

While Cochrane was tightening the jacket he said: "You fellows tried to kill me; now it's my time." When he had me squeezed tight enough he turned me over on my back and went to the cell door. "When you're ready to snitch on yourself, Blacky, just sing out," he said as he locked me in.

I will not harrow the reader with a description of the torture. The jacket is no longer in use and no purpose would he served by living over those three days in the "bag." Every hour Cochrane came in and asked if I was ready to give up the hop. When I denied having it, he tightened me up some more and went away. The torture became maddening. Some time during the second day I rolled over to the wall and beat my forehead against it trying to knock myself "out." Cochrane came in, saw what I was doing, and dragged me back to the middle of the cell. I hadn't strength enough left to roll back to the wall, so I stayed there and suffered. A guard looked in and there was real sympathy in his voice. He said: "Why don't you scream, make a noise? They might let you out; they don't want to kill anybody any more." I didn't want my friends to hear me screaming; I kept still. It wouldn't have done any good, anyway.

On the evening of the second day the doctor came and felt the pulse in my temple. He then ordered me taken out for the night. They took the thing off and I collapsed in one corner. There was a wooden cup of water on the cell floor and I took a small mouthful only, because it would make the jacket so much worse when I was put back in it. My fear of snitching was gone now. The very ferocity of the punishment had made me a wild beast.

I crawled around the cell looking for something I could use to open a vein or artery; I wanted to die. All I found was my shoes. I tried to dig a nail out of one of the heels, but only broke my finger nails. At last I loosened one of the small metal eyes where the shoe is laced and with the heel of my shoe beat it out flat on the cement floor. After rubbing the metal on the floor for an hour I got an edge on it sharp enough to open the skin but it would not cut the vein. Every time I touched the vein it jumped out from under my crude blade. The sensation was something like touching a live wire, like an electric shock. Finally I gave it up and lay down to wait for morning.

I had an opium habit, but suffered so from the jacket that I forgot all about the hop – another proof to me that the habit is mostly mental.

Cochrane came at eight o'clock the next morning. I denied having hop and out came the jacket. All that day I was only half conscious, dopey. I don't think I suffered as much as on the previous day. Some time in the night they released me, and I lay on the floor in a stupor. I don't know how long. Toward morning my mind cleared and I felt that another day would finish me. I decided I would send for Captain Murphy after they put me back in the jacket and ask him to take me down to the bank of the canal where I worked so I could dig up the hop from its plant and give it to him. I was liked by the "cons" and knew he would go with me personally, so my friends could see him triumphing over me. At the canal, instead of giving him hop I intended to throw my arms around him and drag him to the bottom, where we would both "cease from troubling."

The fourth morning Cochrane said: "You're a damn fool; better give up your hop. You can't finish out the day." I waited for him to put me in. He held up the "bag" in front of me. I was sitting on the floor. "Get up," he said. I didn't; I couldn't: I was too weak. With a gesture of disgust he threw the jacket out the door into the corridor. Motioning to a couple of trusty prisoners, he said: "Take him away." They helped me to my cell and into my bunk. I lay there half dead, but victorious. My cellmate came at noon and slipped me a jolt of hop. I took it and felt better. He had not even thrown it away as I asked. "I knew you wouldn't squawk," he said, "so I held on to it."

My three months passed quickly enough and I was released, still feeling the effects of the jacket. When I got out I held up my hand and swore I would never make another friend or do another decent thing. I borrowed a gun and got money. I returned to Folsom by stealth and flooded the place with hop. I went about the country for months with but one thing in my mind, a sort of vicious hatred of everybody and everything. As much as possible I shunned even my own kind – thieves.

Then back to San Francisco again where I fell into a stool-pigeon trap. Captain "Steve" Bunner, who now chases policemen, was then a very plain, plainclothes "dick," chasing burglars and stick-ups. He arrested me. He says I tried to shoot him but that he bears me no malice. I say he got me a twenty-five year sentence, and I bear him no malice; and today, while we are not exactly bosom friends, we certainly are not enemies. I had no money to take an appeal from this stiff sentence, but an attorney came and volunteered his services, saying "I was in the district attorney's office when you were sent to Folsom and I know you got jobbed. I'll take your case for nothing."

While waiting on appeal the great earthquake and fire occurred. All the records in my case were destroyed. I could not be sent to prison, and the attorney could not get me out, so I became a permanent fixture in the county jail.

The old Broadway county jail was a stout structure and resisted the quake, but was fire-swept and abandoned. When the fire threatened, all prisoners were removed to Alcatraz Island and later to the branch jail at Ingleside. I was there over six years and the things that happened there during that time would fill a book.

During the graft prosecution that followed the fire, Ingleside housed the mayor, the political boss of San Francisco, and many of the supervisors. A looting banker was there, many strikebreakers indicted for the murder of union men during the car strike, and soldiers for wantonly shooting down citizens while the city burned. Jack Johnson, the colored heavyweight champion, was with us for thirty days for speeding.

Money was plentiful in the jail. The grocer came every day and we all got enough to eat. The political boss bought many books and founded a library. He also got a big phonograph that was kept going all day and far into the night. I was "appointed" jail librarian, and at once catalogued the books and installed them in an empty cell.

The jail was a cross between a political headquarters and an industrial plant. The political prisoners did politics, and the prisoners whose records were burned in the fire turned to industry.

We got contracts to address envelopes and sublet the work to others. We sewed beads on "genuine" Indian moccasins for a concern downtown. Best of all, we bought cheap jewelry from mail-order houses and sold it at a profit to visitors, giving them to understand that it was stolen stuff we had smuggled in with us.

One by one, those whose records were destroyed by the fire made application to have them restored in order to perfect their appeals. In the reconstruction of those records they lost their valuable points on appeal and one by one they were turned down by the higher court. I made no move, but decided to stay in the jail rather than go back to Folsom, although conditions there had been greatly improved by Warden Yell, who soon put Captain Murphy out and won the confidence of the convicts by treating them on the square.

At last a visiting grand-jury committee reported to the district attorney that there was a prisoner at Ingleside whose case had been pending more than six years, and recommended that something be done with it. He at once put me on the docket for restoration of records.

My attorney had retired and with money I had saved from work and speculations in jail I got a new lawyer. I had all the criminal lawyers in San Francisco doped out like race horses by this time, and my choice was

Sam Newburgh. I had seen him beat some of the toughest cases that ever went to trial. Not only that, I had seen him go down in his pocket and give clients money after he got them out. He never weakened, never lay down, or ran out on a man – money or no money.

Newburgh at once threw down a most formidable barrage of objections and technicalities. The prosecution got busy and, as usual, the defendant was lost sight of in the smoke of battle. I had little hope of actually beating the case; the best I could expect was a new trial and maybe a sentence I could do instead of one that would do me.

But while my affairs were at this stage a new hope appeared. I had made a few new outside friends by this time. One of them especially, a fine, noble woman, who was interested in helping us all, concerned herself to do what she could for me.

About this time Fremont Older, now editor of *The Call*, had helped the late Donald Lowrie, whose writings did for American prisons what John Howard's did for those of England.

This woman, who was one of Mr. Older's friends, wrote him and said:

"By way of thanking you for helping Lowrie I am going to give you another man to assist. He is John Black, at the Ingleside jail. I wish you would see him."

He called at the jail soon, but instead of having me out to the office he came down to my cell, squeezed his bulk through the doorway, and sat down on the edge of my bunk. Waving the guard away, he produced cigars, helped me to a light, and asked, in a voice that rang to me like a twenty-dollar piece, what he could do for me. For once all my mistrust, suspicion, and hatred vanished.

I said: "Mr. Older, I'm afraid you will waste a lot of valuable time trying to do anything for me. I have twenty-five years. I'm guilty. I'm plastered over with prior convictions. The police hate me, the jailers dislike me because I tried to escape, and the trial judge is sore because I've done everything possible to obstruct the judgment."

I told him I was a hop fiend, that I had used it for ten years, and was still using it. I told him I was tired of stealing and tired of living. I told him there was but one thing I could say for myself. I had never broken my word either to a thief or a policeman. I told him if he did help me out I would give him my word to quit stealing. He went away, saying: "This looks pretty tough, but I will try."

He at once saw Judge Dunne, who sentenced me, and suggested probation on the ground of my long confinement and dangerous physical condition.

Mr. Older was the powerful editor of a newspaper and a long-time friend of the judge. He was stared at as if he had gone mad, and his suggestion met with a cold, flat, final turndown. He sent word to me that the judge was adamant and nothing could be done. I saw my case was tough indeed when he couldn't help me, and began planning a getaway.

I will not say there is honor among thieves. But I maintain that the thieves I knew had something that served as a good substitute for honor. I thought over all my thief friends and at last chose one and sent for him. He got me saws, and I cut bars in my door.

On a propitious night he cut the window bars. I was too weak to pull myself up to the window, and he had to reach in, lift me bodily, and drop me on the ground outside.

Strange as it may sound, the fresh, cool night air had the same effect on me that the foul air of a sewer would have on a healthy, normal human. It overcame me. I was not able to walk at first, and my rescuer had to support me on our way to the car line.

Before daylight and before the escape was discovered I was safely planted in a room in Oakland, where I stayed and was nursed back to life, fed and protected by my friend.

After waiting for a couple of weeks for the hue and cry to subside, he stowed me away in a sleeper one night at Richmond on a northbound train with a ticket to Vancouver, B. C.

County constables and town whittlers beat up the jungles, searched box cars and brakebeams; city dicks explored the hop joints and hangouts for me and the reward offered, but I traveled safely as a first-class passenger on a first-class train.

No police officer who knows his business would think of looking in a Pullman sleeper or diner for a fugitive hop fiend yegg with a twenty-five-year sentence hanging on him.

Arriving safely at Vancouver, I took stock and found myself sick, weighing one hundred and ten pounds, with a ferocious hop habit, about ten dollars, and a big pistol – the gatherings of forty years.

Then came a foggy night. Necessity and Opportunity met, and I went away with a bundle of bank notes and some certified checks. The checks went into the first mail box as an apology from Necessity to Opportunity.

Then began the toughest battle of my life. Opium, the Judas of drugs, that kisses and betrays, had a good grip on me, and I prepared to break it. The last words of my rescuer when he put me in the train rang in my ears:

"Good-by and good luck, Blacky. And you'd better lay away from that hop or it'll make a bum of you.

TWENTY-FOUR

I HAD money enough to last some little time, long enough to get my strength back, perhaps. I paid the landlady a month's rent and told her I was a sick man and would be in my room all the time and not to disturb me.

In this way I hoped to account for never stirring out of doors, which I did not dare do. I certainly was a sick man, and looked it.

This landlady was very good-hearted, and, sympathizing with my illness, she did not leave me alone two hours in succession. She sent a Chinese boy every hour or two to see how I felt, and in the morning she would send in coffee and toast and come in herself to inquire how I was.

After the boy had made the bed in the morning, she must come in to see if he had turned the mattress and shaken up the pillows for me. She was so busy helping me out that she nearly landed me back in jail.

I came back to my room from the bathroom one morning, and there she stood staring at a gun I had been keeping under the mattress. She had insisted on turning the mattress herself and found it. She was standing there staring at it like she would at a rattlesnake, and asked me what I was doing with that "awful thing."

I sat down and said to her: "Mrs. Alexander, I bought that pistol to kill myself with in case I get physically disabled. You see, I'm a sick man. I told you I was a sick man, and I have a suspicion I am a consumptive. I don't want to go to doctors and I'm going to let this thing run its course, but if I find I am down and out and done for I'm going to shoot myself. That's what I have it for."

She was all upset with sympathy. She said: "You're no consumptive. You are only run down. You'll be all right in a few months, with good food and care. Let me keep this thing. I'll take it and keep it. Don't get downhearted, you'll be all right."

Of course I had to let her take it. That night I went out and bought another one. I also bought a bag and a few clothes, and I was careful after that to lock the new pistol up in the bag when she was around.

So I settled down to fight it out with my opium habit, at the same time keeping on the watch all the time for the police.

I had been using opium steadily for ten years. For ten years I had never gone to sleep without taking it. I owed to it all the sleep, all the rest and forgetfulness and contentment I had had in that time.

Now I made up my mind to quit. Right away I found I had to pay back every second of sleep, every quiet, restful moment I had got from the opium in the whole ten years.

I was taking about five grains a day. I began to taper down slowly. I cut off a grain a week at the start, then for a couple of months I took only three grains a day.

It would have been a good deal harder to quit if I hadn't had that fear of the jail always before me. That took my mind off the opium. The worst hold the drug gets on a man is the mental hold. It becomes a mental habit. A man has to keep a hard grip on his mind; he has to want to quit, first, and keep wanting to quit all the time, then he can do it.

I could stick the daytime out. I found something to do; I read, or ate, or walked around the room. I did not dare go out in the daytime, for fear I would be recognized by the police or by some stool pigeon. This worry was always on my mind, and in a way it helped, because while I was thinking of that I was not thinking about the opium.

It was the small, still hours of the night that got me. I had to get some sleep and strength for the next day. Every particle of opium I cut off my daily dose cut off just that much sleep. For years in the jail I had slept away all the time I could; I had slept ten or twelve or fourteen hours a day. Now I had to pay back all that sleep I had stolen from myself.

I put in twenty-three hours a day waiting for the twenty-fourth, when I could take my little jolt of hop. Every day when the hour arrived I was tempted to take one more good jolt, so that I could have a decent night's sleep and forget everything for a few hours.

But the last words of my friend who had rescued me were always in my ears. "Lay away from that stuff. It will make a bum of you."

Hundreds of times it was just that memory that tipped the balance, and I would take only what I had allowed myself, no more. I believe now I quit because he said that to me. I felt that if I could not do that much, and it was the only thing he ever asked me to do, I wasn't worthy of the friendship of such a man as he had shown himself to be.

Then I would go to bed and try to sleep. After several hours I would get up and go out for a walk, to get some exercise. I would walk as fast as I could for three or four hours in the darkness, always keeping watch for a policeman or for any one who knew me.

I would walk until I was tired out, because I was still pretty weak, and it did not take much to tire me. Then I would hope to sleep a little.

But in the long, still hours my nerves demanded opium. And I resisted and fought it out till my strength got down to the vanishing point.

Then I would get up and drench myself with whisky and wash it down with absinthe. My room looked like a cross between a drug store and a distillery. I had bottles of tonics, invalid's port wine, whisky and absinthe.

I would take a drink out of every bottle in the room and fall down on the bed or on the floor in a stupor and sleep for a few hours.

In this manner I stuck it out. I took a small portion of hop each evening, reducing it daily according to the system I planned. Finally I got to the stage where I could skip one day's portion and get two hours' natural sleep.

Then I tried skipping two days and got by with it, but on the third day I was tied in a knot with cramps and aches and nothing but hop would put me on my feet.

All this time Mrs. Alexander, my kindly landlady, was urging me to go out in the sunshine during the day. She said it would do me good to get more air, and she could see no reason why I wouldn't do it.

So at last I went out one afternoon.

I went to a little park where it was quiet and lay on the grass. It was so good to touch and smell the grass again that I couldn't get enough of it. It seemed to me that grass was the most beautiful thing in the world. I felt as though I could eat it.

I lay there in the sunshine and ran my hands through it and pulled a blade or two and chewed it. I had not been in the sunshine nor been able to touch anything green and growing for over six years. I wouldn't have spoiled that lawn, put a cigarette stub or an orange peel on it for anything in the world.

After that I went out three or four afternoons a week and lay on that grass in the park. I could feel that I was getting stronger, I could eat with good appetite, and every night I decreased the opium according to my schedule. I finally got the dose down to an eighth of a grain.

Even that amount, even the smallest particle that I could get on the end of a toothpick, would make the difference between sleeping all night or not.

I don't believe in those radical cures. It stands to reason you can't cure in three days a habit that it took you five or ten years to build up. I think any man can cure himself. He must first be cured mentally, he must want to be cured. If he doesn't want to be cured, all the treatments in the world aren't going to do it. You can lock men in prisons and deprive them of hop, and they will come right back and get it again because they don't want to be cured. But the man who wants to quit can.

It took me six months to get the dose down to nothing. Even then for months more the thing might jump out at me at any minute, like a wild beast and tear me to pieces. I would go half crazy for the time, I would be mad to get hold of some hop. But that would last only a few hours, and every time I got through it safe I knew it would be easier next time.

Every minute I was out of the house in the daytime I kept watching for people who knew me. A good many men had been through Ingleside jail in the six years I was there and Vancouver was full of them. None of them ever saw me, because I saw them first. I tried to see every man in the block ahead of me the minute I stepped on the curb.

Cured of the habit now, I went back "on the road," determined to stay in Canada, keep away from big cities and wise coppers, and try to do the twenty-five year sentence outside instead of at Folsom. I traveled east over the Canadian Pacific Railway to the booming province of Alberta. One morning after an all-night ride, I crawled out of a box car in the town of Strathcona, tired, hungry, and dirty. I was not in distress for money, and looked around for a quiet place where I could lay off for a week and rest up. After a breakfast, a bath, and a shave, I walked around a while and located a quiet, respectable-looking place with a "board and rooms" sign. It looked to be a half-private, out-of-the-way place so I went in.

A Chinese boy was dusting up in the lounging room, and I asked him for the "boss man."' He disappeared out in the hall. In a few minutes I heard a heavy step and turned around to face Salt Chunk Mary, the friend of the bums and yeggs at Pocatello. More than fifteen years had passed since she disappeared, yet I knew her instantly. The same, level "right now" look from her cold blue eyes the same severe parting of her brick-red hair the same careful, clean, starched house dress, and the same few short, sharp, meaningful words told me it was she who had broken open the town jail and set me free when no man would turn a hand.

"Oh, Mary!" I cried, and my hand went out to her. I said something about Pocatello and the night I saw her last, and about Foot-'n'-a-half George, long dead, but she stopped me cold. Looking me straight in the eye, she said in a tone of finality that left no chance of an answer:

"You are mistaken; you don't know me. My name's not Mary, and I was never in Pocatello in my life."

When Mary said no she meant it. I went out and away envying that courageous woman who had the strength to leave Pocatello and her life there, and bury herself in a far corner of the North.

After much thought I decided that Salt Chunk Mary had washed her hands of the old life and old associates and was trying to spend her remaining days in peace. I saw her no more, and went my solitary way, pistoling people away from their money – the highwayman's way.

A distinguished chief of police in one of our big cities gave this advice to the public:

"If a holdup man stops you, grab him and yell at the top of your voice."

That was the advice of a policeman; more, the advice of a policeman who was never stuck up. I know something about the stick-up game. I've been stuck up myself. This is the first time I've told about it, and it will be the last. I'm not advising any reader what to do in case of a stick-up. I'm only telling what I did.

As I was walking home one mild midnight up Haight Street, a young man came down the street toward me. He was whistling a little tune, his hat was on the back of his head, and he walked briskly, swinging his arms.

"Ah, ha," thinks I, "here's a young fellow that's just left his girl at her door. She gave him a kiss, and he's happy. He's hurrying home now, and – " my reflections ended. About ten feet away from me his arms swung together and his right hand pulled a long gun out of his left sleeve.

"The real thing," I said to myself, stopping.

"Put up your hands."

I did.

"Turn your face to that fence."

I did.

He stepped up behind me and put something hard against my spine.

"All right, brother," I said meekly. "It's all yours. It's in my left-hand pants pocket."

He found it.

"I've got a watch, brother, that's worth a lot to me; I wish you'd let me keep it. It would bring you four dollars, but it might bring you forty years."

"Huh!" he grunted. He felt for the watch, took it out of its pocket, "hefted" it in his hand, and put it back. "You keep your face to that fence till I get out of the block or I'll 'spray' you with this automatic."

I did.

That's the way I deal with a stick-up man.

There is no way I know of to protect yourself from the starving moron who pounces on you out of a dark doorway, knocks you on the head with a "blunt instrument," and goes through your pockets after you are on the sidewalk. That kind of "work" is unprofessional, unnatural, and disgusting, and does not concern me. The psychiatrist might explain and classify it; I cannot.

After circulating around with my pistol for a few months I was arrested and, almost by chance, identified as a fugitive from California justice. In short order I was brought back to San Francisco.

The first man that came to see me in the city prison was Sam Newburgh, the attorney who had my case when I escaped from the jail.

Two days before I had escaped, the last fifty-dollar payment on his fee had come due. At that time I was almost sure I would escape and get away without any trouble, and I was tempted to defer this payment and put him off until later, because I saw I would have use for the fifty dollars myself.

But when he came out to the jail I paid it to him.

He remembered this, and when I was brought back he was the first man there to see me. To my surprise and delight he told me that my legal status was just about the same as when I had left. My appeal was still pending.

I had some thoughts that Mr. Older might feel that I had abused his confidence in leaving the jail, when he was trying to do something for me. But he knew at the time that I was turned down by everyone and didn't have a chance of getting my liberty, so I hoped he would understand.

He came immediately to see me, and I explained this to him. I said I never would have made a move of that kind if there had been a chance; that I had to do it in order to do myself justice. I said I knew I would not live another two years in that jail; they had all admitted they could do nothing for me, and I had thought I had a right to do as I did.

He said, "I think you did the only thing. It was the only way out for you. I would probably have done the same thing myself."

He remarked that I was looking stronger and healthier. I had gained about thirty pounds in weight. Mr. Older could see in a minute that I had quit the opium. He spoke of it at once.

He said he would see if something could be done for me. He thought it might be possible that the district attorney's office on account of all the complications in the case, would agree to ask for an amended sentence, a sentence of only a year or two, if I would stop fighting and plead guilty.

I said: "If I had thought such a thing possible, Mr. Older, I'd have paid my way back here and given myself up!"

I had little hope that any such thing would be done. I had never encountered anything like it. The next day Maxwell McNutt of the district attorney's office came in to talk to me.

He spoke about my escape, and I told him the reasons for it as I had told the others. I explained that I would not have had to do it if my friends had been able to do something for me in the way of a lighter sentence.

He said that so far as the district attorney was concerned, he thought I had served almost enough time. I was astounded when I heard this. In all my experience I had never encountered a district attorney's office that thought any criminal had served enough time.

This was a revelation to me in the ways of courts and police. It was the first time I ever got any better than the worst of it. I saw myself relieved of that burden of a twenty-five-year sentence. I saw myself coming out in a couple of years with the slate wiped clean.

I realized that Judge Dunne would be taking a chance in giving me a sentence that amounted practically to nothing. He had his place on the bench and his reputation with his fellow judges and the people to consider. If I came out of prison and got into trouble immediately after, I would be double-crossing him.

I saw it was up to me to square myself and go to work when I came out.

After some delay the district attorney and the trial judge agreed to amend the judgment, and a day was set for me to go into court. Mr. Older asked me to make a statement, hoping there might be something in my experience that would throw some light on the criminal problem that might help people to help criminals.

When I got into court I decided not to make this statement until after I was sentenced, because I didn't want any one to feel that what I said was said for selfish reasons, and if I said it before I was sentenced it might appear that I was talking for leniency.

I decided I had got all the leniency that was coming to me, and very much more than I ever expected.

The judge sentenced me to one year. That was better than I had hoped for. The district attorney had suggested it probably would not be more than two years, but here the judge had cut even that in two.

As near as I can recall them, my words were as follows:

"I would like to make a statement before it is too late. I feel that this will be my last appearance in any court as a defendant, and I want to make this statement in the hope that there may be something in my experience that will prove valuable to some one, perhaps some one in authority who has to do with the instruction and correction of offenders, particularly of the younger ones.

"I would not make this statement if I ever expected to appear in court again as a defendant. As criminal as it is, I will consider it as nothing if it prove of value to any one, if my failure would cause some young man to hesitate before it is too late, before he finds himself charged with crime.

"My prison experiences began with a sentence of two years and thirty lashes in a Canadian prison. I could not see that I deserved this flogging, and it seemed when I got it that all the cruelty in the world was visited on me – all the brutality, all the violence. There was a lesson in cruelty I have never forgotten. Fortunately, I had a disposition that hardened with the flogging instead of breaking under it.

"I proved an incorrigible prisoner while there. I broke the rules many, many times in a small way – nothing violent, nothing desperate, but I would talk, laugh, whistle and sing, and that outraged the silence of the system then in vogue.

"I was punished repeatedly on bread and water, the dark cell. The warden was a hard, stern man. His motto was – 'break them first and make them after.'

"Then came the day for the second installment of my flogging and my discharge from prison. I went out with the skin on my back blistered and broken and my mind bent on revenge. I went out of there with a hatred for law and order, society and justice, discipline and restraint, and everything that was orderly and systematic. I had a hatred for courts, jailers, prison keepers, and wardens. I hated policemen, prosecutors, judges and jurors.

"If I had reasoned right, I might have made a better start than I did. But I had no experience to guide me. I planned for revenge and I turned on society to get it, because society furnishes the judges, the jurors, the policemen, the prosecutors. Before I got fairly started on my career of revenge I was back in prison.

"When I went back I learned more brutality and violence. I knew the bread-and-water punishment, the dark cell, the straitjacket and the water cure. I thought violent thoughts, I planned violent plans, and I executed those plans as best I could as soon as I got outside. I suppose a man's actions are the creatures of his thought, and his thoughts are naturally the products of his environment and the conditions under which he is forced to live.

"If you put a boy in prison at the age I was, as prisons were then, he will become a criminal as sure as the day follows the night or the night follows the day. I imagine those conditions were responsible for many criminals of my age or thereabouts, who were considered incorrigible. I won't say confirmed, because I believe there is no such thing as a confirmed criminal. I have seen many miraculous reformations. One man may be reformed through a woman, a woman's plea, a mother's love. Others might be reformed through the assistance and kindness of friends. But still another might be reformed by an act of kindness from some unexpected source. I believe that one who has been brutalized can be turned right by an act of kindness and be regenerated. It looks reasonable.

"When I stood up in this court to be sentenced for twenty-five years, I was a criminal, as I have described. I had learned the lesson of violence in prison, and I believed that I lived in a world of violence, had to use violence, and use it first. I had no more thought of right or wrong than a wolf that prowls the prairie. I hunted because I was hunted myself, and I showed no consideration for anybody or anything because I knew I would receive none.

"I was a habitual criminal. I had formed the criminal habit. Habit is the strongest thing in life, and criminals such as I have described obey the impulse to commit a crime almost subconsciously. So far as the right or wrong is concerned, he gives it no more thought than you would when you walk down the street and open the gate to enter your front door. It is a habit with you.

"The twenty-five-year sentence I received made no impression on me whatever. I expected it, and had expected it for years. It was simply an incident, an obstacle another delay – a violent one, to be sure; but I had dealt the game of violence, and when forced to play at it I am not the one to complain.

"So I went back to the county jail and my lawyer went back to his law. Then came the fire that destroyed the records of my conviction and sentence, and put me in the perpetual criminal class at the county jail. I became more permanent than the sheriff. I saw them come and go, and after years of comparative peace and quiet and fair treatment in the county jail I began to change my views and think different thoughts, and I looked forward to a different sort of life.

"A few friends rallied around and began to plan ways and means to help me. They investigated, found it impossible, and told me.

"The future looked dark, and I was in despair. The day of my deliverance seemed to be receding instead of advancing. I planned to get my liberty in another way, and I did get it, but I got it under such circumstances as to make it impossible for me to lead the life I had planned.

"It was impossible for me to mix with men in the daytime. I was a fugitive. I was hunted again. I had to seek the back streets on the darkest nights.

"In a few months I found myself back in jail in San Francisco. Then something occurred that surprised me more than I can tell. I was told that there was a possibility of my getting credit for the time that I had served in the county jail, that I might get a sentence I would see the end of, instead of one that would see the end of me, and that it might be possible for me to get out and lead a different kind of life.

"This made a greater impression upon me than the twenty-five-year sentence, this offer of help from such a surprising source. At first I thought I was getting the double-cross, but I investigated and found it was true, and what little doubts I had were completely shattered. I did not admit the possibility of any kindness from judges, district attorneys, prosecutors, or anybody who represents the people.

"I now saw that I was wrong, and that it was up to me to build new rules to regulate my conduct in the future, that I would have to formulate a philosophy that would admit the possibility of kindness from such sources; from people who desired to help me if I would help myself.

"I have promised myself, and I promise the court, that when I finish this sentence I shall look for the best instead of the worst, that I shall look for kindness instead of cruelty, and that I shall look for the good instead of the bad, and when I find them I shall return them with interest.

"I am confident when I promise the court this that I will not fail. I imagine I have enough character left as a foundation on which to build a reformed life. If I had no character, no will power, no determination I would have been broken long ago by the years of imprisonment and punishment and I would have been useless and harmless and helpless, a force for neither good nor bad."

Judge Dunne asked me if I had any choice of prisons, and I said I preferred San Quentin because I had already been in every other prison in the state, and I would like to go over there and see what that place was like.

I left the courtroom with that one-year sentence feeling as if I had received a Christmas gift; it was the twenty-fourth of December.

At San Quentin I had a hard time to convince friends that my sentence was cut to one year. The atmosphere there surprised me. There was none of that smoldering hatred of officers ; no hopeless, despairing prisoners; no opium and no scheming to get it in. Everybody was looking forward to parole. There was no brutal punishment. A man's credits were safe. All those changes worked for the best. Prisoners had a chance to shorten their time by good conduct, and their conduct was good.

One of the first "cons" to reach me was my friend, Soldier Johnnie, doing a short sentence.

I hadn't seen him since leaving the Canadian prison, where I got the dark cell for speaking to him. We were comparing notes for a week. It was from him I learned that the Sanctimonious Kid had escaped from Canon City before finishing his fifteen years and that he had gone to Australia, where he was hanged for killing a police constable. In turn, I told him of Foot-'n'-a-half George's death, and of Mary's disappearance into the Far North.

Johnnie finished his time first, and went back to the road, where he probably will live out his life and die unwept, unhonored, and unhung.

I put in my sentence without any trouble and came out in ten months. That was thirteen years ago.

On the boat for San Francisco I saw the bar. At once I felt that I needed a jolt of booze. I got it.

Then I saw the lunch counter. I at once felt the need of a cup of real coffee. I got that. After that, I sat down on a bench and thought it over.

Here I was, physically fit and serviceably sound, walking up to that bar and buying a drink of whisky I didn't need just because I happened to see the bar, and then a cup of coffee just because I saw the coffee urn.

I decided I would have to beware of the power of suggestion. The bar had suggested whisky and the lunch counter coffee, and I fell for them both.

Anyway, I made up my mind that I would close my eyes when I got to the ferry building for fear I might see a sack of registered mail lying around loose. It would suggest days of ease and nights of pleasure, and I might fall for that.

I got through the ferry building and walked up Market Street, as they all do. In time I found myself in Mr. Older's anteroom. There were several men waiting to see him. I looked them over and said to myself, "There's preachers, politicians, and pickpockets in that bunch. I'll be lucky if I don't have to wait an hour."

The young lady took my name and I was the first one in. Mr. Older was there with a suggestion, too; luncheon at the Palace Hotel.

I'm not strong for eating in swell places, but I do like quick contrasts. I had my breakfast in San Quentin, so why not lunch at the Palace?

We had a good meal. While we were eating, Mr. Older suggested that I come down to his ranch for a few days, till I got my bearings again in the outside world and was ready to begin work.

I was glad to do this. It helped get me over the hardest part of the life of the ex-prisoner who intends to go square; the first few weeks out of prison. I went down that night for a week and stayed six months.

I would have been content to stay there always. I was able to do enough on the ranch to pay for my board and shelter, and I liked it. But it was necessary after a while for me to come back to San Francisco and go to work. My room was wanted on the ranch by other men who needed it worse than I did.

Eddie Graney needs no introduction here. I only hope this story has as many readers as he has friends. While he is known and respected for his square decisions as a referee of big fights, I think his fame rests chiefly on the fact that while he has the finest billiard rooms west of – oh, well, west of anywhere – he has not yet learned how to play billiards.

Graney gave me my first job – cashier in his pool room – handling his money. After a few months a better job appeared. With a letter of introduction I saw Mr. B. F. Schlesinger of the Emporium.

"Where did you work last?" he asked.

"At Eddie Graney's."

"And before that ?"

"At San Quentin, in the jute mill."

He knew all about me and put me to work as salesman in the book department. I knew something about books – I had been librarian at the county jail. I was honest – hadn't stolen any of Graney's money. I felt perfectly at ease among the books, and made good. Book selling grew dull later, and I was slated for a transfer to another department. At the manager's office I was told that the only vacancy was on the ribbon counter. I looked in a mirror on the wall and saw a face in it that didn't seem to belong behind the ribbon counter.

I said "Mr. Schlesinger, this is a great life if you know when to weaken. I think this is where I'll weaken."

At lunch time I saw Mr. Older and told him about it.
Fortunately, there was a vacancy at the Bulletin in the circulation department just then and I got the job. I left the Emporium with the best wishes and good will of everybody I met there. When Mr. Older became editor of *The Call* he found a place there for me as librarian; I still have that job.

In thirteen years I have learned to work – some day I may learn to like it. Yet it is so easy and simple and safe and secure that I now wonder how any man coming out of prison could think of doing anything else. The pity of it is that so many ex-prisoners who do think of trying to work can't get it. I take no credit whatever for going to work. I could have done that years before.

I quit stealing and learned working because I was in a hole where I could not do otherwise. I was in hock to friends who saved me from a heavy sentence, provided me with work, and expected only that I stay out of jail. That's not asking much of a man – to keep out of jail. The judge who cut my sentence took a greater chance than I ever did. If I had gone back "sticking up" people, the judge's critics could have said that he, and he alone, made it possible – and that's precisely why I quit.

If I had stolen Graney's, the Emporium's, or the Bulletin's money, they could have said that Older made it possible, and had I been tempted to steal that thought would have stopped me. I cannot say I quit stealing because I knew it was wrong. I quit because there was no other way for me to discharge the obligations I had accepted. Whatever measure of reformation I have won is directly due to Fremont Older and Judge Dunne of the Superior Court. They took a chance on me, a long chance, and it will be a long time before they regret it. Fremont Older has been a rock in a weary land to me, and Judge Dunne has been a shelter in the time of storm.

It has been easy for me. The noble woman who found me rotting in jail physically and mentally is still my friend, I am proud to say. The kindly Christian couple who gave me a home with them in San Francisco and treated me as a son are still my friends. Friends everywhere, to help and advise and encourage. Even friends from the road and the jungles drop into my office and shake hands and say: "More power to you, old-timer. You're sure makin' good. I'm goin' to try it myself some day."

My feuds with the police are dead and buried. No copper has bothered me or obstructed me. Many of them have offered in good faith to help me. And so I say it has been easy for me to go on the square. I speak only of my own experience; others may not have been so fortunate in finding friends.

I wish I could sift out a few grains of wisdom from my life that would help people to help prisoners, and help prisoners to help themselves, but I can't find them. I don't know. All I can say with certainty is that kindness begets kindness, and cruelty begets cruelty. You can make your choice and reap as you sow.

I am not worrying about prisons. If they improve as much in the coming twenty years as they have in the last twenty, they will have to be called something else. While the number of convicts is increasing, the percentage of second and third timers, habitual criminals, is decreasing. That's hopeful, and it's because of more humane treatment, more liberal parole laws, and the extension of road building and other work, that fits a prisoner for the outside, gives him the work habit.

Highway building by convicts is the sanest and most constructive step I have seen. Instead of appropriating money to build a third prison in California, the same money might be expended in road-building materials, and one of our two prisons emptied into the road camps, where the prisoner could be self-supporting and not a dead weight on the taxpayer while in prison, and worse after he gets out.

A certain number of prisoners, say ten per cent, always have and always will abuse probation and parole. The ninety per cent of prisoners who respect probation and parole more than justify the laws under which they are released. Probation to boys and young men should be extended. Paroles to first-time convicts should be more liberal. Paroles to second-timers might well be closely scrutinized, and for third-timers-if the Prison Board "throws the key away on them" they will die off and settle their own problem. I am in the third or fourth-timer class myself, and if I got back into prison and the board sentenced me to life with the privilege of applying for parole after fifteen years, I wouldn't have to look very far for the person responsible for it.

As I see it, the criminals of this generation should cause no concern. They will soon be out of the way. The problem wouldn't be solved by shooting them all at sunrise, or by releasing them all at sunrise. Something might be done for the generation that is coming up. It seems to me there's the place to start – but what to do, I don't know.

I am sure of but one thing – I failed as a thief, and at that I am luckier than most of them. I quit with my health and liberty. What price larceny, burglary, and robbery? Half my thirty years in the underworld was spent in prison. Say I handled $50,000 in the fifteen years I was outside; that's about nine dollars a day. How much of that went to lawyers, fixers, bondsmen, and other places? Then count in the years in prison – suffering, hardship, privation. This was years ago when there was much less police protection.

"What chance have you now?" I would ask any young man, "with shotgun squads, strong-arm squads, and crime crushers cruising the highways and byways; with the deadly fingerprinting, central identification bureau, and telephotoing of pictures; and soon every police station broadcasting ahead of you your description and record? Then consider the accidents and snitches – what chance have you? Figure it out yourself. I can't."

Had I spent that thirty years at any useful occupation and worked as hard at it and thought and planned and brought such ingenuity and concentration to bear on it, I would be independent to-day. I would have a home, a family perhaps, and a respected position in my community. I have none of those, but I have a job, I have two suits of clothes, I have two furnished rooms in a flat. I have as many friends as I can be loyal to. I am fifty years old, and so healthy that when I hear my friends holding forth about their ailments I feel ashamed of myself. I would not turn time backward and be young again, neither do I wish to reach the century mark and possible senility.

I have no money, no wife, no auto. I have no dog. I have neither a radio set nor a rubber plant – I have no troubles.

I borrow money from my friends in a pinch, ride in their machines, listen to their radios, make friends with their dogs, admire their flowers, and praise their wives' cooking.

If I could wish for anything else it would be a little more moderation, a little more tolerance, and a little more of the trustful innocence of that boy who learned his prayers at the knee of the gentle, kindly old priest in the Sisters' Convent School.

AFTERWORD

WHEN *You Can't Win* first appeared in serialized form in the *San Francisco Call* it was called *Breaking the Shackles.* A better title maybe, unless you take *You Can't Win* in a larger sense – not as you can't win at the crime game, but as the defiant creed of rebels and outcasts everywhere. You can't win because the game is rigged and it stinks anyway: because winning in this setup means embracing hypocrisy, corruption and selling your soul. You can't win but you've got to take it like Jack says, "with a smile."

The beauty of Jack's book lies in the way it mixes worldliness and cynicism with hard-won compassion and generosity. What Jack offers are eternal verities like mercy, tolerance, and kindness – notions which have been tamed and cheapened, especially in this richly hypocritical era of "compassionate conservatism." But when they turn up at the end of a long hard twisted path like the one Jack took, their true – and subversive – meaning gets restored. His is also the blackly humorous voice of an outsider – of someone who has grasped the essential rottenness of "the system[1]" and will not be taken in. It's this combination that gives this bad pilgrims progress its peculiar power. I think this is why a lot of people seem to have something like a conversion experience when they read it. Jack got it just right.

So what more can be said about Black that's not in the book? In a letter to Lincoln Steffens he later accused himself of "dealing off the bottom of the deck" in *You Can't Win.* Yet in reading the book it seems clear that Black was forthright in all the ways that count – there's an aura of trustworthiness to it that surpasses that of any other autobiography I can think of.

He did, however, pass over a couple of things that can be gleaned from other sources. He gives one hint when he writes about his experience at Folsom Prison and how after his release he "went about the country for months with but one thing on my mind, a sort of vicious hatred of everybody and everything." In the months before the 1906 earthquake Black was apparently a one-man San Francisco reign of terror until he was caught for shooting a man in a botched holdup in Golden Gate Park and got his 25 year sentence. The book also passes lightly over his six years in the Ingleside jail, telling us only that "the things that happened there during that time would fill a book." He doesn't mention what a good setup he organized for himself there, seasoned wily criminal that he was. He was "king of the opium ring," selling shots of morphine and becoming quite a prosperous bigshot. He was so well connected that when he decided he needed to get out – mostly because he was being devoured by his own morphine habit – arranging his escape was probably not so very difficult.

Glossed over somewhat in *You Can't Win* is the role that Fremont Older played in Black's reform and resurrection. Older was another remarkable guy who deserves to be much better known.[2] Like his friends Lincoln Steffens, Clarence Darrow, Theodore Dreiser and John Dewey, he was an exemplar of a kind of homegrown passionate radicalism that flourished for while in the Progressive era. He used his editorship of the *San Francisco Bulletin* to mount serious and tireless attacks on injustice, privilege and corruption. Older may have been the finest example of the school of journalism that believed the duty of the press was to comfort the afflicted and afflict the comfortable – so unlike the journalism of today devoted to pumping out happy-face corporate sludge and delivering well-heeled readers to their advertisers[3].

Older was most famous for his ferocious years-long battle to bring down Abe Ruef, the "boss" of San Francisco, who ran the town as a giant protection racket, with the entire city government taking payoffs from anyone who wanted to do anything from building a streetcar line to running a gambling joint or bordello. Under Ruef, if an honest cop accidentally got hired he was sent off to a lowly post in the most remote police station. Older eventually triumphed, and Ruef was convicted and sentenced to a long prison term. And then, when Ruef had been shipped off to San Quentin, had his head shaved and been put in convict stripes, Older had a revelation. He realized that it was really the system that encouraged people like Ruef which was corrupt, not the man himself, who was just another smart ambitious fellow out to make a buck. Older scandalized a ladies club by explaining his new attitude:

> What happened to Ruef would not seem to me so cruel if the community had profited by his misery. If his degradation had awakened the people to the true conditions here it might have been worth a human life. But we are still going on in the old way, believing that jails will cure our civic diseases, for which we are all equally responsible. But at least it has been a valuable experience to me, and has done

me a great deal of good, because it has enabled me to discover myself, and to learn that we are all of us guilty, and that we can no longer absolve ourselves by putting men in prison.

It will be a long time I fear, before this view takes possession of the minds of men, but perhaps gradually we will begin to study ourselves more and learn more of the evil that is in us before we can set out after the other fellow. That is the way I feel and hereafter I am going to let the other fellow severely alone, and permit him, if he chooses, to work out his own salvation in his own way... Men and women must want to be good. The feeling must come from within. The legislature can never do it."

Older went to San Quentin and asked for forgiveness from the initially quite skeptical Ruef; they eventually became friends and Ruef's sentence was shortened. This trip to San Quentin awakened in Older an interest in prisoners that eventually led him to Jack Black.

Older was a kind of pessimistic crusading idealist whose operating principle was that everyone was an inextricable mixture of good and bad, that the job was to hunt for and draw out the good. One of his main activities was giving those at the bottom of the heap, the most marginalized and downtrodden people, especially prostitutes and criminals, a hand up. He would find work for them but he'd also give them a voice – by telling their stories in his paper, or even better, by getting them to write their own stories. Here's his first impression of Jack:

Jack Black was only a shadow of a man when I first met him at the Ingleside jail... Only his burning eyes were alive. They flamed out of deep caverns, eager, intelligent, observing, appealing. His hair, hanging over his forehead, was heavily streaked with white; his cheekbones were almost bursting through the tightly stretched skin of his face. Morphine. Ten years of it had wrecked his body.

I had never before met anyone in prison who attracted me mentally. There was real character back of that brilliant mind. His word once given would be kept. Before we had talked ten minutes I would have trusted him with anything I possessed, and, if I could secure his release, he would go straight, I felt certain.

In essence Older set in motion an informal convict self-help society that ultimately involved hundreds of ex-cons. Black, it seems, became crucial to this enterprise, and helped many others climb out of the prison hole. Here's how he explained it in a 1916 letter to William McLaughlin, AKA Brick, then locked up in Folsom prison:

> Mr. Older doesn't claim any miraculous pull or drag, nor does he do any fancy "fixing." When he wants to help anyone, he quotes and points to Lowrie, Buck English, Dorsey, Black ... others too numerous to write about. The ex-cons outside do that .... You will be officially paroled to the State Parole Office but there will be others to look you over who will know more about your comings and goings in a minute than the parole office would know in a month, and if you play the bunk for us you will be amazed at the original and thorough way you will be regulated.

You Can't Win also entirely skips over Jack's career at the *San Francisco Bulletin.*He became something of a bodyguard to Older, who needed one because his paper continued to fearlessly take on the system. He didn't stop at the lower levels of the intricate web of corruption that ran the city and the state; he was willing to go after the magnates and their corporations – in this era the Southern Pacific Railroad – at the top of the pyramid. These people had an impressive arsenal to fight back with, from legislators and media outlets to squads of detectives, and – for the really dirty work – underworld characters. Older narrowly escaped kidnappers and would-be assassins several times. Black went around unarmed – though a tale is told of the time he had to hunt down a man who had threatened to kill Older, stick a gun in his gut and advise him how unwise that would be. Jack's reputation as a tough old con and *his* underworld connections served nicely.

For a brief time Black actually became a crime reporter, and then he was the *Bulletin's* head of circulation when it was involved in a major rivalry with the *San Francisco Call* in 1916 – a circulation war so serious it involved actual street battles between the two papers' "newsboys[4]." In one of these skirmishes, Robert Wall, a *Call* newsboy, shot Black, who was wounded so badly that at first he was not expected to survive. This prompted a remarkable outpouring of eulogies from the many friends he had accumulated in the three years since his final prison stint. When Black was well enough, Wall was brought to his bedside to be identified as the assailant. Jack socked him but didn't say a word. But then, within days, he forgave him. As Jack told the press:

> But for this act I would never have known the full strength of the love my friends have given me. One must be callous indeed to remain insensible to such loyalty and kindness as this. It purged my mind of the last bitter thought. I found I had forgiven my worst enemy – I could forgive even the stool pigeon that indexed me. I don't want anything to happen to Bob Wall. If they prosecute him they will have to do it without my aid. I just want to let it go.

Wall responded by apologizing profusely for his idiocy, and wasn't prosecuted.

After *You Can't Win* came out in 1926 Black seemed to try to get a writing career going for himself. He wrote a play called *Salt Chunk Mary* that was produced in Los Angeles[5]. For a brief time in 1927 MGM was paying him $150 a week to write a prison drama[6]. But more important to him, it seems, was using his small measure of fame to become an ardent spokesman for prison reform. He gave talks all over the country, telling (from his rich personal experience) how harsh prison treatment and capital punishment do nothing to deter criminals; how much better decent treatment, respect, and a serious shot at going straight would work. His message is sadly all too relevant in this lock-'em-up era with its vastly expanded but still thoroughly disastrous prison system.

Jack had become a highly esteemed person. It's almost too easy to find testimonials to what a compelling and impressive character he was – like this one from R.L. Duffus, the Bulletin's main editorial writer:

> Jack was an honest, witty, and communicative man. He also had a fierce sort of pride, which compelled him to mention, some time in any conversation with a stranger, long after he had reformed, that he had once been in prison. I wish I could bring back some of his personality. It was rich and understanding, full of the flavor of earth.

People were impressed by his erudition too, which is less surprising if you know that he had used his prison time to read all the way through the Encyclopedia Britannica three separate times.

The picture of Jack as a literary eminence and upright citizen is too simple though. He had too much of an outsider's sensibility to be seduced into the genteel complacency of the owning classes. He was never comfortable with being a "respectable" citizen. When he was asked by a reporter how he felt about it he said "I don't care for it. Too much hypocrisy. In the underworld you're known for what you are. Besides, by nature I guess I'm a night bird. I like coming out when everybody else has gone to bed. I like cellars." Also, he had to maintain his underworld connections out of necessity, because the code of the "Johnsons" was rigorous. In an article he later explained:

> Many former associates had a right to expect and demand help from me, and of course they did demand it. In the fifteen years that I have been playing Society's game, I have many times had one foot in a jail as the result of trying to reconcile the underworld and upperworld codes...I have been asked to send pistols and explosives and narcotics into jails by men who had a right to demand them because they had done favors for me in the past. Fortunately I had influential friends in the upperworld who understood both codes and helped me to pay my debts in a legitimate way. The man who wanted a pistol was given instead a chance at parole or probation – a chance to make good in the upperworld. Instead of sending opium to the addict who supplied it to me when I was locked up, my friends sent him to a hospital where he could take the cure.
>
> Some of my debts had to be paid in kind, and no one could help me. I owe my life to a thief who risked his life to take me out of jail. He smuggled me saws to open my cell, then came in the night to cut the bars out of the window and lifted me out through the hole when I was so weak from tuberculosis that I could barely walk. He sheltered me and fed me and finally sent me away where I was safe and free to get well. Years afterward, when I had cured myself of the dope habit, served my sentence, and won immunity from the law, and was just beginning to feel a little secure in my respectability, my telephone rang in the small hours of the night. A woman's voice asked if I was "Mr. Black" and said, "I have a message from Eddie and I'm leaving town immediately. Of course you know I can't give it over the phone." I knew a dozen Eddies. I ran them all through my mind. "You don't mean Eddie who took me out of —. "Yes, yes," she interrupted.

"Hurry."

I didn't know what had happened but I realized another debt was due. She gave me an address. Fifteen minutes later I found myself in a shabby, light-housekeeping room with the man who had taken me out of jail a bundle of bloody rags, lying desperately wounded on the dirty carpet. He needed medical attention and money, but more than that, he needed to be shielded from the police. What did I do? What would you have done? Could I turn my back on him and walk away to my secure, respectable position? I couldn't and didn't. He was hidden, nursed back to health, and sent away to safety.

From the late 20's onward the main source of information about Jack's doings is in his letters back to Older. They are full of humility, self mockery, and bemusement. He wrote "This speaking is the softest and easiest racket in the world." His advanced acerbic tendencies never left him either. He wrote things like "Justice is a word that resides in the dictionary. It occasionally makes its escape, but is promptly caught and put back where it belongs." Between pulling down Hollywood money and his fees for talks – he refused to call them lectures except in quotation marks – he wrote that "I am in danger of dying (rich) in disgrace." But these good times didn't last long. By 1929 he was in New York trying to organize a production of *Salt Chunk Mary*. He wrote to Older "I found myself quite well known through *You Can't Win*, and could be going about all the time if I weren't so anti-everything". He sold a couple of articles to Harper's magazine, and wrote to Older after the first one that;

> I was surprised to sell it at all for it's all propaganda against too much law and punishment. I'd have been glad to give the article for nothing because it contains a couple of dirty remarks about New York's Chief of Police and the Baumes law. For *me* to criticize N.Y.'s Police Chief in a high-brow magazine seems dangerously close to success.

This article is so strikingly pertinent to the crime/prison situation today that we've included most of it as an appendix.

Still in New York at the beginning of the 1930's, the play finally opened, though it had been retitled *Jamboree* and it now had a co-author named Bessie Beatty. The *New York Times* critic wrote that there was "enough of this and that in Jamboree to make a good roaring melodrama of the nineties. But Bessie Beatty and Jack Black have just missed putting it in sound theatrical form." It was a flop.

By now the Depression had settled in with full force. Jack was still giving talks on crime and prisons, often under the auspices of The League to Abolish Capital Punishment that Clarence Darrow had started and on the board of which Jack was a member. His letters reported, ominously, that only his lecture fees were "keeping him out the soup kitchens and breadlines." To Older he frequently expressed his desire to get back to California but somehow New York held him. Jack knew that he was welcome anytime at Older's ranch south of San Francisco; he'd spent much time there earlier – in fact it was where he had written *You Can't Win*. He also knew that Older, who was legendary for his generosity and considered Jack to be a great good friend, would have been happy to help him out. His pride, or something else, wouldn't let him ask for charity. Speaking engagements petered out, as did the royalties from *You Can't Win*. "I'm not borrowing money," he reportedly told a friend. "I'm afraid I'll never be able to pay it back."

He had once told his friends that if life got too grim he would tie weights to his feet, row out into New York Harbor and drop overboard. In 1932 this seems to be precisely what he did. Jack vanished. His watch was found in a pawnshop, pledged for eight dollars. This was his dearest possession, a gift from an ex-con that he had helped. For his friends this was definitive proof that he was gone.

— *Bruno Ruhland*

NOTES

[1] The concept of "the system" was in fact concocted just at this time by Jack's friend Lincoln Steffens.

[2] Especially in a town like San Francisco, which prides itself on its history of nonconformists and "characters". In fact, he probably deserves as much credit as anyone for San Francisco being the free-thinking liberal burg that it still is.

[3] For a taste of the one exception we can think of, send one dollar to the Anderson Valley Advertiser 12451 Anderson Valley Way, Boonville CA 95415

[4] This was before Older quit the *Bulletin*, whose owners, always nervous about his crusading style of journalism, became too faint hearted, and moved over to the former bitter rival, the *Call*.

[5] Does anyone know where we can find a copy of it?

[6] We can't find any film credits for him though.

SOURCES

Thanks to Mickey Disend for research. I consulted various issues of the *San Francisco Call* and *San Francisco Bulletin*, *Harper's* magazine June 1929 and February 1930, the Fremont Older papers at the Bancroft Library, Univ. of California at Berkeley and these books:

Fremont Older, **My Own Story**, 1926, Macmillan & Company.
R.L.Duffus, **Tower of Jewels**, 1960, W.W. Norton & Company
Evelyn Wells, **Fremont Older**, 1936, Appleton-Century.

What's Wrong with the Right People?

"THERE'S a lot of law at the end of a rope." That was the gospel of the California Vigilantes when they set out to clean up the crime wave of 'Forty-nine. In the name of law and order they were going to take a short cut, kill a few killers and horse thieves, and make San Francisco safe for business. They were the "right" people of their time, noble gentlemen on a noble mission bent; but like noble gentlemen turned reformers, all down the ages, they got drunk on blood-power. As long as they kept the rope for horse thieves the populace looked the other way, but when they succumbed to the inevitable temptation to hang business rivals and political enemies, this same populace made short shrift of them.

That was a world of ox carts and covered wagons. Ours is a world of automobiles and airplanes. Most things have moved along, but eighty years has made little difference in the methods with which the right people deal with the "wrong" ones. In the main they are facing the crime wave of 1929 with the mental attitude of the Vigilante.

"There's enough law at the end of a night-stick." This has the Vigilante ring to it, but it was spoken by New York's most recent police commissioner at the outset of the clean-up campaign with which he began his regime. The only result apparent so far is a lot of indiscriminate clubbing and shooting by the police and a corresponding increase in murders and crimes of violence.

These are violent days. We are all agreed on that. The question is, who is responsible? Are the wrong people making the right people violent or are the right people making the wrong people violent? Or is it fifty-fifty?

From my seat on the sidelines it looks as though society is trying to out-gang the gangster, out-slug the slugger, and out-shoot the shooter, without pausing to ask whether it won't result in simply pyramiding violence. The right people all over America in press and pulpit are writing and preaching about the wrong ones. Crime commissions and individuals high and low, from the Chief Justice of the Supreme Court to the smallest small-town reformer, are surveying and recommending, and resolving and whereas-ing them. Legislators are legislating, and the police are pistoling and night-sticking. All are preaching and practicing more violence as a cure for crime.

Is there any justification anywhere, in any time, for believing this method will work? I don't find it. I do not pose as an authority on crime and criminals. My testimony is that of a bystander – a guilty bystander, if you like, for I have survived four penitentiaries and numerous county jails ... what happened to me as an individual is unimportant. I am useful only as an exhibit in the case; but if the laws which the right people are making today had been in effect fifteen years ago, I should never have had a chance to stop stealing and learn working. I should probably have been stopped by the rope, the chair, or a policeman's bullet. If I had escaped these I should be a life-timer in some such prison as Dannemora or Charlestown, spitting my lungs out against a whitewashed wall and, like other life-timers, preaching to young offenders the doctrine of "shoot, and shoot first."

Besides being wrong myself, I have known intimately, in and out of prison, almost five thousand wrong ones. This may seem a wide acquaintance, but in jail one has ample time for social intercourse. These five thousand constitute a cross-section of the underworld from which the crime wave bubbles up. They ranged from the petty thief who "snares" a door-mat with "Welcome" on it, to that prison patrician, the bank burglar. The door-mat thief was just as interesting to me as the bank burglar. It wasn't what they did that interested me but why they did it. Some were mental cases, pathological, with bow-legged minds: in prison parlance, "a kink in the noodle." Some were in prison because they had too little money and some because they had too much. Some because of ignorance and some because of over-education. Booze, "hop," jealousy, avarice; all furnished their quota. A few appeared to be there from perversity – just downright cussedness.

The majority were guilty as charged, or of kindred offenses, though here and there one was innocent. Except for those convicted of crimes of passion, none had leaped into a criminal career overnight. Most had arrived by slow and gradual stages, the result of action and reaction. One was there because of a boyhood feud with the neighborhood cop. One because he lost his job in a strike. One because his wife got sick and his children were hungry.

We'll assume that most of them were the initial offenders. They wronged society, and society, not understanding, wronged them back – with interest. The vicious circle that leads from one penitentiary to another had begun. All there stories could be hooked together on one thread: hatred of the police, contempt of the law, and fear and mistrust of the whole legal machine.

II

My own case is typical. Up to the age of fifteen I thought a policeman was a hero, a person to be looked up to and trusted and confided in. Then one evening I was mistakenly "picked up, taken down, and thrown in" by one of them. The treatment I got in jail from him and his brother officers shot that illusion all to pieces.

Every subsequent contact for twenty-five years strengthened those impressions, and it has taken me the best part of a lifetime to learn that the cop is a victim of the same machine which makes the criminal.

I got my first lesson in violence that first night in the jail. For twenty-five years I punished and was punished. I hunted because I was hunted. I showed no consideration for anybody because I expected to receive none. I learned the game of violence thoroughly, from the police, the courts, the prisons. In the end I came to believe that I could survive only by using violence – and using it first.

I know hundreds of reformed criminals and I don't know one who was reformed by a policeman's night-stick, a severe sentence, or prison cruelty. A brutal flogging in a Canadian prison, and, a year after, three days in strait-jacket on a dungeon floor in California, certainly did nothing to turn my thoughts toward reformation.

The strait-jacket was to the prison warden what his rope was to the Vigilante, what the New York Commissioner would make of the night-stick – a short-cut. The jacket had a brief reign and a swift and violent end. So far as I know, every man who was subjected to its ferocious punishment was so hopelessly maimed that he was a derelict for life, or so twisted mentally that he became a homicidal maniac. They left the prison like the little Jewish tailor whose hands were too shriveled to do any honest thing except to catch pennies on the street corner, or like me poisonous and revengeful. This attempt to maintain order by "throwing the fear of God into them" failed as all such systems fail. It culminated in the bloodiest prison break in the history of the United States. Of the twelve men who escaped, six of the most desperate are still at large, with ropes around their necks, and the murders they have committed to keep out of the hangman's grasp are almost unbelievable.

When I left prison, still weak from the effects of the strait-jacket, I swore to myself that from that time on I would be a creature of the night. I vowed I'd never let the sun shine on me, never make another friend or do another kindly act. The prison officials were safe in their prison, and I turned on society for revenge. Within three months I was back in jail charged with robbery and shooting a citizen who refused to be "stuck up." If he hadn't had a good doctor and a good constitution, I shouldn't have lived to discover that the pen is mightier than the jimmy or the six-shooter. If the Baumes Law had been in effect, I should never have discovered it, for that law robs the judge of all discretion. On the fourth conviction it is mandatory upon the judge to sentence a defendant to life imprisonment whether he shoots a citizen or steals a pair of shoes.

For the past fifteen years I have been feeding and clothing myself instead of letting the tax-payers do it, because, at the time of my life when I least deserved it, I met trust and judicial leniency, which gave me hope. The judge who sentenced me to a year when he might have locked me up for life and thrown the key away, took a greater chance on me than I ever took on anything. He stopped my stealing as effectively as a hangman's rope. He gave me my life and I couldn't doublecross him anymore than I could doublecross the friend who once cut the bars in a jail window and gave me my liberty. Loyalty is the only virtue of the underworld, and the judge appealed to that. He put me in a hole where I had to stop stealing and fall into the lock-step of society.

I repeat that I have never known one criminal who was reformed through cruelty. Such reformation as I have achieved is due, initially, to the act of the judge who said, when he sentenced me to a year instead to life:

"I believe you have sufficient character to build a new life. I will give you that chance."

III

The records are full of the cases of men, notorious for their violence, who reformed when their loyalty was challenged. It's the petty criminal, the weak man, without character enough to be very good or very bad, who violates parole, or any sort of confidence. He doublecrosses his fellow crooks and he doublecrosses society. The "worst" man is often the best bet. Frank James, train-robber and killer, threw away his guns when the governor of Missouri pardoned him. Al Jennings now pushes a pen instead of a six-shooter, thanks to Roosevelt's pardon. Emmet Dalton, Chris Evans, Jack Brady, Kid Thompson – all highwaymen and killers – lived out the letter and spirit of their paroles.

Desperate men bereft of hope are potentially violent men. The Baumes and kindred laws which destroy hope are violent laws, and they breed violence. At best they create a blind alley from which the only exit the desperate criminal knows is "Drop him before he drops you." The result – a dead policeman here, a dead citizen there, a dead stool pigeon somewhere else.

Wrong ones and right ones are much alike when their backs are to the wall. They are both apt to get panicky and spoil what might be a polished professional piece of work. A pickpocket with his hooks on a thousand-dollar poke may fumble it. There's too much at stake. The crime-doctors, faced with an appalling increase in crime, are crowded into hasty action by a lot of nervous citizens who want the crime wave stopped overnight. They recommend more laws, when they already have more than they can enforce. They recommend more punishment, when the experience of all the ages has shown its futility. They listen to the hue and cry against "mollycoddling" criminals, and restrict parole, probation, and pardon - the only measures that permit a criminal to reform. To lighten a leaky boat they throw over the biscuits and water.

V

The problem seems too big for any one crime commission, or any number of crime commissions for that matter. But if any one thing seems certain, it is the folly of more laws and more punishment.

Lao Tse, who was a contemporary of Confucius, said, "Govern a kingdom as you would cook a small fish," meaning do not overdo it. "The more active is the legislation, the more do thieves and robbers increase."

A great Chinese Emperor, founder of the Ming Dynasty in 1386, took his cue for abolishing the death penalty from this philosopher. "Almost every morning ten men were executed in public," wrote the Emperor. By the same evening a hundred had committed the same crime. Lao Tse said, 'if the people do not fear death how can you frighten them by death?' I ceased to inflict capital punishment. I imprisoned the guilty and imposed fines. In less than a year my heart was comforted."

England made the same discovery. They didn't stop hanging people in England for sheep-stealing, shop-lifting, or pocket-picking because it stamped out those crimes. They stopped because of the alarming increase in the murder rate. The law made potential murderers out of petty thieves. The extreme penalty failed to stop pocket-picking even in the shadow of the gallows. Men were arrested for picking the pockets of a crowd assembled to witness the hanging of a pickpocket. Once the English hanged people for sixty different offenses. Now they are considering the abolition of the death penalty, even for the only remaining one.

England has proved that violence doesn't cure violence.

It is safe to say that if every voter in America could be forced to witness a hanging or an electrocution, capital punishment would be abolished at the next election. Certainly no one who has lived through one of those black Fridays in prison could doubt that evil walks with the hangman. As the day of execution draws near the prison becomes a smoldering volcano. The convicts grow sullen and short-tempered. Old grudges are opened, old hates revived. Stool pigeons are stealthily slugged; guards are cursed, defied, and assaulted. The dungeons are filled with unruly prisoners "boiling up" with hatred. On those Fridays I have seen the most murderous knife-duels between prison enemies. In the stone quarries at Folsom, men threw thousands of dollars' worth of valuable steel tools in the canals and smashed with sledge hammers pieces of carved and polished granite upon which they had worked for months. In a blind, helpless surge of revolt they destroyed whatever they could get their hands on. In the "diner" I have seen hungry men hurl their food to the floor, refusing to eat "the damned hangman's stew." On this day of legal violence imprisoned men became so violent that the wardens finally hit upon the plan of keeping the "main line" locked up until after the execution. Now men sit in their cells brooding in silence, or make the prison corridors ring with their hoots and curses.

Of one thing the right people may be sure: no prisoner's thoughts are turned to anything of good on such a day.

VI

What, in a nutshell, is my case against the right people? I contend that more laws and more punishment will mean nothing but more crime and more violence .... We need more emphasis on prevention than on punishment .... The secret of the cure of crime – if there is one – is contained in a knowledge of its causes .... The right people are working on the wrong end of the problem. If they would give more attention to the highchair, they could put cobwebs on the electric chair. They lay too much stress on what the wrong people do, not on *why* they do it; on what they are instead of how they got that way.

— Jack Black

From an article in Harper's Magazine, *June 1929*